# If the Spirit Moves You

Justine Picardie is a journalist working most recently at *Vogue* and as editor of the *Observer Magazine*. She is now a full-time freelance writer and lives with her husband and two sons in London.

JUSTINE PICARDIE

# If the Spirit Moves You

PICADOR

First published 2001 by Macmillan

This edition published 2002 by Picador
an imprint of Pan Macmillan Ltd
Pan Macmillan, 20 New Wharf Road, London N1 9RR
Basingstoke and Oxford
Associated companies throughout the world
www.panmacmillan.com

ISBN 0 330 48786 8



13 15 17 19 18 16 14 12

A CIP catalogue record for this book is available from the British Library.

Printed and bound in Great Britain by
Mackays of Chatham plc, Chatham, Kent

*For Ruth*

The savage, it is said, fails to distinguish the visions of sleep from the realities of waking life, and accordingly when he has dreamed of his dead friends he necessarily concludes that they have not wholly perished, but that their spirits continue to exist in some place and some form, though in the ordinary course of events they elude the perceptions of his senses. On this theory the conceptions, whether gross or refined, whether repulsive or beautiful, which savages and perhaps civilised men have formed of the state of the departed, would seem to be no more than elaborate hypotheses constructed to account for appearances in dreams; these towering structures, for all their radiant or gloomy grandeur, for all the massy strength and solidity with which they present themselves to the imagination of many, may turn out on inspection to be mere visionary castles built of clouds and vapour, which a breath of reason suffices to melt into air.

James George Frazer, Book II, 'Killing the God',
*The Golden Bough*

It was not for a long time that I learnt to appreciate the importance of phantasies and unconscious thoughts about life in the womb . . . They afford the deepest unconscious basis for the belief in survival after death which represents a projection into the future of this uncanny life before birth.

Sigmund Freud, *The Interpretation of Dreams*

We die with the dying:
See, they depart, and we go with them.
We are born with the dead:
See, they return, and bring us with them.

T.S. Eliot, *Four Quartets*

GOOD FRIDAY IN the year 2000. Jesus is dead and so is my sister, and I'm running on a treadmill at the gym, watching MTV with no sound on. If my sister were still alive she would be thirty-six in ten days' time. But Ruth died when she was thirty-three, the same age as Jesus. Obviously, I know she wasn't nearly as famous as Jesus was at the age of thirty-three – I'm not *that* crazy, nor inclined to blasphemy under normal circumstances – but Ruth is a little bit famous, because after she was diagnosed with terminal breast cancer I asked her to write a column for the *Observer* magazine, which I was editing at the time. The magazine was called 'Life' and her column about death came on the final page. She only wrote a handful before she died, but many thousands of readers responded to her pieces, which were later collected (along with emails and letters) in a book called *Before I Say Goodbye*. Thus she has a kind of public afterlife – she rose again, in the bestseller lists at least – which is perhaps both a blessing and a curse for those who loved her.

When I think about her now, which is most of the time, it's like rewinding a silent film in my head: I see the crucial scenes in our lives together (holding her hand whilst her twins were born in an emergency caesarean; holding her hand when she kissed them goodbye just before she died two years later). But what I can't hear is her voice in my head, and that silence is driving me crazy.

The treadmill is supposed to be good therapy, and sometimes it works, but not today because Good Friday is the saddest day of the year. I've tried it all since my sister died, in the manner of the sophisticated consumer that I am supposed to be: the gym, bereavement counselling, psychotherapy, anti-depressants, valium, sleeping pills, homeopathic remedies. Prozac is sufficiently numbing to take the edge off the silence (though I'm trying to stop taking it because I wonder if I've been missing something; if the impermeable layer that it provides is in fact now necessary). But still nothing really speaks to me.

I didn't expect silence. We had always talked so much. She was my best friend as well as my sister: a little less than three years younger than me, the child I needed to protect when I was still a child (and my parents scarcely grown-ups themselves); yet I could not protect her now. When we knew that she was going to die, because the cancer had spread to her lungs and her liver, we spoke about how we would always talk to each other, even after her death. Neither of us had grown up believing in a conventional Christian afterlife (and anyway, I had given up on that unkind God after his failure to answer my prayers to save her); but, even so, it seemed impossible that we would ever be separated by silence, that our voices were contained only in our flesh and blood.

Yet in the weeks after her death, I heard nothing. At night there were just my own muffled screams in the pillow when I went to bed; or the memory that I tried to block out but which filled my head of her agonized breath on her last night, as she gasped for all that remained of life. And I could say nothing to her except, 'I love you, I love you, I love you.' 'I love you too,' she whispered, before she slipped away to a place where I could not follow.

Since then there have been times when I have longed to go after her. But today, after I've finished at the gym, I walk back home, back upstairs to the computer in the attic. I'm almost expecting to find an email from Ruth ('message waiting') but there is nothing; just my half-reflected face on the blank screen. I wonder if she is on the other side, looking back at me looking in. I wonder if I could smash a hole in the screen and put my hand through to reach her. I often dream about being with Ruth in a wood. She is a little girl, lost in the wood, and I am on the other side of a glass screen watching her. In my dream I shatter it with my bare fists and reach through, cutting my wrists as I do so, on the broken glass. When I was a child I saw a television adaptation of *Wuthering Heights*, and Cathy's ghost came to a dark window; she was outside, and she smashed her way in, with bleeding wrists and knuckles. Or maybe – though I can't quite remember, maybe I dreamed this – it was a little girl in the house who closed the window against Cathy's ghost, slamming the window down on her dead fingers as they reached inside.

I don't need a therapist to explain this, thank you very much. I need only turn to one of my favourite books, Iona Opie's very useful *A Dictionary of Superstitions*:

> **Death: opening locks/doors and windows frees spirit: 1891**, *Church Times*, 23 Jan. Yesterday, at Willey, in Warwickshire, I buried a little boy three years old. It was snowing hard, yet the parents (of the labouring class) would have both front and back doors of their cottage wide open all the time of the funeral.

So much for communication, then.

## SUNDAY 23 APRIL

WHEN I DREAM about my sister, as I do almost every night, she doesn't say very much. Just before dawn on Easter Sunday, when Jesus is doubtless rising again, I dream that I meet my sister at a party. 'I thought you were dead!' I say.

'No, I just went to America,' she says, looking evasive.

'But I saw your dead body. I went to the funeral and saw the coffin. You were cremated.'

'Hmm,' she says, infuriatingly.

'And what about the children?' I ask her. 'How could you just go to America and leave Lola and Joe? They've missed you so much! And I've missed you so much! How could you do that?'

She turns away.

'Ruth, listen to me,' I say. 'Your husband has got a girlfriend. She's called Anna. They've just moved into a new house together, with the twins. Don't you care? Are you even listening to me?'

She still says nothing. I look at her more closely, at her cropped hair that has been dyed red, and then I realize that this is a stranger, someone pretending to be Ruth.

'You're not my sister,' I say to this woman.

'You *bitch*,' she replies.

After this dream, I think maybe I need some help. A few months ago, a friend gave me the telephone number for a man – a medium, in fact – named Arthur Molinary, who works at the College of Psychic Studies. I liked his name – it made me smile – and I quite liked the idea of going to this strange sounding place. But I had stuffed the number in a drawer. I didn't feel the need to ring him then. Now I can't think of what else to do.

## WEDNESDAY 26 APRIL

I RING THE COLLEGE of Psychic Studies from work. This is a very peculiar phone call to make in an open-plan office, so I try to whisper.

'I'd like to make an appointment to see Arthur Molinary,' I hiss into the phone.

'Mr Molinary is fully booked until 6.15 p.m. on 8 June,' says a business-like woman at the other end of the line. 'Would you like to take that appointment?'

'Yes,' I say, 'but isn't there anything sooner?'

'Well,' she says, pausing briefly, as if scanning the appointment book of a popular doctor's surgery, 'you could come in and see our junior sensitive on 16 May at 6.30 p.m. We've been getting very good results from him.'

'I'll take both appointments,' I say, feeling excited, suddenly feeling Ruth. I can't see her sitting next to me, not literally, but I can see her in my mind's eye, wearing her favourite lavender-coloured skirt and a white shirt from a shop called Ghost.

'See you then,' says the receptionist. 'And we need twenty-four hours notice if you're going to cancel.'

'I won't cancel,' I say. (Later, when I tell my husband, who is a rationalist, about this conversation, he raises one eyebrow and remarks, 'You'd think the College of Psychic Studies would *know* if you were going to cancel.')

## Monday 1 May

It's Ruth's birthday. I've lost my good spirits and sunk back into gloomy, angry silence. Both my parents have stayed the previous night at my house (in separate bedrooms because they are divorced). In the morning, we make small-talk between slices of toast. I wonder whether to tell them about my appointments at the College of Psychic Studies. My father used to be an Oxford don; my mother is a therapist. I can't see spiritualism going down well with either of them, though, as it happens, my paternal grandfather developed an interest in seances after his parents died.

It's kind of an unspoken family embarrassment: poor, sad, silly Louis, who was named Lazar (for Lazarus) but changed his name when he was reborn into evangelical Christianity, joined Jews for Jesus, and started listening out for rapping on the table and voices from beyond.

'Dad,' I say, 'why don't you ever talk about Louis and the spiritualists?'

'Oh, that dreadful rubbish,' says my father. 'How absurd, how truly *ridiculous* can you get!'

My father had the first of several nervous breakdowns just after his mother died; I must have been seven or eight when he was sectioned and sent to a mental hospital near Oxford, where he was given electric shock treatment. (I was not there – how could I have been? – but I remember it as if in a bad dream, standing looking at him from the other side of a glass wall, as he was strapped to the bed, and electrodes attached to him, like Frankenstein's monster, and then the electricity was shot through his brain, and when I cried out, 'Stop hurting him!', no sound came out of my mouth.) Since then, he has had years of therapy, and brutal doses of medication that have left him a little frail and shaky. His father's experiences with spiritualism were, possibly, a gentler way of dealing with grief than my own father's psychiatric treatment; but he might disagree with this observation.

(At the same time that my father was in a mental hospital, I made my brief acquaintance with the Old Testament, when I absorbed myself in a curious Christian denomination, for several months at least, with a school friend. Her father was a distinguished Oxford physicist, but he was also a Christadelphian, which at the time sounded to me like a flower, but is in fact a subsection of the Church that expects a second coming of Christ on earth. So my friend and I sat in the Christadelphian Sunday School in a basement hall on a suburban Oxford street, while her parents waited upstairs for the return of Jesus Christ, and my father wrestled with his demons somewhere nearby.)

As for my mother, she was raised in the rituals of the High

Church by her mother, who had been sent away by *her* mother to a Convent boarding school at the age of four. Perhaps unsurprisingly, my mother had thoughts of becoming a nun as a teenager; but though there is something saintly about her, she did not, in the end, follow in the footsteps of her ancestor, Henry Garnett, a Catholic priest who was executed after the Gunpowder Plot, and later beatified by virtue of the image of Christ that was seen in the drop of his blood that fell from his severed head. Instead of marrying God, my mother discovered my Jewish father and socialism and her own cleverness instead. Their marriage failed. (I grew up associating Easter with my father's concurrent descent into depression; a link which I did not understand until a recent email arrived from him which observed, gnomically, 'There were Pogroms in the Tsarist Empire, usually orchestrated by the Russian police themselves at about Easter time and fuelled by the Catholic priests, to blame the Christkillers who would be accused of murdering Christian children for their blood to make matzos at Passover.') Recently, my father has found some consolation in the rituals of Judaism that he previously rejected; while my mother returned, briefly, to the Church with her second husband (a doctor – a blood specialist, and also a haemophiliac). After the doctor died of Aids, she discovered a different kind of solace in what Freud saw as the science of psychotherapy.

I, on the other hand, search for answers in the *Dictionary of Superstitions*:

> **Bleeding, charm to staunch.** The verse to stop . . . bleeding is the 6th verse of the 16th chapter of Ezekiel, which must be repeated by one of the opposite sex from the patient. 'And when I passed by thee, and saw thee polluted in thine own blood, I said unto thee when thou wast in thy blood, Live; yea, I said unto thee, when thou wast in thy blood, Live.'

After Ruth's death, I seem to my mother to be silent and closed: in need of therapy, probably. But, like I said, my experiences with therapists have not been very successful. The first bereavement counsellor I saw made me irritable, partly because of his twinkly New Age language ('you need a safe place to be held'); and also because he sent me notes on blue paper decorated with pastel bunnies and birds. The second therapist was far better, but we got stuck on my recollection of Ruth's blood phobia (she felt faint – and sometimes fainted, even fitted – at the sight of her own blood). The therapist seemed to suggest that perhaps my sister and I had repressed the memory of our father's suicide attempt: could there have been slit wrists or something? But, as I kept telling the therapist, my father had in fact only taken a minor overdose of pills, though during (or maybe because of) this period of therapy, I was haunted by the unasked for image of him hanging in our living room in Oxford.

Whatever, all this delving into my subconscious soon got to be far too uncomfortable and exhausting. Prozac is so much easier; and anyway, I am bored of myself; bored of grief; bored of hearing my own voice talking drearily, pointlessly, when what I really want is Ruth.

And, if not her voice, then maybe that of a medium who can hear her when I can't? That's what I try to tell my mother, stumbling over half-finished phrases, like my tongue doesn't work, on my dead sister's birthday. She looks at me quizzically. Somewhere in her measured response, I hear the word 'internalized', but not much else. Then she tells me that she, too, has dreamt of Ruth. 'Once she was on the other side of a river, waving to me, but I couldn't cross the river,' says my mother. 'Another time, I dreamt I was driving very fast down a motorway, and I saw Ruth flash past in the opposite direction, in another car.'

'But do you ever feel her presence when you're awake?' I ask.

'Only in my memory and my sense of loss,' says my mother, quietly.

My silence fills the air between us. She wants me to love her more, but sometimes love is edged aside by grief. So my mother leaves, without me telling her that I do love her, I do, even though my sister, whose name is carved upon my bones, whose spirit runs through my blood, is dead. My sister is dead.

Then my husband, Neill, drives me and our children and my father south across London, over Blackfriars Bridge – the bridge that I crossed so many times, to and from the hospice that housed my dying sister – to the far side of the river. We park where the bridge ends, and walk alongside the grey cold water of the Thames. It is May Day. Helicopters hang like vultures above the opposite bank, where anarchists are engaged in a minor riot. There is rubbish washed up on the dirty sand. I think that Neill is angry with me for being sad, on this spring holiday. ('That's pure projection, and you know it,' says an imaginary therapist's voice that sometimes pops into my head when I least want to hear it.) I walk ahead with the children, who are uncomplicated in their conversation, leaving my father and husband in our wake.

Finally, we get to the Hayward Gallery, to an exhibition which has been curated by our neighbour, David Toop, whose wife, my friend Kimberley, killed herself on a wintry morning five years ago. (Kimberley half-believed in spiritualism, and as she sank into despair, hoped that death would free her soul from darkness into light; but that is another story . . .) The exhibition is called Sonic Boom, and it is about sound, but it is also about silence. I stand in front of a work called 'A Procession of Ghosts', made of graceful wires scratching on a huge, smooth white page. Nothing is there to read, and yet there is the faint sound of something being written in the silence. I stare at the blank space and try to imagine Ruth's words on her birthday. But I cannot read anything. The page stays empty and smooth, while the faint scratching of what might be a pen continues . . .

## WEDNESDAY 10 MAY

I'M SITTING IN a plane on my way to Hollywood to interview a clutch of film stars for *Vogue*. I look out of the window, in search of Ruth, as ever. The first time I flew after she died, I cried because of the sky's emptiness. This time, it's easier. Could she not be here in the cabin, her spirit flying from her children's pillows at dawn to be with me again now?

'Are you there?' I whisper silently, mouthing the words.

'I'm here,' says the voice in my head. And after all, I think, why should she be dangled in the clouds beyond this tiny, fragile helix of steel and diesel, when I am inside waiting for her?

I close my eyes and hear her voice as mine.

'Ruth?'

'Yes.'

'I miss you.'

'I miss you, too. But I'm here you know.'

'Can't you just give me a sign?'

'You don't need one.'

'What's heaven?'

'Heaven is a state of mind.'

'And hell?'

'Hell is your unhappiness . . .'

'What it's like for you now?'

'Blue and fast and silver.'

'So where do you spend your time?'

'With the twins, and you, and by myself . . .'

'Remember that dream I had? The week after you died? We met at night in the gardens at Trinity Hospice, and you were lying on a kind of mat, as if you were sleeping. And then you sat up and said to me that you were spending all your time with strangers. I thought of you, like a lost ghost crossing Blackfriars Bridge, to and fro, over and over again.'

'That was before I found myself. I'm better now.'

I open my eyes and I'm crying, 36,000 feet high in the sky, wondering if Ruth is sitting in the empty seat beside me.

'Of course I am, stupid,' she says.

'I *feel* stupid,' I say. 'I'm not as clever as you.'

'Yes you are,' she says. 'You are me.'

## TUESDAY 16 MAY

MY APPOINTMENT WITH the junior sensitive. I'm so nervous I can hardly park the car outside the College of Psychic Studies. It's a grand, nineteenth-century building, around the corner from the Natural History Museum (one wrong turning, and Darwin or Freud could have turned up on the doorstep). Just beyond the entrance hall is a waiting room that doubles as a library, with faded rows of dusty Victorian books, and a brochure that sets out the College's principles. ('Founded in 1884, the College is an educational charity. We seek to promote spiritual values and a greater understanding of the wider areas of human consciousness, welcoming the truths of all spiritual traditions and, equally, each and every individual . . .') I wait, browsing through the forthcoming lecture programme. (Tomorrow night is Dr Edgar Mitchell, who walked on the moon in 1971, yet is now on his way to South Kensington to deliver his thoughts on 'The Quantam Hologram: Nature's Mind', with special reference to 'intuitive, psychic and mystical experiences'.) Before I get much further, my name has been called. 'Justine Picardie. Room four,' says the receptionist.

She points me up the stairs, past the oil paintings of the former presidents and luminaries of the College, past the lecture theatre, to the second floor.

The junior sensitive is a middle-aged man, small and bald and anxious in a carefully ironed shirt and respectable trousers.

'Do you mind if I draw the curtains?' he says, in a soft northern accent. 'It's so light outside, it's blinding.'

'Go ahead,' I say, and we both sit down.

He closes his eyes. 'I definitely feel something,' he says. 'I felt it as soon as you came into the room. My nose is itching and my throat, my throat is sore.' His hand clutches his neck, but his eyes are still closed.

'There's a very high pollen count outside,' I say, unkindly. 'Maybe you've got hay fever?'

He opens his eyes, and looks at me, uneasily. 'You could be right,' he says. 'It could be hay fever.'

He closes his eyes again, and starts waving his hands in the air, paddling them through the twilight in this hot, still room.

'You must remember to breathe deeply,' he says, breathing deeply himself, by way of demonstration. 'In, out, in, out. And swim. When you're stressed, go swimming . . . And you need to drink plenty of water. Lots and lots of water.'

This does not seem to me to be particularly helpful advice, nor does it seem to represent the views of my sister, so I remain silent. He paddles with his arms more urgently, as if swimming to a far shore.

'Clarissa!' he says, finally. 'Clarissa! Does the name mean anything to you?'

'No,' I say, stonily, wishing I could leave right now.

'Hmmm,' he says. 'Well, store that name away for the future.' He breathes deeply again, as if to reassure himself; yet his brow is furrowed and his nose wrinkles like the White Rabbit in *Alice in Wonderland*. (Why 'junior sensitive' I wonder? Why can I not bring myself to ask him what that means?)

I gaze up at the ceiling, feeling foolish and disappointed. What on earth am I doing here? Why would Ruth talk to me in such a peculiar place, anyway, through the unlikely guise of this man?

'I see someone who looks like you and talks like you,' he continues, undeterred. 'Do you have someone in your family who has passed on?'

'My sister,' I say, reluctantly.

'She died of cancer,' he says, clutching at his stomach, leaning against the wall for support. 'I can feel her nausea.'

I feel like punching him on the nose, but I don't. I'm too polite to leave. I listen to his comments on my dead grandparents. ('They like this time of year. I see them eating ice cream. Did they like ice cream? I'm trying to find some proof for you here. Did one of them have their tonsils removed, perhaps?')

Finally, I can go. 'Goodbye,' I say. 'Thank you.'

'Goodbye,' he says, gently. 'Sometimes the spirits don't tell you what you want to hear . . .'

I walk down the stairs, past the pictures of the Victorian mediums, past the posters advertising Dr Mitchell and next weekend's workshop on the path of the soul, and then out of the big front door, where suddenly I laugh, looking up into the summer sky where the pollen swirls like heaven's dust or discarded feathers from angels' wings.

## Wednesday 17 May

The next day, I go into work, and in my morning post is a book and a letter written on lavender-coloured paper.

Dear Ms Picardie [it begins],

I read your article in the *Daily Telegraph*, 25 September 1999, understanding exactly how you feel about your sister Ruth's death two years ago. Your remark about your longing for 'her advice and unique understanding of our shared past' is especially poignant.

Your story struck such a chord with me that I decided to send you my book, Voices From Paradise. I won't talk any more in this letter but let the book speak for itself. I feel it can help you not only by expressing shared experience, but in a practical way too.

Please read it and if you feel it adds up, unbelievable though it all may seem at first, perhaps you'll recommend it in whatever way you feel is appropriate.

With kindest regards,
Judith Chisholm

The subtitle of the book is 'How the dead speak to us', and despite my disappointing experiences with the junior sensitive, I take the book home with me and read it. It proves to be so very absorbing that I miss *ER*, which is my favourite thing on television, just as it was Ruth's too (the unreal blood seemed not to disturb her when we watched it every Thursday night together before she got ill, and afterwards, and not long before she died, lying side by side on her narrow high hospital bed; though by then her brain tumour meant that she could not follow the dialogue. 'What are they talking about?' she complained. 'What are their voices *saying*?')

Judith Chisholm is a former *Sunday Times* journalist (the paper where I first started as a reporter, though she left before I arrived), whose son died unexpectedly at the age of thirty-six. The book begins as a moving account of her grief, and then describes her experiences with mediums and seances, before leading to a precise exposition of her belief in something called the electronic voice phenomenon, or EVP, which is, she claims, a means of recording the voices of the dead. By way of support, she cites Sir Oliver Lodge, the inventor of the spark plug, a former principal of Birmingham University and President of the Society for

Psychical Research from 1901 to 1903. ('The dead live in etheric wavelengths which operate at much higher frequencies than ours,' wrote Lodge in *The Outline of Science.* 'Our physical world is working on vibrations that are up to the speed of light. The etheric world operates at frequencies far in excess of the speed of light.') She also points to the views of Thomas Edison who, after inventing the light bulb and the phonograph, turned his attention to building a machine that would allow the dead to speak to the living. 'I am inclined to believe that our personality hereafter will be able to affect matter,' wrote Edison at the age of seventy-three. 'If this reasoning be correct then if we can evolve an instrument so delicate as to be affected or moved or manipulated by our personality as it survives in the next life, such an instrument when made available ought to record something.'

Judith Chisholm's book concludes with a set of instructions on how to record the voices of the dead. 'You need: A tape recorder (variable speed is useful as some of the voices are very fast and need slowing down); a new tape; a remote microphone, if your tape recorder will take one, which should be hung up somewhere for maximum efficiency (a remote mike helps cut down background hiss); a quiet room and, very important, a positive, expectant, cheerful, loving attitude of mind.' She also recommends recording after sunset on the night of a full moon, preferably during a thunderstorm: though not for any reasons relating to myth or superstition, but because of electricity and magnetism and something called 'the gravitational effect'.

> Not long after Jesus raised Lazarus from the dead, 'Then came there a voice from heaven . . . The people therefore, that stood by, and heard it, said that it thundered: others said, An angel spake to him.'
>
> St. John, Chapter 12, verses 28–9

## THURSDAY 18 MAY

I HAVE FINISHED READING the book. It is dark outside. The children are asleep upstairs. There is a full moon, and a thunderstorm has just moved on. 'Have you got a tape recorder and a microphone?' I ask my husband.

'Why?' he says. I do not answer, but he knows what I'm thinking, and he looks at me with disbelief and worry and exasperation. But he loves me, so he goes and fetches the tape recorder and the microphone and a blank cassette and sets them up for me on the kitchen table. 'I'm going upstairs,' he says. 'Call me if you need me.'

I light a candle and switch off the lights. I turn on the tape recorder and whisper into it, in case anyone hears me. But then I remember that I want Ruth to hear me, not to mention Kimberley and Oscar and Adam and Simon and Jon – all my friends who have died in the last few years. 'Um, is anybody there?' I say. 'I would very much like to talk to somebody. I feel like so many people have died recently, it would make more sense to conduct my social life in the spirit world . . .'

Silence. I leave a gap on the tape, as instructed in the book. ('With the open-mike method, you will not hear any discarnate voices at the time of recording, only on playback. Leave gaps in your own speech in order for there to be space for a response on the other side.')

Silence. I believe in this. I do. I have a positive, expectant, cheerful, loving attitude of mind. There is a full moon outside. There has been lightning and therefore masses of electricity. My sister is going to talk to me. She is going to leave me a message on my tape. I know this to be true. I do.

I switch the tape off. I rewind it. I play it back.

I hear my voice on the tape . . . and nothing else. There is nothing. But there must be something. I rewind it and play it again.

Silence. I consult the book. 'Play your tape back. Listen very carefully. At first it's hard to distinguish anything other than the background hiss of the tape recorder, which you can never completely eliminate, and the sound of your own voice. As the discarnate voices usually imprint at a level below that at which we expect to hear them you have to try to listen to all levels on the tape – listen through it. This is extremely hard at first, but becomes automatic later on. The voices can be whispered. At first they usually are. They are sometimes very fast, often curt, often seemingly banal in their utterances. There is great economy of words yet what is said usually has more than one meaning. Sometimes prepositions and auxiliary verbs are left out. Usually one to three words are imprinted at first. If you hear something that may be an 'extra' voice, run the tape back and listen again – and again.'

I run the tape back. I listen again, and again. Still nothing. I go upstairs and get my husband. 'Can you listen to my tape, please?' I say. He puts on some headphones and listens to it. I watch him listening but I cannot hear anything.

His eyes fill with tears but he does not speak.

'Did you hear something?' I ask.

'Only your voice,' he says, finally. 'There's only you. You know that, don't you? It's only you . . .'

## Monday 22 May

I rang Judith Chisholm after the failure of my experiment in EVP and now I am driving through the fading light to her house in East London. I don't know what I will hear, but I know I have to see her. 'Are you cracking up?' says a poster for the Samaritans, behind the broken glass of a bus shelter. No, I am not cracking up. I feel calm. I turn left off the main road, to Judith's street, which is long and narrow. At the end of it lie the Hackney marshes, the kind of place where ghosts would live, I think, if ghosts were to live anywhere. I knock on Judith's front door. She lets me in. She is probably the same age as my mother, but my mother's hair is a paler red, fading to a gentle grey, whereas Judith's is the colour of blood. She shows me into her front room, which is painted dark green. There is a crucifix on the wall and glass vats of jewel-coloured homemade wine on a side table. The house smells of damp cats, or city roses in the rain. Her youngest son – her surviving son – comes into the room. His name is Vic. He is an electrician; a thin man, and very pale. He has been expecting me. 'It's so amazing,' he says. 'You lost your younger sister. I lost my older brother. That's not a coincidence. That's a one in a million chance.'

I say nothing. I am silenced by this house. Judith brings me a cup of tea, and half-way through drinking it, I lurch into a question. 'Do you believe in heaven?' I say, trying to concentrate on looking at her, rather than Christ hanging on the cross on the opposite wall.

'Spirits go through stages,' says Judith, unperturbed by my clumsy attempt at conversation. 'I think some of them go to purgatory. Some of them may even go to hell – not in the hell fire and brimstone sense, but in terms of mental torture. But they do *go* to hell, those who deserve it. And purgatory is—'

'Like a waiting room,' cuts in Vic, 'or at least that's what I heard, anyway.'

'Vic, please, go and play with your computer,' says Judith. 'Two people can't do this. We can't both talk to Justine.'

'OK,' says Vic, mildly. He looks at me and holds out his hand, which I take. 'I'm sure we'll meet again.'

Judith tells me about her EVP experiments. She has been engaged in them for seven years, she explains, at first in search of her dead son, who said a little; but now he can't get a word in edgeways, because the voice that fills her tapes is that of a man called Jack

Hallam. She used to work with Jack at the *Sunday Times*. He was the picture editor. He believed in ghosts, and wrote books, collecting stories about other people's ghosts. He died in 1986.

'Time is a curious thing,' says Judith. 'I've heard remarks that suggest that spirits are aware of the passage of time. I heard Jack say, 'It's a long time since I heard from Chisholm – that's what he calls me, Chisholm. But I don't think he's aware that fourteen years have passed since his death.'

'Do you think he's in heaven?' I say.

'I think that he's in purgatory,' says Judith. 'The evidence seems to point to that.'

Judith's evidence is on her tapes of Jack's voice. She has hours and hours of it. And for every minute of tape, she says, she has to listen to it twenty or thirty times over. It is exhausting, she says. She is so exhausted by her experiments that often her head hurts. Yet now I am here, at last, an independent witness to these endeavours, and she is going to play me some of the tapes; but I will need to read her transcript, too. 'It's not like ordinary speech,' she says. 'You need to accustom your hearing. You may not even hear it. I have an extraordinarily wide range of hearing. I can hear things that other people can't.'

We go upstairs to the first floor, to her study, where she keeps her cassette player and her notes and her Dictaphone: her little door to the other world, where Jack Hallam is always waiting. Because once Jack found Judith, he couldn't be silenced.

The walls of the study have been scraped back to the plaster, but a few faint scraps of the old layers of wallpaper remain. I am frightened, briefly. The room is silent yet filled with my expectation, so heavy and thick that it seeps like a stain around us. And then Judith Chisholm plays me the first recording she made of Jack Hallam's voice, on what was then a brand new Dictaphone (a Panasonic recorder which cost £89, much to Judith's dismay, yet an entirely necessary expenditure, she says, even in this cash-strapped household). I hear a whispery scratchy sound through the speakers – the sound of an empty pen on paper, of shallow gasps, or rats in the attic, a tap at the window, a ghost in the machine. 'Can you hear him?' she says, urgently.

'I don't know,' I say.

'Listen,' she says, and rewinds the tape. But I still can't hear the words. So she rewinds it again. This time I ask her to tell me what he is saying. And I think, maybe . . . I think maybe I hear a voice. I read her transcript while I listen to the tape. It says:

13 October 1999
Key: Sp = Spirit

Sp: Hallam knows
Me: Having just recently bought this . . .
Sp: Yes
Me: I don't actually like it . . .
Sp: We do like it
Me: But is it useful to you? Can you come through on this and would you like me to keep it? I'm just going to leave this next bit of tape empty so you can perhaps speak on it . . .
Sp: Now, Hallam's content. Hallam can progress. We need Hallam to know. Hallam needs someone who can help him. Tell him! Go and find Hallam! Go and get Hallam!

She plays me other tapes, and shows me other transcripts. In one, she asks Jack Hallam why he has been sent to communicate with her; could he please explain 'the plan'. 'There is no plan,' he replies. She wonders if she is missing something, because sometimes, despite her experience in these matters, even she finds it hard to understand all of the words. And sometimes they scare her. Her notes of an EVP session that took place on 12 January this year relate that she can't tell if the spirit voice is saying, 'Let's kill her' or 'Let's keep her happy', or maybe, 'Let's keep Hallam' or 'Let's kill Hallam'. She plays the tape to me. 'What can you hear?' she asks.

'I don't know,' I say, again, unwilling to engage with what is happening here. ('You are repressed,' interjects my imaginary therapist, with characteristically unhelpful timing.) Judith scrabbles around her study to find other tapes, searching for them with her glasses perched on the end of her nose like a storybook academic (the Professor Higgins of the psychic world, whose own perfect enunciation serves only as a contrast with that of these recalcitrant, belligerent ghosts).

Yet, as she plays me snippets of the other tapes, I think I *can* hear the word 'Hallam'. I *do* hear a voice saying Jack Hallam, though it sounds as if it comes in a dream. I tell Judith that I can hear Jack. 'Let's make a recording together,' she says. 'Let's do an experiment.'

'OK,' I say. She turns on the Dictaphone. She speaks into it. She gives the date, and says that she is here with me to make a recording. She speaks to Hallam, because he is always ready to speak to her. 'I hope you're not angry with me for . . . I don't know what for, but I hope you're not angry with me anyway,' she says to Jack, very gently. 'Have you got anything you would like to say to us?'

She leaves a space. The silence fills the space. 'Justine, would you like to say something?' says Judith. I take a deep breath. 'I wonder if Ruth, my sister, is with you and could . . . speak to me?'

There is another silence. 'I hesitate to cut in,' says Judith, politely. 'I hope I'm not cutting across what's being said but as we don't really know where you are Jack, if it is Jack who's speaking, we're not sure whether Ruth is there as well . . .'

After five minutes or so, she turns the Dictaphone off. She rewinds it. She plays it back. This time I hear voices. I know I hear them. I can't make out what they are saying, but there are voices, as faint as moths banging against a light bulb, fingernails at the door. I hear the sound, but not the words. I cannot read the words because there is no transcript. I do not understand. I cannot hear Ruth's voice. But I do hear a man's voice – Jack Hallam! – saying, hoarsely, '*Ruth!*' I gasp, frightened by the sound. The voice that says 'Ruth' makes her name sound like it has been torn in half. I feel that I have been torn in half.

Judith is alive, excited, wired. 'That's Jack!' she says. 'It's definitely Jack! I recognize everything about him! He always hogs the recorder! He's so stroppy . . . But if he's there, they're all there. It stands to reason, doesn't it? It proves that there is life after death.' I look at the walls where the paper has been scraped away, where the plaster crumbles, but I say nothing.

'You needn't worry about your sister any more,' continues Judith. 'She's OK. That's an amazing thought, isn't it?'

But I can't hear *her*. I hear Judith but I can't hear Ruth. I'm dog-tired, dead-beat, half-asleep, swimming against the tide. Judith wants to rewind the tape, over and over again, but I'm too tired to listen, too tired to cross this bridge. She wants to do a transcript, now, with me, but I say no, I have to go home. So she makes me a copy of the tape, and we say goodbye.

I drive home, fast. I take my tape into the kitchen, where Neill is sitting at the table. 'How was it?' he asks.

'Listen to this,' I say, 'just listen to this. I *heard* the voices.'

I play the tape out loud to him. But there is nothing to hear, apart from Judith's voice and mine. 'There's nothing here,' says Neill.

'There is,' I say. 'Well, there was. It must be a bad copy . . .'

I play it again. I play him the bit where Jack Hallam says 'Ruth!' But it doesn't sound like her name any more. 'That's the sound of a chair moving,' says Neill, 'or the click of the components of the machine, or your breathing. It's just your breathing . . .' I am silent. My face isn't moving, but he looks at me as if I'm crying. 'You need to get some sleep,' he says. 'You've got to get some rest now. You'll feel better in the morning . . .'

. . . Alas!
Our dried voices, when
We whisper together
Are quiet and meaningless
As wind in dry grass . . .

T.S. Eliot, 'The Hollow Men'

## Thursday 1 June

Judith has transcribed the tape we made at her house last month, after much work. She sends me a finished transcript, which has several spirit voices, all talking together. 'It's Chisholm,' says one of the spirits. 'Both of them have suffering hearts,' says another. The spirit transcript continues: 'Let's help them.' 'I don't know how.' 'Let's take them to heaven and show them him.' 'Show them in heaven serving up her son with ground nuts.' 'Babylon.'

I go to bed reading Judith's transcript, over and over again, searching for clues, but I'm still lost. It doesn't seem to make any sense. Maybe it's about Judith, not me. I'm an interloper in her tape recorder; Jack Hallam doesn't want to talk to me. I fall asleep thinking of squirrels; of squirrels and Judith and hoards of nuggets, nuts, squirrelled away for the winter; for later, for dark nights. Judith's nuts.

I sink and surface through the night's sleep. I'm burning up. I can't think straight, sleep straight, go anywhere at all. Outside, the clematis leaves are tapping on the window. I feel sick, stuck, struck dumb in the dark, counting squirrels. Nuts.

At last, towards dawn, the squirrels stop running around my head. I dream that I am on a bicycle, cycling over Blackfriars Bridge, away from North London to south of the river. I am visiting Ruth's children, Lola and Joe, and her husband Matt and his American girlfriend. They have just moved into a new house that Ruth has never seen. It takes me for ever to get there, and when, at last, I reach it, I am hot and cross and thirsty and dusty. I can't find anywhere to leave my bicycle, and Lola looks sad and Matt looks anxious and where, exactly, am I supposed to sit? Then, in my dream, I see Ruth standing by the kitchen sink, to show me where I can get a drink of water – and for the first time since her death, I see her not as sick Ruth, dying Ruth, but Ruth as full of life as ever. I know that she is dead – that no one aside from me can see her ghost – but she looks happy, and spirited, and she flashes her brilliant smile at me, and tosses her pre-cancer halo of dark curls. She says nothing, and I am silent, too, but it doesn't matter. I have seen my sister . . . My sister has seen me.

> **Water, running: cures. 1625**, T. Jackson, *Originall of Unbelief.* This upon mine owne knowledge . . . I can relate; of two, sent more than a mile, after the Sun-setting, to fetch South-running Water [for a cure], with a strict injunction, not to salute any either going or comming.
>
> Iona Opie and Moira Tatem,
> *A Dictionary of Superstitions*

## THURSDAY 8 JUNE

AFTER MY DREAM of Ruth, the date with Arthur Molinary seems less pressing; yet now it is here, after all this waiting, and why waste the appointment? But this time I feel no sense of excitement as I climb the stairs, past the lecture theatre, to the second floor of the College of Psychic Studies. Inside room four, Arthur waits for me, a glass of water on the table before him, the sun shining through a wide open window. He gestures me to sit at a chair opposite him, and looks at me, through his pebble spectacles, his head cocked to one side like a magpie. And then he begins to speak, and at first all I hear is the echoes of other voices in his voice: Jewish, Italian, Spanish, northern English, merging and shifting and separating again. I say nothing. He pauses, as if listening to the silence, and then starts talking again. 'Your sister comes so close, she gives me goosebumps,' he says. 'Can you picture opposite your bed? She walks towards you from there every night, to say goodnight to you. You must have been more than sisters, you must have been very close friends. I know she comes every night . . . She talks to you as you fall asleep.'

He keeps talking, and I drink in his words. 'Your sister couldn't have loved you more than she did,' he says. 'Words cannot express her love. It's like a silent communication. And while you live, and she's on the other side, there will always be that bridge – she'll always be meeting you half way.'

'What does she want me to do?' I ask.

'She wants you to be happy,' says Arthur Molinary, with a small shrug of his shoulders in his buttercup cotton shirt.

He tells me other things, too: things I already know ('She had two lumps in her breast, and then her brain was troubled, she was confused and her legs grew weak, she couldn't walk . . . and when she died, she couldn't breathe, her lungs filled up . . . she died in the night, in the end, and in the morning you sat and held her body'); and things I didn't know. ('While you sat with her body, she woke up in brilliant sunshine, and she went out into the garden outside, into the light, and picked you a flower.') Then he says that she says that she is going cycling.

'She loved cycling,' I say. 'She was always riding off on her bike.'

'So she's still enjoying herself in the other world,' says Arthur, cheerfully. After a small pause, he asks me a question. 'Your sister says, why don't you believe in God?'

'Well, *she* never used to,' I say, evasively.

'She does now,' he says, with another slight shrug of his shoulders. This somehow seems to me unlikely, though I do not say so out loud.

And just who's talking, anyway? Is it the extraordinary Arthur Molinary, or my silent voice that he is listening to, or my sister's? Does he hear my thoughts or hers, or is he simply stating the obvious here? And does it matter, anyway, because I am her and she is me and she lives on inside my head and in my heart and courses through my blood, like life itself, there for anyone who looks to see.

At home that night, I listen to the tape that Arthur made for me of our session. There is much that is wondrous; there is also some that is inconsequential. (My dead grandmother says that I must tidy my house; my sister says that I should eat more Marmite, for the vitamins; that I drink too much water, which is flushing the vitamins away. What *is* it with the water, anyway?)

Mostly, though, he is sensitive. He is a very senior sensitive, after all. As I listen to the tape, my faith ebbs and flows, like the tide, like the river. But still I love my sister. And my sister loved me . . . And now I know, at least I think I know, that after all, after all of this, in the end there is a beginning. And there is life after death, because I am still living. I tell that to my husband as we lie in bed at the end of the long day. He listens to me and then says, 'Have I ever told you about my friend, Tony King, who killed himself? He walked into the River Thames and drowned. It was after the death of his mother, but also he heard voices in his head. He was schizophrenic . . .'

'Well, I'm not mad,' I say, 'if that's what you're suggesting . . .'

'I'm not suggesting anything,' says my husband, evenly. 'I'm just telling you about Tony . . . I'm sure I've told you this before – his mother died of a bee sting, and on my mother's birthday, he gave her a glass jar with three Roman nails in it that he had found on the shore of the river. He loved the river.'

'How did he know they were Roman nails?' I say, as if we're in court, not bed. 'That sounds too symbolic, like they were the ones used to nail Christ to the cross, or something.'

'I don't know if they actually were Roman,' says Neill, 'but that's what he believed them to be . . .'

'Go on,' I say, 'I'm listening.'

'A couple of years after Tony died,' he continues, steadily, 'you and I played on a Ouija board one night with some friends . . .'

'That doesn't sound like you,' I say, 'the great sceptic, and I don't remember anything of the sort . . .'

'It was our first New Year's Eve together,' he says; and then I do recall the scene, but only that: no words, no story.

'I still felt guilty about Tony, I suppose,' continues Neill, 'and I missed him. Anyway, I asked him where he was, and the board spelt "home". I said, "Where's home?" And he said, "the sea" . . .'

'So you do believe in something,' I say, point-scoring while missing the point, trying to keep a small note of triumph out of my voice.

'I don't believe in one thing or the other,' he says. 'But it made me feel better, that's all.'

'I'm feeling better now,' I say.

'I know,' he says. 'I'm glad.'

## Sunday 11 June

Pentecostal Sunday in the year 2000. The voice on the radio at breakfast this morning tells me that this is the day of the coming of Jesus's spirit: fifty days after he ascended to heaven, his spirit returned to his disciples on earth, just in the nick of time, just as they were sinking into despair as they waited for a sign in an upstairs room. I sneeze, once, twice ('bless you, bless you') and then switch off the radio, as if an allergen is emanating from within the machine.

In my upstairs room, an email has arrived from my father. He composed it yesterday as an early birthday present for me; a reconsideration of his father, written at my request. 'Your grandfather Louis was evangelized into an inspirational form of Christianity by a highly unorthodox class teacher when he was about nine or ten,' my father has written. 'He wept at the account of crucifixion . . . He was soft and sentimental, easily moved to tears . . . Later, people pitied me for having such a naive father and didn't blame me as much as him for my "meshuggassen" – madnesses . . . As well as going to seances he went in for aura-seeing, through violet-tinted motorcycle glasses,' my father continues crossly, though maybe he is smiling, as I do now, grateful for these fragile threads of memory that bind us together, the family ties transmitted from his computer screen to mine. 'I was shown the invisible aura of myself and others at the age of about eleven, and I knew from then on that my father belonged to the world of strange cults, which gave him the sense of belonging . . . Of course, he despised Freudian insights into his very evident mechanisms of denial and projection of his deep unease.'

There is more, but it's enough for now – I don't want to stay in with God on the radio or Christ on the computer (or Freud, which is where I know my father's birthday message is heading). So I send him a quick email back, telling him that I love him. Today the sun is shining, like yesterday, like tomorrow, and we go to the park: my husband and my children and some neighbours. The boys play football together, while I wander over to a gathering on the far side of the park, with my dead friend Kimberley's daughter, who is also my son's best friend. The local churches have congregated on the dried grass of the old bowling green for a Pentecostal celebration; Juliette and I hover at the outskirts, unwilling, or maybe simply unable to join in the hymns, because we don't know the words.

Some of the people around us are blind or in wheelchairs; deaf or lame or maimed. A woman walks towards us, and hands me a hymn sheet and order of service. 'HOLY SPIRIT WHO ARE YOU?' is printed on the page, and then the words to the hymn, 'Shine, Jesus, Shine'. I can see the choir and the congregation are singing, but their voices are lost in the open air. I can't hear the words, so I read them instead. 'Lord, I come to Your awesome presence/ from the shadows into Your radiance/ by the blood I may enter Your brightness . . .' Unfortunately, God doesn't speak to me, again, and I feel slightly embarrassed, as if I'm intruding. I glance down at Juliette; but she's not looking at me, she's looking at all the people around us, watching quietly, calmly, without saying a word.

'Shall we go?' I ask her.

'I don't mind,' she says, and then meets my eyes and smiles. I take her hand and we walk away, across the park, while the voices of the congregation drift into nothing behind us, drift away into the wide open sky, into the clouds and the blue where the dust swirls and the silence reaches all the way to the end of everything, where the dead wait, and speak in the beat of our hearts.

> So, if I dream I have you, I have you,
> For all our joys are but fantastical.
>
> John Donne, Elegy X, 'The Dream', *The Elegies*

## Tuesday 20 June

> All I can do is tell the truth. No, that isn't so – I have missed it. There is no truth that, in passing through awareness, does not lie.
>
> But one runs after it all the same.
>
> Jacques Lacan, Preface to *The Four Fundamental Concepts of Psycho-Analysis*

Today is my birthday. I was born in 1961, in my parent's flat in Hampstead. They had been married for eight months, and had known each other for less than three months before they got married. The summer before my birth, my mother met my father for the first time, when she saw him playing Ariel in an outdoor production of *The Tempest.* He ran across the water towards her. (Later, she told me that it only looked as if he walked on water; in fact, there had been a ramp submerged beneath the apparent waves.) So there they were, just twenty-two years old, and suddenly I arrived, a month early, feet first in an undiagnosed breech birth, and yellow with jaundice. My father was writing plays by then, as well as acting, and it can't have been easy, in a one-bedroom flat with a crying baby. I have a photograph from that time, where he is sitting looking at me, his unexpected daughter, with a perplexed expression on his boy's face. We left London for a while, when I was still a baby, and lived in a rented cottage in the middle of nowhere, so that he could have some more peace and quiet. My mother told me later that it was very lonely out there in the muddy English countryside, and she often wept over my bucket of sodden nappies, longing for escape.

My earliest memory is of going on a plane to South Africa with my mother, to visit her parents, who were living in Cape Town at the time. She was heavily pregnant with Ruth, which means I must have been two. When we were there, we went swimming in the sea, and afterwards I hid in a wardrobe at my grandparents' house while a church parade went past outside. (I always liked wardrobes as a child, long before I read C.S. Lewis's books about Narnia; and when I did discover his stories, with their revelation that escape lay just beyond the back wall of a wardrobe, I spent even more time sitting inside pieces of furniture, searching for the world on the other side.)

After the wardrobe and the sea, Ruth was born. My mother went to hospital one day and then she came back. I went upstairs, and there was a baby lying in a crib in the bedroom. I told my mother that I had found a baby, and she said, 'Yes, that's your new sister.'

Despite the urgings of therapists over the years that I must have felt jealousy towards Ruth, I never remember feeling anything other than love for her. My baby; my sister; my comrade. Ruth and me, me and Ruth, arms linked together against the rest of the world. She had curly dark hair and a wide smile. When other people were around, she always pretended to be brave, and roared like a lion at strangers, even if she was frightened. But I knew that she was scared, too, so that made me brave on her behalf.

We moved back to London from the country, and one day, in the park, she ran away and fell into a lake (the same lake that my father had run across, as Ariel? That's how I like to remember it, anyway). An old lady jumped in after her, but my mother rescued them both. We walked home to our flat in Marylebone High Street, Ruth dripping between us, my fierce, sweet sister.

When I was seven, my father got a job as a lecturer at Oxford University, so we moved there; first to another flat, and then to a tall thin house in a place called Jericho. Ruth and I slept at the very top of the house. Often I was frightened that someone would come up the stairs in the middle of the night, to get us; maybe a ghost or a bad man, a murderer, carrying a knife dripping with blood. Sometimes I had nightmares that I was being chased by the knifeman, but I couldn't run fast enough, and he always caught me, stabbed into my flesh. When I woke up, and couldn't go back to sleep again, I lay with my eyes closed, because if I couldn't see the ghosts or the bogeymen, then they couldn't see me.

One day, after school, I came home and my father wouldn't let me into the house. He said I was an anti-Jewish spy sent by the Catholic Church. I went for a walk instead, and waited for my mother to come home. There was a little door at the end of our road that led into the gardens of an Oxford college. I liked going there, to hide behind the trees and watch the ducks on the lake. There were special ducks, called 'Mandarins'. I never saw them anywhere else.

Not that day, but soon afterwards I think, my father had to go to hospital, for the electrical treatment. He was supposed to stay there, but he came home one night when he wasn't meant to, and smashed a window, and there was blood mixed up with the broken glass. He was shouting and crying at the same time, and my mother was weeping. I hid with Ruth in the corner, where he couldn't find us. I didn't tell anybody at school. It was our secret.

Another day after school, when my father wasn't living with us any more, and my mother was out, Ruth slipped and cut her face on a step down to the kitchen in the basement. She bled everywhere, blood gushing down her face, and I knew that she had to go to hospital, so I took her there (surely not? someone else must have driven us). She had stitches above her eye, and a little scar that stayed there for the rest of her life, to remind me that I hadn't taken good enough care of her that day.

Many years later – about three years ago, in fact – I told Ruth that I wouldn't let anything bad happen to her; that I wouldn't let her die, because I loved her so much. It was summer, and the days were long, but by then the tumour in her breast had spread to her lungs and her liver. She had more chemotherapy – poison, drip, drip, dripping into her veins – as I sat next to her, holding her hand, watching the blood drain from her face. But it didn't work. She died.

Today is my birthday, and I am another year older, though my sister is dead.

## Wednesday 21 June

The longest day of the year; the briefest midsummer night, when magic should happen for everyone who waits for it, where anything might come crashing through the sky. (When I was a child, and lost my first few milk teeth, I knew that it was not a tooth fairy who came into my room in the dark, bringing a secret sixpence, but Aslan: a longed-for yet ominous visitor; the lion who ruled Narnia. A fairy would be too small to come so far.)

Tonight I dream the dream that keeps coming back to haunt me. I am in our house – a different house from the one we actually live in – and as I climb the stairs to the top of the house, I know that something, or someone, is waiting for me. There is a room up there that I have not found before – a wrecked room, that needs rebuilding, but I'm too frightened to go inside it, because a ghost is on the other side of the door. It is not Ruth's ghost – just an evil spirit that fills the room; invisible yet terrifying; saying nothing, though I know it is there. Sometimes, in this recurring dream, I walk through the door and discover that there is a whole new wing to the house, with a series of uninhabited rooms, each more dangerous than the one before. Some of the rooms are piled with dusty furniture; others are empty, aside from the silent spirits. At the far end of the house – the place I never go to – I know that a madwoman waits, or maybe a madman. Sometimes it is a lunatic child, locked away in a tower room; whatever, the crazy person has nothing to do with me; does not belong to me. I will not go there.

## THURSDAY 22 JUNE

> Then Jesus said unto them, Verily, verily, I say unto you, Except ye eat the flesh of the Son of man, and drink his blood, ye have no life in you. Whoso eateth my flesh, and drinketh my blood, hath eternal life; and I will raise him up at the last day. For my flesh is meat indeed, and my blood is drink indeed.
>
> St. John, Chapter 6, verses 53–55

TODAY IS THE Feast of Corpus Christi; a day, according to the noticeboard outside our local Catholic church, dedicated to particular veneration of the Eucharist; a time to remember the holiest of Sacraments, which is the Sacrament of the Body and the Blood of Christ, who died to save our sins.

Occasionally I worry that I will die of breast cancer, but I don't often think about it (though I am this morning – of all mornings – which must be blasphemous, sinful, and entirely irrelevant on the occasion of Corpus Christi, when the holiness that surrounds the saved should be drifting out of the aisles of our local church, towards my house, perhaps, and up into the clouds of summer; but I don't seem to be able to help myself, and neither does Jesus, for that matter).

I know that I am probably 'high risk' – as the geneticists say – but it seems to me that Ruth did the dying for both of us. In medical terms, I am known as a 'surviving sister'. Even in a high-risk family, someone has to survive. The month after she died, I developed a lump in my left breast – but it was nothing, nothing but a bit of harmless gristle; grown there in grotesque sympathy, or symmetry, of the useless kind.

Where in our blood lies the code for breast cancer? What triggered it in Ruth, and not in me? Why do we not share this secret?

It must have been just about this time of year, three years ago, that I took her to another London hospital, for a second opinion on her terminal diagnosis. It was a clear midsummer morning outside, though the windows were closed to the outside world as we sat in the waiting room for an eminent professor of oncology. At last, when we were ushered into his consulting room, he seemed almost embarrassed to see us; as if the dying had no place here. He talked about chaos theory, about patterns of hereditary cancer in the Jewish community and mathematical models of the apparently random disease; but still, he could offer no hope. Afterwards, Ruth said, 'I used to think, "why me?" Now I think, "why not?"'

'But why not *me*?' I thought, though I did not say it out loud.

By then, I was beginning to learn to keep secrets from the sister I had once told everything. Sometimes, I was lost for words. I felt like I was searching for the answer to a puzzle – that the clues might be found in our flesh, perhaps, or in our cloudy history – but now I think the pieces of the puzzle are still missing; and even if I found them, it wouldn't help. The answer – the truth that I am searching for – is that Ruth's death is a mystery. It's as simple as that.

Not that it stops me searching, in circles that lead me back to the place where I started. Maybe I'm looking for both of us, after all.

## Saturday 24 June

> 'Shall I ever be able to read that story again; the one I couldn't remember? Will you tell it to me, Aslan? Oh do, do, do.'
>
> C. S. Lewis, Chapter 10, 'The Magician's Book', *The Voyage of the Dawn Treader*

I have a telephone appointment with Rita Rogers, who is probably the most famous medium in this country, in part because she did readings for her friend, Princess Diana, and also because of her work for the police in murder investigations. She has agreed to talk to me this afternoon (we have a mutual acquaintance); even though her waiting list is well over two years (and she is trying to do a little less work these days). I've been given a time to ring her at home in Derbyshire; her phone is engaged when I first try, but I keep hitting the redial button until she picks it up.

Rita says she doesn't know my surname, and she doesn't want to know it, either – 'I don't like having names and things, I don't want too much information from you.' Something told her she had to give me a reading, she says. 'I get fifty letters a day from people wanting readings. If I took every appointment I was asked for, I'd be booked ten years in advance. But I knew I needed to speak to you.'

For twenty minutes or so, she simply chats to me. 'I've spoke to spirits since I were four years old,' she says, 'and I'm going to be sixty next year. But from the age of four, I've known that people don't die – I hate that word *die* – people pass over.' She inherited the gift from her Romany grandmother; it runs in the blood, she says. Then Rita tells me a bit about Diana. 'She said, "Why does my presence bring people trouble?" Di thought she brought bad luck.'

'I know the feeling,' I say, but don't elaborate.

'It was like the princess and the pauper when she came to my house,' continues Rita. 'But she was never grand. All she needed was coffee and bananas – she loved them, you know.'

'Did you foresee her death?' I ask (not telling her that when Diana died, three weeks before my sister, Ruth said, 'I'll be next').

'Well, Di came up to see me with Dodi in a helicopter, not long before they died,' says Rita. 'He wanted a reading from me, and I must say, I've never been so cold and chilled as when I was doing that reading with Dodi. He sat on the settee with both his hands on the back of his head. He was a man of few words, was Dodi. All of a sudden, I got his mother in spirit, and his mum was giving a warning. I said, "Always keep your own driver, Dodi." And I mentioned a tunnel, water, and France – I asked him to avoid all those things, because I knew there was going to be a dreadful accident. He thought I meant the tunnel from France to Switzerland. So I did warn him – but I wasn't meant to stop him.'

She sighs, a small sigh, down the telephone, over a hundred miles away. 'The afternoon before they died, Di rang me from Paris at 4 p.m. I said, "Di, come home now." She said, "Oh, Rita,

I can't." I said, "I wish you were coming home, Di." And I did wish it, I did. Still, what's meant to be is meant to be. I feel she's happy now, and that's all that matters.'

Then, in the same conversational manner, she says, 'I'm getting a gentleman and a lady, on your mum's side. The lady's name is Patricia, and the gentleman is Frederick. They had ancestors, of the Catholic religion.'

'My maternal grandparents were called Patricia and Frederick,' I say.

'I know, dear,' she says. 'They've already told me that. And I'm getting an initial R . . . Ruth. She's with your grandparents, too. She's saying she had beautiful curly hair, but it went thin, when she had the cancer. She wants you to know that it's grown back again, and she's sending her love to everybody . . . She's very close to you. She's been blowing on your face, to let you know she's there. And she flutters around her children all the time. She adores those children. She says to you, be sure that they have good shoes.'

Now that Rita has got going, she keeps talking, without waiting for me to reply. She talks and talks, in a gentle, soothing monologue. 'Your sister Ruth loves to write stories,' she says. 'She reads stories to the spirit kids. And she says you've been very loyal to her. She wants you to know that she was afraid of dying, but now she's fine. And Michael, who's Michael? Oh yes, she says it's your dad. He has a very unsettled mind, buzzing away like a live wire, full of electricity, he is. There was a bit of a distance between you girls and him – your mum and dad are separated, they're not soulmates, are they? – but Ruth keeps an eye on him now. She says, you and he must make your peace with each other. He won't be around for ever, you know . . . He'll be popping off one day.'

I listen, while she speaks, and then pauses, as if she's hearing someone I can't hear. 'Now there's another lady here for you,' she says. 'She's called Kimberley, and she's saying you've got her daughter, Juliette, in the house right now.'

'I do,' I say, gulping, because Juliette is upstairs, playing with my children.

'Well, this lady Kimberley is saying, "Thank you". She was very down before she passed on – I don't think you could get any lower than she was. But she's in the light now, and having a wonderful time. Ooh, they're both talking at once, these two, Kimberley and Ruth, they've both got so much to say. And your grandmother, too, Patricia. She's saying her oldest son, your uncle, is called Richard. He's the good Catholic. And then there was your mum, and her twin brother, whose name begins with T . . . oh yes, Timothy.'

The names keep coming – of the living and the dead – in a quiet, domestic litany. There's nothing earth-shattering, except for the fact that most of these people have apparently been resurrected from the grave, down the phone from Derbyshire. (Or maybe her mind reads mine? Or does she voice my unspoken words; the words I cannot admit out loud?) I don't know what to say. I don't know who to say it to. (Should I be talking to Ruth, as if Rita wasn't there; or vice versa?) At the end, when it's time for Rita to stop, she says, 'If they're dead and gone, then who am I speaking to? I'm certainly not talking to myself, that's for sure.'

'Thank you so much,' I say.

'That's all right, dear,' she says. 'Bye bye.'

I put the phone down. I don't even understand how a telephone works – not the mechanics of how two voices are joined together from all those miles apart. I don't understand this, either. Later, when I tell a friend of mine about the experience, he says that maybe Rita could have looked up all this information about me on the Internet; or, more likely, read about Ruth in the past. I tell him that she didn't know my surname. 'That's what you think,' he says, darkly.

'Well, my grandparent's names aren't on a website, and nobody knew that Juliette was in my house during the reading,' I say. 'There'd have to be hidden cameras and spies in our road. Frankly, the conspiracy theory seems just as far-fetched as the fact that Rita Rogers can talk to the dead.'

'So you're a believer now?' says my friend, looking surprised and also slightly disapproving.

'Oh, I don't know,' I say. 'I wish I did. I wish Ruth would just talk to me, out in the open. It would be so much easier.'

'The voice of the converted,' says my friend. For a moment, I don't know whether he's talking about Ruth or me.

## Thursday 3 August

I am sitting in this house in Norfolk, a place so quiet that I can hear the cold tap dripping in the kitchen, the damp apple wood spitting on the fire, the dog sighing in her sleep. My younger son, Tom, is asleep in a bedroom upstairs with Juliette. Neill is in London. Jamie, my older child, is faraway in America with Neill's mother. Lola and Joe are also in America with Matt and his partner, Anna. It is close to midnight. I am the only person awake in this house; maybe the only one for miles around in the empty night country . . .

I think suddenly of Ruth. She consumes my body so completely that I feel adrenaline pumping through my blood, and I catch my breath, I can't breathe properly, I'm panicking, here in the quiet. At the same time, I look through the window into the dark outside. There is a handprint on the glass.

'Ruth?' I say.

There is no reply.

'Ruth, for God's sake, what are you doing?'

'Nothing,' says a voice in my head, but I don't know whether it's hers or mine or someone else's entirely.

'Nothing?' I whisper into the silence. 'You need to do

something.'

'I'm fading fast,' says the voice.

'Not for me, you're not,' I reply.

'Let me be,' says the voice. My heart is pounding, pounding. 'Let me be, let me be . . .'

I close my eyes, and I see Ruth closing her eyes too, like she did when she was dying, when she couldn't breathe any more, when she was fighting for breath through the oxygen mask on her face. The back of my neck is cold, as if someone is blowing night air onto it, as if the closed window has opened behind me. I am frightened. I say it out loud. 'I'm scared.'

'Of what?' says the voice in my head.

'Of Ruth . . . of Ruth's absence,' I reply.

On the ceiling of this room, there is the dark shadow of the smoke of some long-gone candle. Only the candlestick remains.

Is this all there is? Is this it? I am back where I started again, in the shadowlands, in the ashes.

## TUESDAY 15 AUGUST

TODAY IS THE Feast of the Assumption, the day when the Virgin Mary was taken up into heaven: not just her soul, but her body too. I remember this, I'm sure I do, from my childhood visits to the Christadelphian Sunday School. But what does the assumption refer to, I wonder? The ascent to heaven itself, or the supposition that the event had occurred? (When I seek clarification on this point from my friend Lola, who is a good Catholic godmother to my niece Lola, who was named after her, she says, 'The Feast of the Assumption celebrates when Mary was bodily assumed into heaven, when her body was glorified.' But then my mother's older brother, Richard Garnett, who is also a devout

Catholic, sends me an email with a different interpretation:

> The catechism of the Catholic Church teaches that it is the feast celebrating the Church's assumption that Mary, when 'the course of her earthly life had been completed, was taken up body and soul into the glory of heaven, where she already shares in the glory of her son's resurrection, anticipating the resurrection of all members of his body,' i.e. the community of believers.

When I read his final phrase, I realize that I am not yet a believer, nor in limbo still, but floating in a most unsatisfactory way. Could that be what the Church means by a lost soul?)

Later, I am walking home with Tom in the early evening, and just as we reach the end of our road, I see a young man walking towards us. He is wearing a purple anorak, and blood runs from his eyes, down his cheeks, like tears. In his hand, he is carrying a knife, which is also dripping with blood. Two other people pass him, and he screams at them, waving his knife. They run away. All this has happened in a few seconds, maybe less. I wonder if I have gone mad – if I am imagining things, because we should not have bleeding men wearing purple in this neat little road – and then I pull Tom close beside me to hide behind a neighbour's hedge, and we kneel down low, so that the man cannot see us, though who knows if he can see anything though his tears of blood. After he has passed by, we run down the road to our house, and once inside, I put a chain across the front door, to keep us safe.

'Mummy, close the curtains too,' says Tom, his face pale. 'The man might look through the windows.' I draw the curtains, and Tom climbs on to my lap. 'It's OK, sweetheart,' I say. 'It's OK. He can't see us.'

'We saw him,' says Tom.

'Yes, but he didn't see us,' I reply.

**Bleeding, charm to staunch. 1610,** MS book of physic. 'There were three Maryes went over the floude; The one bid stande, the other stente bloude: Then bespake Mary that Jesus Christ bore, Defende gods forbod thou shouldest bleede anye more . . .

Iona Opie and Moira Tatem,
*A Dictionary of Superstitions*

## SUNDAY 20 AUGUST

LOLA AND JOE'S fifth birthday. They are still in America. (Not long before Ruth died – just after the twins' second birthday – she wrote a note to herself in her sweeping, generous hand, though her writing was less sure by then, because of her brain tumour. 'GOALS,' she wrote. 'Lola and Joe's first day at school. Lola and Joe's fifth birthday.')

This morning, in the half-light before dawn, I dream that Ruth is lying in a bed in an empty room. She is very still, very quiet, very pale. 'Ruth?' I say. She doesn't answer. She is sleeping, though she may be close to death.

'Ruth,' I say, 'if you don't feel well enough, you don't have to go to America.'

'I don't feel well enough,' she replies.

I stroke her face, and then I notice, at the side of her bed, a woman, standing in shadow. All I can see is her naked back – and then her hand. She is holding a pill – a pill that will kill my sister. I knock it out of the woman's hand, and push her away.

Then in my dream, Ruth has gone, but my mother stands in the empty room. In her hand is a letter from Ruth. 'Ruth is in America,' says my mother. 'She has a brain tumour, but she is still alive, though she has forgotten about us all – about you, about me, about Lola and Joe. She has a new life now.'

Afterwards, in my dream, I am on an aeroplane. I don't know where I am going. It is hard to breathe. I need oxygen. There is someone beside me. I cannot see her face. She thinks she is thirsty – we are both thirsty, but I know we need oxygen, not water. We are gasping, gasping for breath, and the girl beside me, whose face I cannot see, reaches for a cup of water, and she drinks it, but it is not what she needs, it is the wrong cup, she drinks it and it kills her, like a draft of swift poison. People are watching and they laugh, they do not help her, and I cannot help her, I cannot breathe, I am dying, too. By chance, I reach out for the right thing – the thing that will save me – an oxygen mask, like the mask on Ruth's face when she died (though that did not save her). I fasten the mask over my face and I live. I live. I am the survivor.

I wake up, still gasping for breath. It is Lola and Joe's fifth birthday. I am still alive, but my sister is gone. I reach into the drawer beside my bed for a packet of pills. I swallow a tablet of Prozac – just one, that's all it takes – gulping it down with a glass of water.

~

## Saturday 26 August

I am going with the children to St Ives, in Cornwall, for a holiday. Neill is staying at home to work. It is the first time I have returned to the town since I was a child, when we went there one Easter with my friend the Christadelphian, and her father the physicist and the rest of her clever family. On the train today, I prod the memory of that last trip, which I have not wished to dwell on before. For a long time, it made me feel hot and sick whenever I tried to remember it, so I stopped thinking about it. Now, though, it just seems strange and faraway. It was cold, then. We stayed in a cold house, but my father was feverish with rage. Everyone was anti-Semitic, he said. They wanted Jews like him dead. And we were witches, too, he said, Ruth and me and my mother, evil Catholic witches, born into her evil Catholic family. At night, he didn't sleep, and he didn't want us to sleep either. During the day, he saw people on the street who were going to kill him. Anyone who wore purple was the enemy, sent to destroy him. I don't remember anything else about the holiday. It seems so odd that it ever happened at all.

Now, thirty years later, I am determined to be happy, but it is hard to get this right. When the sun shines, and the children swim in the sea, and I sit watching over them, I feel fine. I'm OK. Then it rains, and the sea turns grey, and the little chalet we are staying in is cold and damp and draughty, and as the smell of something lost and rotten rises from the drains, I smile at the children, but they know I may be drifting in the wrong direction.

'I'm missing Dad,' says Jamie, on the fifth day, when it is raining hard out of the thundery sky, and the weatherman is predicting gales. 'Can we go home now?' says Tom.

'Not yet,' I reply, still smiling. 'I know, we'll go to the museum, and look at the paintings. It will be fun.'

They look at me doubtfully, but follow me down the hill, through the graveyard that overlooks Porthmeor beach. 'Do zombies come out here at night?' says Tom.

'No,' I say.

'It's scary,' he says, as Jamie peers at the headstones in the rain.

'No it's not,' I say. 'Graveyards are gentle places.'

At the bottom of the hill, we reach the Tate Gallery. 'This wasn't here when I was a little girl,' I say, as we walk inside. Upstairs, it is crowded with other people who have sought refuge from the rain, but I want my children to see the paintings of Alfred Wallis, whose St Ives is as grey and dark as mine. His little ships are tossed on the charcoal sea, beyond the graveyard where we walked today, beyond the chapel of St Nicholas, who cannot save the sailors in a storm. (The curator's notes beside the paintings explain that Wallis was seen by his contemporaries as 'a man locked up darkly in himself'; aggressive and tormented by the voices in his head. After his wife died, he did not go upstairs again in their house, but lived, slept and painted in a downstairs room. In the 1930s, he began to hear a female voice – the 'Douty Mighty' – who scolded him for his sins. Sometimes he stayed up all night, arguing with this and other spirits; during the day, he tried to set his mind at rest by clearing the chimney – from which the spirits emerged – of what he described as 'wires'.)

Afterwards, I buy ice creams for the children, and half a dozen Alfred Wallis postcards for myself. Later, I flick through them, half-searching for hidden reasons about why I have come back to St Ives, or why my father went mad here, though I can see that looking for answers in this place might be a sign of my own madness; and anyway, I'm not sure if the things I find are clues or red herrings.

~

## Saturday 16 September

It is the day after Jamie's eleventh birthday. He is having a party this afternoon. In the morning, while I am washing up, Tom stands on Jamie's new birthday skateboard in the kitchen next to me, sucking a 'Loveheart' sweet, wearing his Pokémon pyjamas.

'There are swings in heaven,' he says, indistinctly, still sucking his sweet.

'What?' I say, confused.

'I. SAID. THERE. ARE. SWINGS. IN. HEAVEN,' he repeats, very loudly and slowly, as if to an imbecile.

'Do you think they have bicycles in heaven too?' I say.

'No, of course not,' he says. 'Bicycles would fall through the clouds.'

'What about the swings?' I say.

'The swings are fine,' he says.

'Who told you that?' I ask, worried that my death obsession may be affecting him adversely.

'Angus, of course,' he says. Angus is his best friend. I go over to Tom, to kiss him, but he still has his sweet in his mouth, and pokes out his tongue to show me. On the Loveheart is the message, 'MEET ME'. I'm considering whether to take this as a sign from Ruth, though I can see that in doing so I might be moving into more dangerous territory. (My imaginary therapist suggests that finding messages in confectionery is one of the first indications of schizophrenia . . .)

## FRIDAY 22 SEPTEMBER

HALF PAST MIDNIGHT. Three years ago, Ruth was nearly dead. 'Not dead,' says the voice in my head. 'Just changing.'

'No, not dead,' I agree, looking at the flame of the candle I have lit for my sister tonight. It does not flicker; it burns so brightly.

'Oh my darling, oh my darling, oh my darling Clementine, thou art lost and gone for ever, dreadful sorry, Clementine,' sings Ruth's voice in my head, singing the song she always sang as a child; the song she sang to my children, and later to her own, even when she was too sick to lift them in her arms. (I can't remember the whole song, only bits and pieces, but they go round and round my head: 'In a cavern, in a canyon, excavating for a mine, dwelt a miner, Forty-niner, and his daughter, Clementine. Oh my darling, oh my darling, oh my darling Clementine, but I kissed her little sister, and forgot my Clementine . . .')

A few months before she died, she lay on this bed with me – the bed I am lying on now alone. She cannot be far away from me tonight. She must be close. I hear . . . the clock, just the clock. I switch the light off. The candle flame fills the room.

I fall asleep, and dream that I have been given my sister's telephone number where I can ring her now, right now. I write it down, and when I wake up, I am sure it is there by the side of the bed. I look, but can see nothing. It is still dark, so I switch the bedside light on, but there is nothing. 'What's wrong?' says Neill, sleepily.

'Nothing,' I reply.

## Monday 2 October

Judith Chisholm is having a party. I am invited, along with the rest of her friends, most of whom have some involvement with EVP or other psychic matters. Tonight, her house seems lighter than when I came here before, and Judith is glowing; her spirits have lifted.

Inside the living room, I am introduced first to Mike, a divorced British Telecom engineer who lives in Dagenham with his teenage daughter and a snake, who is fed on frozen mice ('Well, we thaw them first,' says Mike, who is a stickler for detail.) Mike, like Judith, spends a great deal of time conducting experiments in EVP, but, unlike her, he says that he gets his best results in receiving the spirit voices when he plays his tapes backwards. He tries to explain to me why this should be so, but his science loses me, so I sit and listen while he discusses EVP with Judith's son Vic, who brings his knowledge as an electrician to the subject. 'The most important thing, is that the spirits need background noise to come through,' says Mike. He and Vic tell me about Dr Konstantin Raudive, a Latvian psychologist and former student of Jung who made thousands of recordings of 'spirit voices' in the 1950s and 60s, against a background of white noise from a radio tuned between stations. Then they talk about Nikola Tesla, the turn of the century scientist who invented alternating current electricity generators. 'He was on to something,' says Mike, 'he was working towards EVP.'

'It's all to do with magnetism,' says Vic.

'Ultrasonic receivers,' says Mike.

'Do you think ghosts ride bicycles?' I ask, during a brief pause in their conversation, but they look at me as if I am completely mad, so I excuse myself, and join another group on the other side of the room. These people are: Judith's friend Andrea; Andrea's mother, who is a Jehovah's Witness; Andrea's American boyfriend Scott, a former FBI agent who has recently moved to London to be closer to Andrea; and John, who used to be a prison officer at Strangeways, but is now the editor of *Psychic World*, and the author of *Psychic Pets*. 'I've seen spirits since I was a child,' says John, 'but my parents told me never to talk about such things. So I kept quiet – and it made me sick.'

Andrea's mother, however, says she agrees with John's parents; that this stuff should be left well alone. 'Spiritualism is the work of the devil,' she declares, which leaves a slightly uneasy silence. We are joined at this point by Joe, who believes in fairies, and Desmond, an ebullient medium from Belsize Park. Desmond does a demonstration of spirit writing for my benefit, holding a notebook at arm's length, with his head turned in the opposite direction, while his hand scrawls something illegible. 'See?' he says. 'Yes,' I say, though I'm not quite clear what it is I'm supposed to be seeing, and I ask Desmond instead about whether ghosts might ride bicycles but he says he's not sure. 'They can play musical intruments, though,' he adds, and tells me about how he had the ghost of Ivor Novello in his flat last night, patting young men on the bottom with his invisible hands, and tinkling cocktail tunes on Desmond's piano.

By 11.30 p.m., the party is still going with a swing, and everyone is tremendously cheerful, even Andrea's mother the Jehovah's Witness. 'You look so much happier than when we first met,' I tell Judith, just before I leave.

'Well, maybe it's you that's made me happy,' she says, 'coming along here and taking an interest, believing in me and everything.'

As I drive home, I'm still smiling, and when I get back, I switch on my computer, and decide, on the spur of the moment, to send Ruth an email. I send three: one to Ruth@heaven.com; another to Ruthie@heaven.com; and a third to Ruthie@heaven.co.uk.

'Are you there?' I type. 'I miss you. All my love, Justine.'

I send the messages, and wait for a reply. I keep checking my inbox, but it is getting very late, so I go to bed, though I'm wide awake and wired. After a few sleepless hours, I get up again, in the middle of the night, and switch the computer back on. There are two messages waiting. I open them. The first one says: 'Name service error for domain heaven: host not found.' The second says: 'The following addresses had transient non fatal errors.'

Maybe I can find the right address, if I just keep looking?

## Friday 6 October

I ring my mother and ask her how my father is. She would be perfectly entitled to tell me to ring him myself (they're not married, after all), but she doesn't. 'It's the Day of Atonement,' she says, 'so I expect he's in synagogue, atoning for his sins, whatever they might be.' I don't respond, so she says, politely, 'And you, how are you?'

'I'm wondering if ghosts ride bicycles,' I say.

'Well, I don't know if I can help,' she says, as patiently as ever. 'But I do have a recurring dream that I'm riding a bicycle up a hill, with you on the back seat and Ruth sitting in the basket, and my mother and father on the cross bar. It's such a struggle. I'm always trying to get somewhere, but I never arrive.' She pauses, and then continues. 'You may not remember, but when you were very little, you used to ride your bike on the street outside our house, round and round in circles. Ruth was still a baby then.'

## SATURDAY 14 OCTOBER

> . . . no matter where we die on earth, each of our tunnels leads to exactly the same entrance on The Other Side. This entrance is in the quadrant that geographically corresponds to the west coast of our North American continent, and it's there that our Spirit Guides, angels, and other loved ones come to joyfully welcome us Home.
>
> Sylvia Browne, *Life on the Other Side: A Psychic's Tour of the Afterlife*

RUTH'S BOOK IS being published in America, and I am going there: to speak for Ruth; to search for her, also . . . I have dreamt so many times now that she is there, in the new world, waiting for me. So I am flying to New York (and maybe I will find her there). Aside from the interviews I must do on Ruth's behalf, I have made two private appointments in Manhattan. The first is to see a woman, a highly sought-after singing teacher; though I am hoping she will produce ghosts for me, rather than Broadway tunes, because she also channels spirits in her spare time. The latter of her talents comes highly recommended by a friend of mine (a business-like person, not the sort you would expect to search for ghosts; but I've discovered that the most unlikely people share my obsession, all with good reasons of their own). The second appointment is to meet a lawyer named Dale E. Palmer, who is pre-eminent in the field of EVP in America. We have exchanged several cautious emails (the American Association of EVP researchers to which he belongs seems more secretive than its British counterpart); and it now turns out that Mr Palmer will be visiting New York at the same time as me: which must signify something – something auspicious – because actually, he lives in Indiana, and does not often visit the East Coast. I have high hopes of these meetings; but first I have to get to New York, and this does not seem an easy thing to do.

When I say goodbye to Neill and the children, my heart is pounding, I'm panicking, but trying to seem calm. They drop me at the entrance to the tube station, and I'm frightened that I'll never see them again, which is ridiculous, of course. (When Ruth said goodbye to Lola and Joe and Matt, on the night that she died, did she know that this was the end, the last kiss, the last touch? 'This is not the end,' I said to her, before she lapsed into final unconsciousness. 'You'll still be with us, and we will be with you, I promise.')

It is raining outside; the rivers of southern England are overflowing; the water is rising to levels that have never been seen before, and I'm leaving my children behind. I must be mad; but it's too late to turn back. I am going to America. I am going there.

The aeroplane takes off through the autumn sunset, and for a few seconds, my spirits soar, here in the sunlight. But then we're in the grey cloud, and I can't see anything; I can't hear anything; my ears are blocked and popping. I can't hear Ruth.

'Ruth?' I say, inside my head.

'Yes,' she says.

'Where are you?

'With you.' The voice in my head – her voice, my voice, who knows what voice – starts singing. 'Oh my darling, oh my darling, oh my darling Clementine, thou art lost and gone for ever, dreadful sorry, Clementine . . .'

'That's not very helpful,' I say.

'I'm further away,' she says. 'You're further on.'

'Don't leave me,' I say.

'I'm not,' says the voice in my head. 'But you've got to live by yourself, without me.'

'I don't want to.'

'I know.'

'What will I do without Arthur Molinary? He lets you speak to me.'

'Speak for yourself.'

'This is not good enough.'

'This is all there is . . .'

She is gone. I cannot hear her. The pressure in the cabin is rising (or is it falling? either way, I don't think I'm thinking straight). I scrabble for my headphones – there is a movie I could watch called *Frequency*, which stars Dennis Quaid as a man who tunes into his dead father's voice on his old ham radio. I turn the dial to the correct channel, but I still can't hear anything. Then there is an announcement. 'Due to static, we will not be showing the film on Channel 2.' Channel 2 is the one I want. Channel 2 is the ghost channel. I can't watch the film, and my sister won't speak to me.

'I *am* talking,' she snaps. 'Just listen, OK?'

'I am listening,' I say.

'One, two, buckle my shoe, three, four, open the door.'

'Oh, that's really helpful,' I say. 'Wonderful. Thanks a lot.'

'Scraps and rubbish,' she says. 'Stuff and nonsense. Just make it up for yourself.'

'I am doing,' I say. 'And it's not getting me anywhere.'

I stare out of the window, as we fly west to America. On the edge of the sky, in the place where we are going, there is a faint red blur of the setting sun. Night is falling, but the light grows brighter in the west. Out here, it is darkness; ahead, there is daylight. To reach America, we must go back in time. I am going back there, to where the sun is rising in the west.

On Channel 2, a different film is showing, called *Field of Dreams.* In it, Kevin Costner is reunited with his dead father, and a team of ghosts play baseball on the cornfield in front of his farmhouse.

'It's so beautiful here,' says one of the ghosts. 'For me, well, it's like a dream come true. Can I ask you something? Is . . . is this heaven?'

'It's Iowa,' says Costner.

'Iowa?' says the ghost. 'I could have sworn it was heaven.'

## Sunday 15 October

> In reality we are weak, hence the heroes of fairy-tales are strong and unconquerable; in our activities and our knowledge we are cramped by time and space, hence in fairy-tales one is immortal, is in a hundred places at the same time, sees into the future and knows the past. The heaviness, the solidity and the impenetrability of matter obstruct our way every moment: in the fairy-tale, however,

man has wings, his eyes pierce the walls, his magic wand opens all doors . . .

Sandor Ferenczi, *Stages in the Development of the Sense of Reality*

THIS MORNING, AFTER I have talked about Ruth on a morning TV show for three minutes precisely, her publishers have arranged for me to go on a sponsored walk to raise money for breast cancer research, with a group of young women called 'The Young Survivors Coalition'. We meet in Central Park, under a blue sky filled with pink balloons. Everyone here talks about living; about cancer cures and beating the disease. It seems impolite to mention the dead. (When Ruth knew that the cancer had spread from her breast to her lungs and liver, she said, briefly, that she felt like 'a failure'. 'It's not your fault,' I said. 'No one could have fought harder than you.' 'If anybody mentions "positive thinking" again,' she said, 'I'm going to punch them.')

In the afternoon, I catch a cab to the Upper West Side, to an apartment block very close to the river, where I am to meet Jeannie the spirit channeller; the genie of New York. She has curly auburn hair, like a halo, calm brown eyes, and the face of a worn, Botticelli angel who has found herself unexpectedly transported to this city. There are cherubs and seraphim of all kinds (plaster, plastic, ceramic, cloth) decorating her music room, which is where she leads me for the channelling session. Her day job, she says, 'is teaching people to find their voices'. On the shelves opposite the sofa where I am sitting, there are books about stagecraft. ('Actors on Acting'; 'Producing Theatre'; 'Stage Makeup'.) Lace curtains filter the streetlight outside. There are trailing green ferns on the table beside me, and a large ceramic frog. On the far wall, a printed text says, 'I came to live out loud.'

Jeannie explains to me that she has a spirit guide called 'Shiang'. She will go into a trance, and then Shiang will speak through her, to give me guidance and advice. Shiang speaks

English, says Jeannie, 'because I speak English'. If he spoke in his native tongue – whatever that might be – Jeannie would not be able 'to vocalize it'. However, I will be able to hear the change in her voice when she is channelling Shiang. 'The pattern of my speech will change when he is present,' she says. 'We refer to Shiang as a he, but I'm not so sure that he couldn't be a she. Shiang also consults other guides and teachers and passes on their thoughts. But they're not very good on specifics – names, dates and so on. These entities' time frame is enormous. Plus, they have to translate a vast textured multi-dimensional image into linear language.'

Jeannie closes her eyes, and settles back into her chair. The room is silent, apart from the clock and the sound of her breathing. She sways slightly, and then starts speaking. At first, I have to stifle a giggle – like a child in church, or school assembly – because her new voice (Shiang's voice) is so unexpected. She (or he) speaks English, but with a Chinese accent, and what sounds to my uneducated ear like a Brooklyn tang. 'Hong Kong Fooey,' sings Ruth's voice in my head. 'Shut up,' I hiss, silently.

Shiang tells me that Ruth was a sea captain in another life. She had to fight her way through pirates and storms, across oceans to unexplored territories. Also, in *another* other life, we were sisters in medieval Europe, and I died first, leaving Ruth to grieve for me. Throughout the centuries, Ruth and I have always loved each other. Now that she dwells in the land of the spirits, she loves me still; just as I love her.

There's some more stuff: about learning to let go; about going with the flow; that kind of thing. It goes over my head, but in a nice, peaceful way. Then Jeannie bends forwards, and comes out of her trance. 'Boy, that was a long, long journey,' she says, shaking her auburn curls. 'I have to contain the vibration of the beings – this profound energy squeezing itself into my little consciousness. Then when Shiang leaves, I feel empty for a moment. But it's never draining, it's always restorative. This is the source of all energy – like a refreshing mountain stream . . .' Jeannie gives me a book which she thinks I will find helpful (Sylvia Browne's *Life on the Other Side: A Psychic's Tour of the Afterlife*). I give her $120, which is her fee for the session.

Outside, it is raining in the dark, and I catch a cab downtown back to my hotel. The cabdriver is listening to a Spanish radio station. When I speak to him, he does not understand me; we conduct our transaction in unsuccessful mime language instead. In the lift at the hotel, two men have a conversation in what might be Dutch; the other man in the lift raises one eyebrow at me, almost imperceptibly, and one corner of his mouth curls. I'm not sure what he's trying to say. I get lost on the fourteenth floor, and have to retrace my steps back to the lift shaft and consult the floor plan. Then I find my room, but the key doesn't work, and by the time I get in, it's too late to call Neill in London. He will be sleeping, five hours ahead of me. I lie on the bed, and gaze at the ceiling. 'This is the tower of Babel,' I say, out loud, but no one is listening. It strikes me, perhaps, that I am being over-dramatic. I chose to come here, after all. I take a sleeping pill, and put some earplugs in, and pull the quilt over my head. The city is very noisy, even in the middle of the night.

> Now the whole earth had one language and few words. And as men migrated from the east, they found a plain in the land of Shinar and settled there . . . Then they said, 'Come, let us build ourselves a city, and a tower with its top in the heavens, and let us make a name for ourselves, lest we be scattered abroad upon the face of the whole earth.' And the Lord came down to see the city and the tower, which the sons of men had built. And the Lord said, 'Behold, they are one people, and they have all one language; and this is only the beginning of what they will do; and nothing that they propose to do will now be impossible for them. Come, let us go down, and there confuse their language, that they

may not understand one another's speech.' So the Lord scattered them abroad from there over the face of all the earth, and they left off building the city. Therefore its name was called Babel, because there the Lord confused the language of all the earth; and from there the Lord scattered them abroad over the face of all the earth.

Genesis, Chapter 11, verses 1–9

## Monday 16 October

The Hall of Records, the Hall of Wisdom, and the Hall of Justice are the first buildings to greet us on The Other Side. Directly behind them rise the Towers, two identical structures, tall and contemporary in architecture, reverent monoliths with massive facades of white marble and blue glass. Waterfalls whisper down the walls, misting the jasmine that scents the air around them and promising the exquisite serenity that waits inside their etched golden doors . . . The eternal pastel light of The Other Side, filtered through the Towers' blue glass, creates a peace and a heightened infusion of God's love.

Sylvia Browne, *Life on the Other Side: A Psychic's Tour of the Afterlife*

I WAKE AT 5 A.M., that half-time between day and night, and I'm not sure if I'm asleep or awake; if I'm talking out loud or in my head.

'So Ruth,' I say, 'what's this about the bicycles on the other side?'

'The wheels are circles,' she says.

'You're going all mystical on me,' I say.

'You're the one who's into magical thinking,' she says, tartly.

'The first time I rode a bicycle by myself, I couldn't believe how fast I went, how free I felt . . .'

'Exactly,' she says. 'Now get some rest.'

**6.15 a.m.** I can't sleep so I switch on the television. A bicycle streaks across the screen. 'Think about bikes all day long,' says a voice. Then a word appears on the screen: 'Guardian'. I know it's an advertisement for something, but I'm not sure what, exactly. I wonder if I'm supposed to see this as an omen, of some sort, for the day. (Postcards, sweets, television advertisements – these days, I take signs wherever I find them.)

I've arranged to meet Dale Palmer at his hotel at 8.30 a.m. It's only a few blocks away, so I walk, clutching my umbrella, trying not to bump into anyone in the rush-hour tide. Dale's hotel is overlooking Times Square: a tall skyscraper, with dozens of people passing through reception, and a waterfall in the midst of it all. I take the gold and glass elevator to the forty-fifth floor, which is where Dale is staying with his family. It goes up so fast that my ears pop, and I'm not sure if I can hear properly. I get out of the elevator, and walk along the corridor. On one side, the wall is waist-high, fringed with what may be real plants (though it seems unlikely); and I peer over the edge, down into the chasm below, hundreds of feet down to the ground floor. On the other side is the entrance to Dale's room. I knock on the door.

The man who opens it is silver-haired, blue-shirted; and he looks, I think, like the Wizard in *The Wizard of Oz*. We shake hands, and then the man – Mr Palmer, I presume – shows me into the hotel suite. It is very large, very plush; an anonymous eyrie, high in the sky. A sign next to the telephone says, 'Connect to the world beyond your room.' Dale's granddaughter, Kelly, is sitting at the head of a mahogany table: slight, silent, composed. I shake hands with her, and with Dale's wife, Kay, and his daughter-in-law, Kelly's mother, Linda. He explains that his son Hunt, Linda's husband and Kelly's father, died suddenly three months ago of a mysterious virus. The trip to New York has therefore been planned to cheer everyone up. They are going to see a Broadway show, and have lunch at Rockerfeller Plaza, and then they're going out to dinner. 'This is the make-Linda-laugh initiative,' says Dale. But Linda still looks bleak, and retires to another room with Kay.

'Kelly will take notes, and tape our meeting,' says Dale. 'She works as a translator back home.' He has already asked me to email my questions about his EVP research in advance, and has prepared written replies. He hands me five closely printed sheets of paper. 'Those are your answers,' he says, and takes a seat opposite me at the table.

'Shall I read it now?' I say, slightly taken aback at the silence in the room.

'Go ahead,' says Dale. Kelly, meanwhile, remains motionless.

I start reading. 'Questions: How did you first hear about EVP? When did you start investigating it? What equipment do you use?'

'Answers: Willis Harmon, late President of the Institute of Noetics Sciences, and I were friends . . . My research into Egyptian history had convinced me that communications among dimensions of reality is possible and was actually taught as an art in the Ancient Mystery Schools. In 1994, I told Willis that clearly communications were possible and theoretically should be possible with the proper electronic equipment. Willis asked me to check into the matter and report back to him.

'Immediately, I began a search, which led to Sarah Estep, the Dean of all experimenters in the US, who had already been communicating with a reel-to-reel tape recorder for twenty years. The equipment she uses is relatively simple. Sarah Estep says: "When using an open reel-to-reel tape recorder, I use a TEAC. I always use a microphone, with a metal funnel over the head. That helps make the voices louder. The tape recorder is connected to my Numark Stereo Tape Deck Tone Calibrator-Mixer. You can also use that to help amplify the voices . . ."'

I stop reading. I'm only half-way down the first page, and I'm already confused. 'Um, do you mind if I read this later?' I say. 'I'm finding it hard to concentrate.'

Dale inclines his head, very slightly. Then he gestures towards the paperwork, and says, 'I'm a trained lawyer – I was the District Attorney in Indianapolis for some years.' That's why he prefers to keep things precise: 'My first task as a prosecutor was to separate the real from the unreal.' It is a skill, he says, that he continues to use in his investigations into the spirit world. 'There are in the world some valid mediums – of that I'm reasonably sure. There are also, I suspect, some who aren't. I've seen more unconvincing mediums than convincing ones. You have to search for a long time.'

I can't follow everything he is telling me: he talks rapidly about the Ancient Mystery Schools, and the lost art of communication with the dead. 'Plato almost tells us how this is done. I'm sure he was a graduate of the Mystery Schools. Master Jesus was, too . . .' Now, however, he believes the future lies in electronic communication with the spirit world: 'Logic suggests that if you as an individual can sit in a room and sense those things, then there have to be electro-magnetic waves that you can detect with the right equipment.'

This is where Dale comes in: he is not a medium, nor can he hear the current experiments in EVP (or EDP – for Electronic Disturbance Phenomena, as he prefers it to be known), as conducted by Judith Chisholm and Sarah Estep, because he is somewhat deaf. But he does have the money and the enthusiasm to set up a computer research project in his hometown – Plainfield

– in Indiana. 'My family foundation will provide all the funds,' he says.

The project is part of GAIT, which stands for Global Association of Instrumental Transcommunication (an organization that Dale set up with Sarah Estep in 1997). Dale's foundation is called the Noetics Institute, Inc, (NII). 'It is our hope and our plan that we have software like no other in the world,' he says, referring me back to page four of his document. 'We have electrical engineers working in several different areas of assigned research. One is working to create software that will enhance the level of voices so that everyone, even the hearing impaired like me, can hear them.

'Phase two of the GAIT plan is to develop equipment for conveying images among dimensions of reality. Erland Babcock, a retired technician from MIT and the University of Massachusetts, is our leader on images. Erland has already recorded some faint, barely discernible images.'

'Ghosts on the computer screen?' I ask.

'Erland has shown me film in which he can see images,' says Dale.

'But can you see them?' I say.

'I can't identify them specifically,' says Dale. 'Do you ever look at the clouds and see pictures in them?'

'Yes,' I say.

'Well, it's kinda like that.' I feel like I'm getting lost in some sort of maze here. Dale can't hear the spirit voices, nor can he see the spirit images, but he seems to know that they are there. My face must betray my confusion, because then he adds, 'The thing you've got to bring to the table is that you're not going to comprehend what we're doing until you take a quantum jump in mind set. We are so body set in our thinking. But our body is just like a suit of clothing or an automobile that we buy or we use for a very short period of time.'

I'm still looking confused, so Dale draws a dot on a blank piece of paper. 'Over 99 per cent of an atom is empty space,' he says. 'There's the nucleus' – and he points to the dot. 'I suggest you think of the atom as being like reality.' He points to the dot again. 'The physical universe is the dot – that's the limit of our vision at this time.'

'Hmm,' I say.

'You and Kelly are lucky,' he says, smiling at his silent grandchild. 'You may get to see so many new things – like the doorway that will go from one dimension to another. I think it may go through the zero point field . . .'

'What about emails?' I say. 'Could I send an email to my sister? Or you to your son?'

He directs me back to page four of the paperwork. 'There it is,' he says. 'It's all written down there for you.'

I start reading again, from the paragraph he has marked. 'It is our hope and plan to create a Website early next year where anyone in the world who has a computer and is on the Internet can log on and do his or her own experiments free of charge. One will also be able to store in the computer a private identification code. In the coming years, after transition, one can communicate back to this dimension and reveal their personal private code. This can then be verified at the NII Computer Center.'

'Does transition mean death?' I say. Kelly flinches slightly. Dale nods. 'So Ruth could send me a message – a private code – and I would know it was her? Via the computer?' Dale nods again.

'That's amazing,' I say.

'I have the computer,' says Dale, 'but I do not yet have it programmed. This will be a very big job.'

Dale has other plans, too. 'NII has invited Dr Edvaldo Cabral, Professor of Electrical Engineering at the University of São Paulo, to write his theory of Emotons in English. It will be on the Website and will show the world the science behind all of these events. It explains all of the so-called psychic phenomena.'

'I still don't think I understand,' I say.

'Machines are not chaotic,' he says, pointing to his tape recorder. 'They have order . . .'

'I wish you could have met my grandfather,' I say. 'I didn't really know him, but I have a feeling you would have got on with each other. He wrote poetry – he won a Bardic chair for his poems in a competition – and he was a spiritualist, too. I don't think the rest of my Jewish relatives approved.'

'Technically, I'm a Methodist,' says Dale, 'but really, I'm sort of a Buddhist in my views.' He smiles at me, and unexpectedly, I feel tears pricking behind my eyes.

'I'd better go now,' I say.

'Come back tomorrow,' he says. 'We can have breakfast together.'

I stand up and hug him (I'm not sure why – he has a grave formality, and I'm usually more hesitant than this – but it seems like the right thing to do). He feels very solid, very stable, very real inside my arms. 'Thank you,' I say. 'I'd really like to come again . . .'

I say goodbye, and take the lift down forty-five floors, back down to the ground again. Then I find a cab, because I've got another television interview to do. On the way, the driver has a long, complicated conversation, to an invisible companion beside (or inside) him. Once, this would have disturbed me. Now, it seems perfectly fine. I wonder if I'm lapsing into insanity, like my father, or my grandfather, for that matter. If so, it's not too frightening, after all. Maybe madness is just a staging post on the journey to the other side.

Dear Professor Freud,

. . . Occultism is another field we shall have to conquer . . . There are strange and wondrous things in these lands of darkness. Please don't worry about my wanderings in these infinitudes. I shall return laden with rich booty for our knowledge of the human psyche. For a while longer I must intoxicate myself on magic perfumes in order to fathom the secrets that lie hidden in the abysses of the unconscious . . .

Kindest regards,

Most sincerely yours,

Jung

8 May 1911, The Freud/Jung Letters

## TUESDAY 17 OCTOBER

I'VE GONE BACK to Times Square to meet Dale and Kay Palmer, and this time he hasn't provided a printed list of answers to my questions, which seems to be a mark of some kind of faith. It's 8 a.m. – lunchtime in London, breakfast in New York. We're eating in the restaurant of his hotel, around the corner from the glass and gold elevator to the forty-fifth floor. Dale is telling me about his long-ago childhood: he was ten months old when his father died in 1933. 'My mother could find no employment, and in August 1936 I was placed in a foster home, when I was just under four years old.'

'Did you see your mother again?' I ask.

'I saw her from time to time,' he says.

'That must have been very hard for you,' I say, 'and hard for her, too.'

He nods his head. 'You have to remember this was southern Indiana in the thirties,' he says. 'There were no good roads, no telephones, no electricity, no food. Every Friday, my mother had to walk four or five miles to the Poor Relief Fund to get us something to eat . . .' Dale had a sister, Laura, who was four years older than him, and who stayed with his mother. 'My sister and I were very close,' he says, 'but she died in 1960.'

'You've had a lot of death in your life,' I say.

'There is no death,' he replies, his grave face turned to mine. 'Master Jesus himself said that. You have to change your way of thinking – you have to think of this brief visit to New York City as life – it's such a temporary thing. You're here for a few days, and then you're going home.'

'I find it hard to think that way,' I say, because there seems no reason in pretending to be something other than who I am to this man. 'I can't stop wishing that my sister was still alive.'

'It doesn't mean that I don't miss my son terribly, *terribly*,' he says.

'Have you communicated with him since his death?' I ask.

'I've felt him,' says Dale, slowly, 'but actual communication, no . . . And you, does your sister speak to you?'

'I'm not sure,' I say. 'Maybe when I'm on aeroplanes. But maybe it's just my voice in my head . . .'

'No, I think there has to be some way she's manipulating your environment in the aeroplane,' he says. 'You're far away from the grossness of the earth. What you have to remember is that if everything is a form of vibration, we're at the lowest level here. When a human being goes through transition, the vibratory rate increases. I'm talking about physics – I'm not talking about mediumship.'

'But have you ever heard the voice of a dead person?' I ask.

'Only the one time,' he says. 'It was an EDP experiment, and I said, "Is Dr Raudive there?" The reply was, "He's here." That was all – but that was all I needed. The thing is, I'm hearing impaired, as you know, so I have to get the technology right, before I'll be able to hear these voices. At the moment, some people can decompress them with their mind – but only by listening to the tapes ten or twenty times.'

We finish our breakfast, and Kay takes a picture of Dale and me together, smiling for the camera, and then we wave goodbye. The Palmers are going home today, back to Plainfield, Indiana (a name that I've fallen in love with; a small, clean town that I imagine surrounded by fields of corn and dreams). I've got two more days in New York, but I almost wish that I was going with them, flying further to the west. I still don't know why I feel so drawn to this odd yet sweet-faced man: transference, a therapist might say; a confusion with my unknown grandfather Louis, who dreamt of the dead mingling with the living, floating through his seances, peopling the new world of Johannesburg where he had come as a small boy, leaving the old world of Russia behind. I have no photographs of Louis, and only one faint, faraway childhood memory: of a silver-haired man, in a large room that overlooked a strange city, sitting on his carved wooden chair, with me, tentative, at his side.

## WEDNESDAY 18 OCTOBER

I AM APPEARING ON a television channel called Oxygen, and I feel like I can't breathe. I'm sitting in a small room, with two huge computers in front of me, and Ruth's face on the nearest screen. The producer is showing me a montage of pictures of Ruth, and then I have to say something about her, and the fight against breast cancer, which will be recorded as an introduction to this particular segment of the show. 'This is a very Oprah segment,' says the producer. I look blank, so she explains that Oprah Winfrey owns Oxygen. I start crying, not noisily, not so that anyone can see me, because it's dark in here, apart from the light of Ruth's face on the computer screen. It's the first time I've cried for months, and I wipe the tears with my hand, and lick the salt away.

I do the voice-over, and then they take me to the hospitality room. Uma Thurman is being interviewed before me, and I watch her on the huge television monitor that hangs above the table. Yesterday, the show featured a roller-blading chimp. 'Was the chimp happy in front of the cameras?' I ask the producer's assistant, as she escorts me to the studio where the interview will take place. 'I don't know,' she says. 'It was difficult to tell what the chimp was feeling.'

I'm going to be interviewed live by a rather beautiful blonde singer, who I think I recognize from MTV. She runs through the questions with me, before the cameras turn to us.

'I'll start by asking you how old your sister was when she succumbed to the disease, OK?'

I look blank again, because I don't understand what she means. 'Do you mean when she first found out that she had cancer?' I say.

'No, when she . . . um . . . passed,' says the interviewer.

Then I realize that she's talking about when Ruth *died.* 'Sorry,' I say, 'sorry, I got confused . . . it's just no one seems to want to use the word "dead".'

'I guess that's an American thing,' says the interviewer.

A couple of times, she calls me Ruth. I don't mind. Ruth's friends call me Ruth, by accident, even now, three years after her death. It often happens. Sometimes they catch themselves, and apologize; more often, they do not hear the mistake, and I say nothing. My sister and I had almost identical speaking voices, apparently (though when I try to summon up hers now, it's gone). What does her voice sound like? I want Ruth's voice, my Ruth's, not mine.

The interview is soon over. Afterwards, I don't know what I said. I feel like I'm sleepwalking. 'That was *excellent,* very clear, very moving, very good,' says the producer. 'Thank you so much.'

'Thank you for having me,' I say, like an obedient child.

Later, that evening, there is a big, glamorous party to celebrate the publication of Ruth's book, and to raise money for the Young Survivor's Coalition. Miss America comes, or Miss USA: I can't remember which. The women that I met at the sponsored walk –

the survivors themselves – are all here, wearing hot pink feather boas. They give me one to wear. I take it, and put it around my neck. The feathers tickle, scratch a little, even though they look so soft. 'Ruth would have liked this,' I say. 'She loved parties. She loved pink.' I wonder if she is in this room tonight, floating amongst the pink balloons, hovering above the red velvet banquettes, buoyed by the bubbles of champagne. (Better than being outside in the endless, heavy rain . . . ) I hope she is, seeing all these people that are here for her. I want to cry, but I laugh instead. This is a party, after all. This is her party.

> The Bororo bury their dead twice: a brief initial burial takes place in the village plaza where for several weeks relatives water the corpse lavishly, in order to hasten the process of decomposition. When decay is sufficiently advanced, the grave is opened, and the skeleton is washed until all trace of flesh has been removed. The bones are painted red, decorated with mosaics made from feathers glued together with resin, placed in a basket, and ceremoniously dropped to the bottom of a river or lake, 'the abodes of the souls.' Water and death are therefore always connected in native thought. In order to procure the one, it is necessary to undergo the other.
>
> Claude Levi-Strauss, *The Raw and the Cooked: An Introduction to a Science of Mythology*

## Thursday 19 October

On the plane home, somewhere above the Atlantic ocean, I read the Sylvia Browne psychic guide book given to me as a parting present by Jeannie the spirit channeller. 'You may find this of use on your journey,' she had said; and she's right, it is a very interesting book. Once I start reading, I don't want to stop. Sylvia says that the spirit world – or 'Home', as it is also known – is closer to us than we think: a mere three feet above our own earthly ground. We can't see it, because 'its vibrational frequency is much higher than ours'; though as far as the spirits are concerned, 'we're actually ghosts in their world, sharing the same space but unreal by comparison, since it is in the spirit world that all beings are completely and fully "alive".' On the Other Side, it never rains, because the weather is 'a constantly calm and clear 78 degrees'. Spirit people don't need to sleep, though they do have bodies: with hearts and lungs and so forth, but 'on the opposite side from where they're located in our bodies on earth, an exact mirror image of the human anatomy'. Sadly, there is no reference to whether spirits ride bicycles on the Other Side. Sylvia says they usually get around by 'projected thought', but from time to time, they ride in 'a kind of combination golf cart and hovercraft, atomic-powered and open-sided, that moves along several inches above the ground'. Spirits also enjoy 'non-contact sports' which take place on the Other Side in 'magnificent athletic stadiums, golf courses, tennis courts, ski slopes, glistening with eternal artificial snow, perfect waves for surfing crashing onto pure, white shores, and accommodations for every other form of organized exercise . . .'

Sylvia's book, which regularly features on the New York Times Bestseller List, along with her several other volumes concerned with spiritual matters, provides very clear instructions about how to 'open the way to some beautiful encounters with the Other Side as often as you like'. Fortified by a glass of in-flight red wine, I read the instructions several times, and prepare myself for the way forward.

This is the place that Sylvia says to summon up, behind closed eyes. 'You're approaching a pair of huge, gleaming brass doors, intricately etched and ornate, the most beautiful you've ever seen . . . Inside, you find a perfectly oval room . . . The floors are hardwood, with white rugs as soft as clouds that soothe your bare feet as you walk slowly across them . . .' There's more to see in the room: candles, jasmine, a white grand piano, an ocean breeze, two white brocade chairs, and the white light of the Holy Spirit. 'You settle into the left chair, so that the chair to your right is empty . . . From the stillness to your right you notice movement, and you turn toward it. A figure steps forward and takes a seat in the empty chair beside you. You're not afraid, knowing no harm or darkness will approach the divine light that protects you. The figure waits, patient, still and open. You're blessed by its presence. Finally, softly, you speak . . .'

I am concentrating on the room, shutting out the plane, feeling only the white light, trying to smell the scent of jasmine instead of the stale, recycled air. I'm sitting on the left-hand chair. A figure approachs. I am not frightened. I look to see who the figure is. It is Anna Wintour, the editor of American *Vogue*. Damn. I do not think she is my spirit guide: she is not supposed to be in the magic room – this is not the point at all. So I drink another glass of red wine, and start again. I open the big brass doors; I walk to the left-hand chair; I wait for my spirit visitor. I wait . . . and wait . . . until I might be sleeping. And then a figure approaches. It is Louis, my dead grandfather. He won't sit in the white brocade chair. He wants his own chair, his carved wooden Bardic chair. He has nothing to say to me. He does not say a word.

## Saturday 28 October

> Love itself functions as a kind of 'borderland' between health and sickness for the human soul.
>
> Sandor Ferenczi, *Love Within Science*

It is the children's half-term holiday, and we have come to Wales for a few days, to stay in a converted barn near a village called Battle in Brecon. It is raining so hard that the field outside has turned into a sea of mud. Even our hopeful dog does not want to go for a walk. Instead, we drive to Hay on Wye, a place that contains more bookshops than people today, and hide there from the rain. The children spend a great deal of time choosing books: Jamie finally settles on a second-hand hardback from a damp shop near the town's castle; a large tome entitled *Air Disasters: Dialogue from the Black Box.* On the front, there is a picture taken on 4 November 1993, of a China Airlines Boeing 747 that had skidded off the runway at Hong Kong Airport, and into the sea, overshadowed by the city's waterside ramparts of tower blocks. ('It was the sudden gusts of wind and the rainwater on the tarmac that had affected the plane's brakes, to the extent of making it veer unstoppably to the left upon landing.') Tom wants a book that unfolds into a three-dimensional board game, entitled 'Ghost Hunters!' ('Make your way around the pop-up haunted castle. But beware! The ghosts are out to get *you* first!')

I don't argue with their choices, but inside, I'm feeling guilty. I am not a good enough mother. I thought I had protected them from the death in our lives, but I have not. I have got lost somewhere, in a dead end, and taken them with me, and now they need compasses and signposts to find their own way out.

I chew my nails on the way back to Battle, while the children doze in the steamed-up car. We skirt the outskirts of Brecon, and then cross the bridge over the River Usk. 'They'll have to close the bridge soon,' says Neill, when we're half-way across. 'The river has burst its banks.' I clear a hole in the misted window, and peer outside. The brown water has nearly reached the top of the bridge itself, and the paths on either side have disappeared.

'Oh, God,' I say, 'I really don't want to get stuck here.'

'We won't,' says Neill. 'There's always a way round . . .'

## SUNDAY 29 OCTOBER

MY PARENTS ARE coming to visit us here today. Although they are divorced, they have both ended up living in Wales, around the corner from each other. My father has only just moved back to this country from South Africa, where he has spent the past thirteen years. I sometimes wonder if he returned here, to a wet island that makes him miserable, to repair the damage of Ruth's death; to rebuild the burnt-out wasteland of our family life.

They arrive in time for a late breakfast, and I cook eggs and bacon and sausages, to fortify us against the day ahead. It is still raining outside, sheer sheets of water. I tell my father about the trip to New York, and my meeting with Jeannie the spirit channeller, and Dale Palmer. He looks sceptical. 'But, Dad, didn't you hear voices in your head?' I say, venturing on to dangerous ground.

'Yes,' he says, with a smile, 'like all the best people.'

'Do you remember our trip to St Ives,' I say, 'when we were little?'

He keeps smiling, though maybe it's a grimace. 'Going away with a bunch of Christians would be enough to drive anyone mad,' he says.

'But were you schizophrenic then?' I ask.

'I was deluded,' he says.

I can't meet his eyes. I have said too much, and now it's his turn. He won't stop talking: about why his father was mad; about why Jews are oppressed; about his role as the madman in the Jewish community. He is grinding his teeth, and my stomach starts hurting so badly that I have to leave the room. When I come back, a few minutes later, he is still talking, gesticulating wildly, while Neill sits listening at the other end of the table.

'We have to leave,' I say. 'There's been a flood warning on the radio, and the weather report is predicting a Force 10 gale tonight. There's already winds of ninety miles an hour.'

'You're leaving so soon?' says my father, crestfallen. 'I thought we were going to have a nice cosy afternoon together.'

'I'm sorry,' I say, 'but I've got to pack.' I go into the next room, where Tom is playing his haunted house game by himself. I can still hear my father talking through the open door.

'My father Louis heard voices in his head,' he says, 'but he chose to give them a spiritualist meaning. He couldn't face up to reality, ever. I told him to read Freud, but he preferred Madame Blavatsky . . .'

'Is your stomach still hurting?' says Neill, when we're safely in the car, as he begins the long drive home.

'Less than it was,' I say. 'I couldn't deal with my father. I couldn't understand what he was saying. Maybe I didn't try hard enough. I don't know . . .'

'I think what he was trying to say was that his mental illness has a place in Judaism,' says Neill. 'There is a name for it – "meshugassen" – and it is accepted in him, because of his father's madness. He feels accepted, within the structure of the Jewish community.'

I sigh, but say nothing. The clocks went back in the early hours of this morning – British Wintertime, again – and it will be dark by 5 o'clock this afternoon, though the sky is already the colour of granite, because of the storm. Neill drives steadily east across the country, skirting broken riverbanks, avoiding flooded roads. I offer to read the map, but the children have fallen asleep in the back, and soon, I'm drifting too. I think of Ruth, walking into the sea, on our last holiday together in west Wales. It was six weeks before she died, and she knew that the cancer had spread to her brain. 'I might as well swim far out, and not come back,' she had said to me at the time.

'Please don't,' I'd said. 'The sea is too dirty here, anyway.' (As children, we had camped in the sand dunes behind the beach for several summers in a row, when the sea was still clear and clean, and then one day my parents had a terrible argument. 'What were you doing in the water?' said my father, over and over again to my mother, as I lay in the tent with my eyes screwed shut, pretending that I couldn't hear anything, my arms wrapped tightly around my sleeping sister. 'I wasn't doing anything!' said my mother. 'I don't know what you're talking about. You're crazy, you're driving me crazy.' After the argument my mother had to go home to Oxford, and we stayed with my father in the sand dunes, and then our tent blew away in a Force 10 gale. The summer was over. I can't remember what happened next.)

I don't know why we wanted to go back to the same beach, when Ruth was dying, but we did, in search of something, I don't know what; the past, I suppose. That final day of our final holiday, on the beach where we'd played all those years ago, we walked into the sea together, into the head-high waves. 'Come on,' she said to me, 'let's swim.'

'The current is too strong,' I said, 'and it's so cold.'

'Don't be scared,' she said, and swam out through the waves. I followed her, then, to make sure that she came back. Our children were building sandcastles together on the beach. At the end of the day, when the sun was falling in the sky, we watched as the incoming tide swept the castles away.

Today, on this muggy winter afternoon, when I half-wake in the car, I realize that the road map has slipped from my hands. 'I've lost it,' I say to Neill, still half-asleep.

'Don't worry,' he says. 'I know the way.'

'But I lost the map when Ruth died,' I say, to myself, rather than to him, my voice hidden by the sound of the windscreen wipers. 'And I still don't know where I'm going.'

## Tuesday 31 October

> Hallowe'en, the night which marks the transition from autum to winter, seems to have been of old the time of year when the souls of the departed were supposed to revisit their old homes in order to warm themselves by the fire and to comfort themselves with the good cheer provided for them in the kitchen or the parlour by their affectionate kinsfolk. It was, perhaps, a natural thought that the approach of winter should drive the poor shivering hungry ghosts from the bare fields and the leafless woodlands to the shelter of the cottage with its familiar fireside.
>
> James George Frazer, 'Balder's Fires', *The Golden Bough*

There is a blue sky in the morning – the first for days – but I'm feeling unsettled, as if yesterday's clouds are still hanging over this house. I dreamt last night of my father – talking, talking, but I couldn't follow what he was saying to me. In my dream, I wandered away from him to a sea wall, where I sat and watched the waves, until a rag doll was washed up into my hands. I took the limp doll, and woke up, feeling cheated.

Today is Halloween; tonight is the time when the veil between the living and the dead is at its thinnest. I want to tear it down; to tear out the tightness in my chest; to rip away this longing, this silence, this dark nothing that occupies me.

'Ruth.' I say her name out loud in the empty kitchen. 'Ruth.' The only sound is the wind that wails outside. 'Ruth.'

I have called her three times. She is silent; though when I close my eyes I can see her wry smile.

I leave the house and walk to the tube station, down the streets where the sound of footsteps are deadened by the fallen leaves, down again into the underground, where no one talks, except the sad mad man who mutters on the platform, skirted by everyone else around him, including me. At Hyde Park Corner, I come out again into the brief weak autumn sunlight, and walk to Belgrave Square, where the windows of all the big white mansions are blank and blind as I look up towards them.

Number 33 houses the Spiritualist Association of Great Britain. I've been thinking about coming here for months now, ever since a friend of mine told me that daily demonstrations of mediumship take place at 3.30 every weekday afternoon. Today seems as good a day as any to visit this place . . . no, more than that, today must be the best day of the year to come. As I push open the big black front door, I'm excited again; the same way I felt as a child on my way to a friend's birthday party (and I've come here for a social gathering of the dead, I suppose). The lady at the reception desk takes my entrance fee – £4 – and points me towards the sweeping staircase. 'It's on the first floor, dear,' she says, 'through the door on your left.'

Inside the upstairs room, which is in half-darkness as the curtains are still drawn, there are many rows of flip-up seats – a hundred or more, as if in a cinema. I take one near the front, beside a notice on the wall which says: 'This Hall Is Named In Memory of Sir Oliver Lodge FRS – a great leader in physical and psychic research.' It's a good omen, I decide – because Lodge was not only the inventor of the spark plug, but also cited by Judith

Chisholm as a forerunner in the search for a scientific means to communicate with the dead.

There are three old ladies in the audience, and two grey-haired men. One more woman arrives, wheezing deeply, and sits beside me. She is wearing a pink hat clamped to her head, and a pink coat, over a pink velour track suit, with mauve appliqué flowers on the front. I would guess she is in her eighties.

The medium appearing here today is called Julie Johnson. She, too, is wearing a pink top – though her outfit is more muted than my neighbour's (neat tweed skirt, tan tights, flat black shoes, sensible sweater). She stands on the raised platform at the end of the room, and opens the curtains behind her. 'There, I'll let in the light,' she says, cheerfully. There is a grand piano to one side of her, and a lectern in front, between two large, elaborate flower arrangements of the type one might find in a church. I study the flowers, trying to work out whether they're real or fake, but it's hard to tell (one moment I'm so convinced they're real that I'm sure I can smell the scent of decay coming from the vases; the next, I can almost see the dust on the fabric leaves.) Julie talks quickly to us, offering up a prayer of peace and harmony in the same brisk tones that a chairwoman of the WI might give thanks to a visiting speaker. 'I'm just the telephone between you and your spirits,' says Julie. 'But I can hear them, see them, sometimes even smell them.'

She half closes her eyes – and, for a moment, I think she looks like a blind person – and when she opens them, she points to a stony-faced woman on the other side of the room to me. The woman is wearing black. 'I can see a cuddly, homely looking lady in the spirit world,' says Julie to the woman. 'She has a velvety red chair, and she crochets bits and pieces for her home. It must be lovely to be able to make such nice things. Oh, and she keeps her house very tidy, very neat. Does that mean anything to you?'

The woman in black nods, though her face is still immobile. 'Now I see you riding donkeys on a beach with this lady,' says Julie. 'Ah, happy days . . . you had such fun. Does that mean anything to you?' The woman nods again, though this time her face is melting. 'She loves you very much,' says Julie. 'She's your auntie, isn't she?' Two tears run down the woman's face, and I can't stop myself looking at her, but when she sees my face turned in her direction, I feel embarrassed, and stare at the ceiling, as if I'm looking for guidance in the crystal chandelier. There are large damp patches on the ceiling, as if all the tears cried in this room have risen towards the sky, but somehow got caught up in the plaster instead.

Then Julie turns to me. My turn! I sit up straight, excited again, concentrating on the memory of Ruth's smile, willing her to make a dramatic appearance today – it's Halloween, for God's sake – right here in Belgrave Square. 'I see your grandfather,' says Julie, 'your mother's father.'

'Oh,' I say, feeling faintly disappointed.

'He's showing me all his plans and documents and papers,' she says. 'Was he a lawyer?'

'No,' I say, trying not to sound truculent, 'a civil engineer.'

'Well, he's worried about Timothy,' says Julie. 'Does that mean anything to you?' As a matter of fact, it does. Timothy is my mother's twin brother, though she never speaks about him, or to him. She has said, occasionally, that he was their parents' favourite, but nothing very much more than that.

The Timothy reference is rather impressive, but even so, I'm disappointed – where's Ruth in all of this? But Julie has moved on again, and I'm catching snippets of other people's stories, other people's spirits. It's like listening to someone else's incomprehensible dreams – though the details are familiar; the stuff of domestic life, rather than gothic tales of death. Julie tells the lady in pink beside me that the spirits know she's been worried about the guttering outside her house. 'But don't worry, you're going to get it sorted out, and you can use that chap who's already given you a quote for the job. He's cheap – and he's very trustworthy.'

After dealing with the building problems of the lady in pink, Julie turns her attention to the anxious-looking grey-haired man behind me. 'I can see a spirit sitting right beside you, sir,' she says, 'and from the look of him, he's your father.' A small smile lights up the man's face. 'Your father says you've got a hobby that you could turn into a job,' continues Julie. 'You've been feeling a bit down – a bit betrayed, almost, at work – but your father says, don't worry, everything is going to turn out fine.'

These homely ghosts continue to dish out soothing advice – about haircuts, travel arrangements, new houses, holidays. It's the kind of chat that my mother's parents were so good at – quiet, gentle homilies that came with milky tea and digestive biscuits. My grandparents would feel at home here, I think, if they were to feel at home anywhere in this noisy world. Maybe I should listen out for their soft lost voices more often . . . instead of allowing my longing for Ruth to drive everyone else from my head?

After an hour, Julie draws the meeting to a close, and thanks us and our attendant spirits for being here today. She leaves at an anxious trot, muttering about her next appointment, and I'm half-tempted to run after her, and ask for more; to follow her in case she knows the way to slip through a wrinkle in time; a secret rabbit hole that leads to the wonderland of the dead. But the lady in pink is having trouble getting to her feet, so I help her up, and then carry her plastic shopping bag for her. 'My name's Elsie,' she says, between wheezes. 'What's yours?'

'Justine,' I say.

'That's a pretty name,' she says, taking my hand in hers.

'Do you come here often?' I ask, as we walk slowly down the stairs.

'Not as often as I'd like,' she says. 'I find the journey rather difficult. But it's always worthwhile. And, you know, I *have* been worried about my guttering.'

Before I leave, I make an appointment to see Julie in two days' time – a private reading, just her and me (and no one else's spirits hanging around and obscuring the view). By the time I get home, the children have scooped out a pumpkin, and are getting changed into their Halloween outfits. 'We're devils,' says Tom, 'but kind of ghosts and vampires too.' They have fake blood smeared around their faces, and their faces are pale with excitement and white powder. They go out on to the street, joining a throng of other children dressed up in the dark. 'Trick or treat!' they cry. 'Trick or treat!'

I dish out treats for all the children who come to our door clutching lanterns and plastic pitchforks in their hands – white chocolates in the shape of ghosts; red sweets that look like blood-drenched teeth; green jelly babies and liquorice eyeballs. Later, at bedtime, while I'm sitting with my youngest son as he's drifting into sleep, he asks, 'What's the trick, now we've had our treats?' But he's asleep before I have time to answer. My oldest son is sleeping too, though his tape of *Harry Potter* is still playing, as it does every night on an endless loop, until I switch it off.

I have laid my ghosts and devils to rest tonight. That's what I tell myself, anyway.

## WEDNESDAY 1 NOVEMBER, ALL SAINTS DAY

An email arrives from my father. He writes:

> Grief: In normal grieving the lost person is hallucinated as a vision or misperception or, more usually, as a voice. If you look at Freud on mourning and melancholia in relation to childhood loss of attachment, you may discover the processes whereby a child's/mourner's anguish in her loss leads to wish-fulfilment – a hallucination of the loved one . . .
>
> All the ancestors are alive to the shaman/witchdoctor/exorcist and are alive to the living relative who has angered them in not showing enough respect for the recently and long-lost dead, the punishment of which is spirit possession, horrible

> delusions and hallucinations. The voices of conscience in the modern, rationalistic person are of course the sophisticated relics of the collective voice of the subject's ancestors, especially the recently dead. Religious rituals can free one from lost souls: eating the Host, the body and blood of the God who died so that you can internalise him – He enables you to carry the burden of guilt over death because you have eaten Him and he therefore sanctifies you.
>
> In depression which is the excessive extension of grief, Freud and Melanie Klein thought that the lost loved 'object' is sadistically internalised – 'eaten' and thus assimilated . . . by means of being internally digested. Cannibalism was the triumphant digestion of the dead enemy and we have a fantasy that something we did may have contributed to the loved one's death so we placate our fears by eating the loved one, having her inside oneself. We thus feel that she is not dead and she speaks to us . . .

Have I eaten my sister? I do hope not. I go and find my husband to ask him whether he thinks I have become a cannibal, at least as far as my dead sister is concerned.

'No,' he says. 'I think it's the other way round – you have been consumed by grief for her.'

~

## Thursday 2 November, All Souls Day

> 'Lord, grant them eternal rest'; Requiem aeternam dona eis, Domine

> . . . it is a widespread belief that the souls of the dead

> revisit their old homes . . . and on that solemn occasion people prepare for the reception of the ghosts by laying out food for them to eat . . .
>
> James George Frazer, 'Feasts of All Souls',
> *The Golden Bough*

EARLY THIS MORNING, in a warm cocoon of sleep and central heating, I dream of Ruth. I'm standing in a queue for tea and biscuits and cake with other women who I do not know. Then I see my sister across the room, smiling at me. I reach out to her – and we hug each other. I can feel her body in my arms, warm and soft and real. 'I miss you, I miss you so much,' I say, as I rest my cheek against hers. 'How can I live without you?'

Before she speaks, I'm woken by Tom tapping me on my face. It's such a struggle to surface from that dream embrace, into the ashen dawn; but when at last I wake, it is as if my child's touch is the answer to the question.

After I've taken the children to school, I go back to Julie and Belgrave Square. The rain is even heavier today; there's thunder and lightning overhead, and the dark morning sky is so wild that it looks like it might split open (when I was a child, maybe five or so, hunched in the back of the car with Ruth, while my parents sat in the front arguing about why we were lost – and we were lost, all of us, that day and others – I saw the same dark sky, but a ray of light shone from the clouds. 'That's heaven,' I whispered to Ruth. 'What's heaven?' she said. 'It's magic,' I said. 'We'll go there together one day.')

Inside number 33, all is not well at the Spiritualist Association. Julie is late. She is not here. She is out of contact, and who knows where she might be? ('Why don't you know? You're all supposed to be psychic!' I want to shout at the receptionist, but suppress this as being unhelpful in the circumstances.) Worse still, Julie's colleague, who is also supposed to be giving readings today, is in casualty. 'He slipped on the leaves,' says the receptionist, shaking her head mournfully. Meanwhile, there is an irate caller on the phone. 'Why are people so aggressive?' she says, looking increasingly aggrieved.

I sit down to wait on a little gilt chair with a red velvet seat outside the Arthur Conan Doyle room, next to the notice board. I'm about to make a note of the next Spiritualist lecture, which will take place on Friday, 17 November ('Why do the Selfish always seem to Succeed and does it Matter?'). But I'm diverted by a second receptionist – a young man – who has put another caller on a speaker phone, for the benefit of his colleague. 'I want to bring my own minidisc recorder for my sitting with the medium,' says the man on the other end of the phone, his voice booming across the entrance hall. 'It's very important, do you understand?'

'That's no problem, sir, I can promise you,' says the receptionist, while his colleague giggles. I'm feeling slightly shocked – this is supposed to be a caring, sharing place, after all – but maybe I'm not supposed to have overheard the encounter, because after the male receptionist has dealt with the agitated caller, he comes over, looking cross, and tells me I shouldn't be sitting here, I should be in the waiting room.

The waiting room is down the corridor. It has three chairs in it, and three woman are already sitting down, so I remain standing, and read the sign on the wall. It says:

> NOTICE TO THE SITTERS
> Every notice is in the nature of an experiment.
> It is not possible for a medium to give specific evidence required by the sitter.
> A medium's work is to try to provide evidence of survival and not to predict the future.
> Refunds can only be given if the medium is told, personally, before leaving the room.

The room is painted bruised green, and filled with a stifling air of anxiety, like a hospital waiting room. There are no windows; just a clock and the chairs. 'Is it normal to be able to overhear every word of the conversation next door?' says one of the women. She refers to the voices that come drifting across the corridor, where another sitting is in progress. 'Who's Mary?' asks the unseen medium. There is a murmured response from his client. 'Now I'm hearing an Elizabeth, probably a Betty,' continues the medium, 'something to do with nurses?'

After forty-five minutes, Julie is finally here. 'So sorry to keep you waiting,' she says, looking flustered. 'I've come all the way from Tunbridge Wells, and the trains are terrible, terrible – and I didn't get home till one in the morning last night, and then I was up again first thing, through all the rain, terrible, *terrible.* I've been working sixty days on the trot, you know, morning, noon and night.'

I'm beginning to feel guilty for being here – as if I'm imposing on an overwrought junior doctor who's about to sink with exhaustion – and things get worse when a straying spirit Elizabeth turns up in this room, too, instead of staying next door, where she doubtless belongs. 'Does the name Elizabeth mean anything to you?' says Julie.

'Um, no,' I say.

'Well, she's here for *you,*' says Julie, looking perturbed at my failure to recognize the visiting spirit. 'She's a very educated lady, you know.'

After ten minutes, we've got no further, and Julie suggests we bring our reading to a close. 'Oh no, please don't,' I say, feeling even more guilty. 'Actually, what I'd really like is some form of communication with my sister, Ruth.'

'Wanting someone in particular often gets in the way,' says Julie, looking disapproving. 'Look, you can have a refund.'

'I don't want a refund,' I say. 'But maybe we should give up on Ruth, and you could try my friend Kimberley instead? She often went to a spiritualist church, you know, before she died. I'm sure she'd like to get in touch with me.'

'The thing is, it's Elizabeth who wants to talk to you,' says Julie.

'I don't *know* an Elizabeth,' I say.

Julie closes her eyes, as if in despair. 'Elizabeth definitely knows you,' she says.

'OK,' I say, 'so what about my grandfather, Louis – he was a spiritualist, too.'

'Oh, yes,' says Julie, looking relieved. 'Now, he had something to do with sheep, didn't he? And he lived in a house next door to a church – in Wales, perhaps?'

I don't have the heart to tell her that Louis was a Jewish teacher turned poet who lived in a top-floor flat in the middle of Johannesburg. So I just nod while she chats about the sheep and the church and a basement room, where I could find a picture of Louis if I looked hard enough. (I don't have a basement, either, but I'm not going to argue about that.)

'Well, it was worth persevering in the end,' says Julie. 'I'm glad we got somewhere, dear.'

After I leave the Spiritualist Association, I check my mobile phone, which I had switched off just before my appointment there, to be confronted with an urgent message saying that Kimberley's daughter, Juliette, is ill in hospital with appendicitis, and I need to get there immediately, because her father, David, is out of the country for a few days, working in Japan. As I run towards Hyde Park Corner, I decide never to visit another medium, never *ever* again. (Surely, if I ever needed evidence of the futility of this venture, here is my proof on All Souls Day.)

Later, much later, as I'm waiting for Juliette to come out of the operating theatre, I ring my husband and tell him about today's communication failure. 'Hmm, yes, it does seem to have been a bit of an oversight,' he says. But I want to tell him that actually, despite the fact that Kimberley was a definite no-show this morning, I'm beginning to feel that maybe she's here now, hovering with me in the hospital, silently, as it happens, alongside David's partner, Eileen (whose mother also killed herself – which means just how many ghosts are there in this hospital waiting room tonight?). In the end, I decide not to tell any of this to my husband, at least not over the telephone. I'll wait until later, though later is a long time coming. Time slows down here, in the way it used to drag when I was sitting with Ruth in her hospital; the minutes drifting into hours, day into night, until you can't imagine ever getting outside again. I eat a Mars bar, and read Eileen our horoscopes from someone else's abandoned newspaper. (Mercury is retrograde, which is bad news for both of us, apparently.)

After Juliette finally wakes up from the anaesthetic, I lean over her pale drowsy face and kiss her. 'I love you so much, sweetheart,' I say, and take her hand in mine, while Eileen holds her other hand. This child is warm and real and constant – as alive as my sister in last night's dream; as sweet as her mother's smile in the photograph that is pinned on the wall next to Juliette's bed at home; as loved as any child can be, by her father and Eileen and me and the ghosts that surround us all, tonight, at the end of this long, long strange day.

## SUNDAY 5 NOVEMBER

'REMEMBER, REMEMBER THE fifth of November, gunpowder, treason and plot,' says Jamie, marching around the kitchen at 9 o'clock this morning. 'Mum, what date did your ancestor get his head chopped off?'

'I don't know,' I say.

'Probably straight away,' says Jamie, 'or was he tortured first?'

'I don't know,' I say.

'Why don't you know?' he says. 'He's your ancestor, isn't he?'

I realize that I have no one to ask about Henry Garnett – the lost, dead priest of my mother's family, beheaded because he refused to reveal the names of those men who had confessed to him their involvement in the Gunpowder plot; subsequently beatified when the face of Christ was seen in a drop of his blood that fell to the ground after his execution. Everyone who might have known more about the legend that surrounds him is dead, too. Anyway, I've got to make pancakes for Juliette's favourite breakfast now that she's back home after her operation, and Jamie's going to his karate class, and then Kimberley's mother arrives to see Juliette. 'Kimberley always made very good cakes and biscuits,' says her mother, watching me mix the pancake batter.

The conversation drifts between half-drunk cups of tea, while the rain sluices down the windows. 'When does the pain go away?' says Kimberley's mother to me, quietly.

'My tummy is feeling better now,' says Juliette, at the far end of the table.

'Did they cut it open?' asks Tom. 'Was there blood?'

'A friend of mine took me to a spiritualist church in Bayswater,' says Kimberley's mother, 'but I can't say anything happened.'

As the voices thread in and out of each other, until they make no sense, I wonder, could I be losing my grip? (And who wants a grip, anyway?) Batter, I think, is the better way forward, as I make another batch of pancakes for the children to eat; mixed up out of ordinary ingredients; fluid, and ready for unremarkable, everyday transformation.

## THURSDAY 23 NOVEMBER

RITA ROGERS RINGS, unexpectedly, half-way through the afternoon, and much to my delight. 'Hello, dear,' she says. 'Rita here.' I don't like to ask why she's rung today, in particular. (Rita knows all, and who am I to question her wisdom?) She begins with a story about a reading she did for a mother whose daughter had died, 'And I knew nothing more than that, dear, nothing, but as I started the reading I said, "Oh no, your daughter was murdered." And she was, dear, raped and murdered, and I saw the whole thing as I was talking to this poor mother, it happened in a park, and the girl screamed but no one heard, and the man put his hand over her mouth, oh, it was terrible, terrible . . .'

As she is telling me the story, I hear a thin scream down the phone, as if it is coming from her end of the line.

'What was that?' I say, interrupting Rita mid-flow.

'What?' she says.

'That scream, I heard a scream.'

'Oh, that would have come from the spirit, dear,' says Rita, as if this was nothing out of the ordinary. 'It happens sometimes, when I'm on the phone.'

'But I *heard* it,' I say.

'Yes, that's right,' says Rita, 'anyway—'

'Is that what the spirit voices sound like to you?' I ask, interrupting Rita again. 'Not in your head, but outside, as if they're beside you?'

'Yes,' she says, 'in fact, I've got two voices trying to talk to me at the moment, your sister and your friend Kimberley in one ear, and it's quite difficult to follow everything, what with you talking at the same time in the other ear.'

'What are they saying?'

'Something about a John. Do you know a John?'

'No,' I say. 'No . . . I mean, yes. I have a friend called John with cancer. And I had another friend called Jon who died in May, of a brain tumour. Ruth knew him, too, but Kimberley didn't.'

'Goodness, what a lot of dead people you know,' says Rita. 'It might not be him, but another name that begins with J. The spirits are worried about this person, who's a bit poorly.'

'Jamie? That's my older son. But he's not ill . . .'

'No, not him,' says Rita.

'Juliette?' I say. 'Kimberley was her mother . . .'

'Juliette!' says Rita. 'Yes, that's probably who it is. She's been poorly, hasn't she?'

'Yes, she has, actually,' I reply. 'She's had appendicitis.'

'Well, her mum must have been worried about her,' says Rita. 'Nasty thing, appendicitis.'

'Rita,' I say, changing the subject abruptly, because I'm trying to fit everything into this unexpected conversation, in case she's about to disappear again (and out of my life entirely, like an unreliable fairy godmother), 'do ghosts ride bicycles?'

'Yes, dear,' she says, 'they do ride bicycles. They like fishing, too. There's water there on the other side, and they go on boats. They have boats and buildings and bicycles – they live like you and I – and there are horses, and the bicycles, yes.'

After the conversation has ended – just as I've put the phone down – I hear a crash from the kitchen, and Cate, my children's much-loved nanny who picks them up from school two days a week, is standing surrounded by broken glass and blood and vinegar. 'I don't know how it happened,' she's saying, clutching her wounded hand. 'This bottle of vinegar just came flying out of the cupboard and somehow it's cut me . . .'

We wrap a towel around her hand, and I drive her to hospital, because the bleeding doesn't stop. On the way, I'm gabbling about Ruth's blood phobia, which isn't very helpful of me but I'm frightened, too. ('She'd always faint at the sight of her blood,' I say. 'Well, I'm feeling a bit dizzy myself,' says Cate.) Then I tell her about my phone call with Rita. 'You'd think the spirits might have warned us that you were about to have a terrible accident, instead of just going on about a poorly person whose name begins with J,' I say, crossly.

'My real name is Julia,' she says, half laughing, half crying, 'it's just everybody calls me Cate. Maybe they were trying to warn us?'

'Well, why can't the spirits be a bit more specific?' I say. 'It's just so vague and unhelpful – like the last time I had to go to this hospital, when Juliette had appendicitis, and all I'd been told by a medium *that very same morning* was that someone called Elizabeth wanted to talk to me. Why couldn't the spirits have just said, "Juliette is very ill. Go to the hospital now." Surely that would have been the sensible thing to do?'

We get to the hospital, and I shepherd Julia/Cate into Accident & Emergency, leaving a trail of blood in our wake. On one side of us sits a young mother with her white-faced, listless baby; on the other, a weeping girl hangs her head down low, grinding her fists into her poor swollen eyes. 'Oh, fucking hell,' I say, looking around this strip-lit waiting room full of the lost and damned. 'Bloody spirits,' and then I stamp off to find a nurse, while people stare at me as if I've lost my mind.

I can't find anyone to help, though I do persuade one grumpy nurse to give me a bandage, and when I get back to Cate, she is bleeding even more profusely, so I wrap the dressing around the wound to try and staunch the flow. 'Can't anyone *help*?' I say, but it seems to be up to me, and the blood is still soaking through the bandage, so I go and find a bigger one from the grumpy nurse, and some surgical tape, which I use to make another equally inexpert dressing.

'I didn't realize that my blood would look so red,' says Cate, paler by the second, gazing at the red splashes and drips around her on the hospital floor. It's not a big wound, but it's a very deep one – you can see the flesh, which is unexpected. (When I was with Ruth during her caesarean, I saw nothing of the cut, because I was looking into her eyes, and she was frightened. 'Sing me a song,' she said, 'tell me a story.' I sang nursery rhymes, and then told her about the picnics we would have on a beach with our children; a bonfire with baked potatoes and toasted marshmallows. 'And chocolate biscuits,' she said, 'don't forget the chocolate.') I wonder how long it would take to bleed to death here, waiting for a doctor: five hours? Six?

'What if I had Aids?' said Cate. 'Not that I do, but they don't know that, and there's all this blood everywhere, and no one doing anything about it.'

Eventually, someone looks at the wound, and then X-rays it; and finally, after another hour or so, I leave her waiting to be stitched up, watched over by her husband John (John!), who has just arrived here from work. 'Maybe that was the J?' I mutter to myself, as I drive home alone, 'though it seems unlikely. Anyway, that's it, I've had enough. Enough. No more mediums. I'm going nowhere, going mad, going round in circles.' ('And you're talking to yourself, too,' says my imaginary therapist. 'I think that's becoming a problem . . .')

Later that night, I'm feeling confused, and I've still got no one to talk to, because Neill is out and Ruth is ignoring me. So I search the distant reaches of the Internet, burrowing further and further away from home, browsing through the endless Websites of American psychic mediums offering telephone sessions costing upwards of $200 for half an hour (and even so, they're booked up until next year). Eventually, I discover a more promising Net destination – 'The Living Energy Universe' – which is devoted to the work of two American academics in Arizona, Professor Gary Schwartz and his wife, Dr Linda Russek, who are conducting laboratory tests into the accuracy of mediums. They're not available to speak to tonight, but I do send an email to their Director of Mediumship Research Committee, a renowned Californian medium named Laurie Campbell. (I ask her whether she might ring me if she has the time, because I need to speak to her about all the dead people in my head, not to mention the copious quantities of blood that appear in my life when I least expect it.)

By now it's two in the morning, and I'm roaming into obscure Catholic Websites in search of more information about Henry Garnett. (It turns out he was a Jesuit, though that's as far as I get.) I feel that it's about time something started making sense – the blood, the dead, the whole damn lot – but everything is a mess. My eyes are beginning to water with tiredness, and there's nothing on the screen that is clear, nothing to guide me, just blurred typescript from strangers on the other side of the world. Beyond that, silence.

## SUNDAY 26 NOVEMBER

I DREAM OF RUTH, again (where are these dreams leading? I suppose if you still love someone, the love has to go somewhere, find a means of expression, even if the one you love is dead, gone, disappeared into the dark . . . I feel as if I'm leading a double life: half by day, half at night; though sometimes the two get confused). In the dream, we are standing on the top floor of a tower block, in the reception area to someone else's office. She doesn't say very much to me, but I tell her how glad I am to see her, how much I've missed her. She looks well – no cancer, no brain tumour, her hair is long and dark and curly again. But she looks wary, too. She tells me she is living in America.

'Can I have your phone number there?' I ask, politely.

'I don't really want to give it to anyone,' she says, looking over my shoulder into the distance.

I'm furious with her, but I don't want to say anything – I'm frightened of revealing how angry I am with her; and I feel like crying, too, because she doesn't love me any more; she doesn't want to talk to me. There are crowds of people around us – a river of strangers, I had not realized there were so many – and somehow I'm pushed away from her. I keep walking, slightly ahead of her – I have no choice but to carry on moving – and then before long, I lose her. I am in a lift going down to the ground floor. I catch a glimpse of her on the other side, as the doors close between us. And then she has disappeared.

When I wake up, on another dreary, sallow Sunday morning, Neill is looking like I am feeling: anxious, hollow-eyed, grey-faced. 'What's wrong?' I say.

'I had a terrible dream,' he says. 'I dreamt I was with someone – a woman, not you . . . a singer, I think, though I couldn't see her face. We were in a garden, and then suddenly, she disappeared.'

'Where had she gone?' I ask.

'She was dead,' he says. 'I just knew that she was dead, though I didn't see her die. And there was a man standing there, where she had been standing – a very ordinary looking man – but I knew that he was Death. And having taken this woman, he had come for me. Then I woke up – it was dark outside and Tom had climbed into bed with us – but I could still hear this man's voice. He knew I was thirsty and he said, 'Do you want to go downstairs and get a drink of water, and you can die there, alone in the kitchen? Or do you want to die now, with your son beside you?'

'And you thought you were awake?' I say, shaken by his dream.

'I *was* awake,' he says. 'But I just lay there, until dawn came, not daring to move.'

'It was just a dream,' I say, trying to reassure him, as he has so often reassured me. 'You were only dreaming . . .'

## WEDNESDAY 13 DECEMBER

I HAVE MADE AN appointment to visit the library of the Freud Museum in Hampstead; the house in Maresfield Gardens that Freud moved to, after his escape from Vienna in 1939. Although I have read his work (how could I not, with a therapist for a mother; and a father who could cite the Oedipus Complex at breakfast?) I have resisted Freud for many years – a childish reaction to my parents' belief, I suppose. (My denial must have been as disturbing for my father to deal with, as his own previous refusal to accept his father's spiritual beliefs. These arguments and intransigence seem to have been passed down in my family's blood . . . ) Now, however, I feel sufficiently irritated by the anodyne language of spiritualism to need a dose of Freud, instead. But I'm not looking for what it was that my father found in Freud – the knowledge that everything we need to know about ourselves is contained inside our own heads, as opposed to a mystical, magical world on the outside. Instead, I want proof that Freud did, in fact, have an interest in the occult; and more than that, that Freud knew in private – even if he did not choose to admit to it in public – that the unconscious is sometimes beyond the reach of rational medicine or materialist science. Where that will get me, I don't really know. (If it's back to spiritualism, then I will have gone round in circles. But these days, I don't seem to be able to do anything other than that.)

I half-remember these streets, from long ago. (I was born very near here, in a road called Frognal, where my parents rented their first flat together, and learnt how to live in a strange city, with a baby that they had not expected so soon in their lives.) When I reach Maresfield Gardens, I feel the same rising bubble of excitement in my throat that I felt when I went to the College of Psychic Studies for the first time. Buildings contain secrets, just as people do; this is a place where doors can be opened to different worlds.

I've visited a virtual version of Freud's house before, on the Internet (a land I find myself floating through, increasingly, night after night, searching for something in lieu of Ruth; searching for a glimpse of what lies beyond the computer screen, on the other side of the glass).

Now I'm in the real house, climbing the stairs to the attic floor, to the Freud library: the place where ghosts live between the lines of books. I feel sure that if I can find the right book – or the right ghost? – I will know the answer to everything. I will make sense of the confusion around me, within me. Instead of losing myself, I will have a real destination. Or something like that.

The letters I want to read are those between Sigmund Freud and his collaborator in psychoanalysis, Sandor Ferenczi. It was Ferenczi (a Hungarian doctor who was seventeen years younger than Freud) who encouraged his mentor not to lose sight of the occult – or that which lies beyond the edge of the expected – in Freud's determined attempt to establish psychoanalysis as a science. In his essay entitled 'Spiritism', published in 1899, Ferenczi wrote:

> Nowadays, most of the so-called intelligentsia have already absorbed as part of their education the principles of atomic materialism. The world is none other than an infinite mass of indivisible particles of different sizes, their vibrating movements creating light, warmth, electricity, and so on. Human consciousness itself is but an effect of certain brain conglomerations. Oh, what a task befell our physics teachers who were under obligation to present these ideas to us with absolute conviction. How easy everything seemed to us, if we just heeded their pronouncements: between sixty and seventy atoms (since then ten new elements!), eight to ten vibrations of the ether. This is the essence of the

> world. Mad is the one who ventures to speak of congruence, of spirit, of metaphysics . . .

Since then, Ferenczi – who did venture to speak of spirit and clairvoyance – has been condemned by some, more orthodox analysts, as 'mad'. But Ferenczi seems to me to have made an important observation when he wrote, in the same essay, 'I do believe that at the heart of these phenomena there is truth, even if it is a subjective rather than an objective truth . . . The spiritists are in possession of alchemical gold, of a hidden treasure; their science has every chance of yielding a rich and unexpected harvest from a terrain which is, as yet, uncultivated: that of psychology.'

And whereas my father saw Freud as representing scientific reason – the rationalist at the other end of the spectrum to his father, my grandfather, the irrational spiritualist – then perhaps what I am searching for, in this library, is a compromise between those opposing positions. Freud's map of the unconscious mind may also contain the as yet unknown. And if an analyst can sometimes be a medium, and vice versa, then my father and grandfather (not to mention my mother the therapist and me) could at last find a common ground. Maybe there is room for all of us in this attic. Maybe we will make peace with each other here.

But first, I must also find clues in someone else's history. (My junior school teacher in Oxford – a kindly man named Mr Hood, who seemed very old in those days, but was probably the same age then as I am now – taught the class that we could build on the past to make a future. We constructed Roman villas in cardboard boxes: it seemed so simple, really; and even though I wasn't sure how the future would fit into the box, I spent hours decorating mine, making smudged, sticky mosaics out of old Readers Digests, planning elaborate extensions at night when I couldn't sleep.)

The letters in the attic reveal that in August 1909, Freud, Jung and Ferenczi sailed to America together – from the old world to the new one – where Freud gave a series of lectures. Soon after they returned to Europe, Ferenczi wrote to Freud, on 5 October, to tell him, 'America is like a dream.' But what really engaged their attention turns out not to have been this trip abroad, but the one that Ferenczi made when he was back in Budapest, to visit a medium, Frau Seidler. Infuriatingly, the first part of Ferenczi's letter to Freud describing this experience is missing: even though I had convinced myself that I would discover it in the library here. But I do find Freud's reply, written on 11 October 1909, concerning the mysterious Frau Seidler:

> . . . she seems to have interpreted the images of ships and travelling symbolically in connection with a death; as perhaps she might have done correctly in other cases, because she would not have known she had a real traveller to America in front of her . . . Should one now, as a result of this experience, commit oneself to occultism? Certainly not; it is only a matter of thought transference . . . In the meantime, let us keep absolute silence with regard to it.

On the whole, Freud continued to keep silent in print about anything that might detract from the scientific respectability of his work. Yet in his personal life, he seems to have veered towards magical thinking at times: making sacrificial offerings of his favourite possessions to save his children from disaster; and placing a peculiar emphasis on the significance of the numbers 28 and 23 in his life. His friend and biographer, Ernest Jones, who was a convinced sceptic, wrote:

> In the years before the great war I had several talks with Freud on occultism and kindred topics. He was fond, especially after midnight, of regaling me with strange or uncanny experiences with patients, characteristically about misfortunes or deaths

> supervening many years after a wish or prediction. He had a particular relish for such stories and was evidently impressed by their more mysterious aspects. When I would protest at some of the taller stories Freud was wont to reply with his favourite quotation: 'There are more things in heaven and earth than are dreamt of in your philosophy.'

Jones continues, in his now (sadly) out-of-print biography that is kept at the Freud Museum, that when his mentor's late-night stories revolved around 'visitations from departed spirits, I ventured to reprove him for his inclination to accept occult beliefs on flimsy evidence. His reply was: "I don't like it at all myself, but there is some truth in it", both sides of his nature coming to expression in a short sentence . . .'

After I've written down some sentences from the letters and photocopied a few pages of the Jones biography, I leave the attic room, and wander around the rest of the museum. I don't quite know what I'm going to do with these bits of paper. They are evidence for . . . what? That weird stuff happens to all of us? Or that Freud – the man my father held up as the pinnacle of rational exploration of human irrationality – might have had something to talk about with my magical-thinking grandfather, after all?

I leave the museum, and walk along the road, concentrating on not talking to myself out loud, forgetting where I am going. Somewhere, I take a wrong turning, and end up not by the tube station, where I thought I was heading, but outside a shop that I have never seen before. It is completely unexpected, yet so familiar, that I begin to laugh. 'JEWS FOR JESUS' says the sign outside, in big letters – a family joke writ large. When my father had talked about his father joining this organization, I'd never actually thought that it existed but rather that it was a fantasy – an after-midnight story – a metaphor for my grandfather's peculiar shift of faith.

I hesitate, and then walk into the shop. The woman inside looks pleased to see me. 'Can I help you?' she says.

'I don't know,' I reply.

'Where do you worship, dear?' she says.

'I don't go to church,' I say.

The woman looks perplexed. 'Where do you live?' she says.

'Crouch End,' I say.

'Oh, there's a lovely church near you,' she says, 'up there on the hill. I'm sure you'd be very welcome there. They'd make you feel at home.'

'Actually, I wanted to find out about my grandfather,' I say. 'He joined this organization many years ago.'

'I'm not sure I can help you with that,' she says. 'I think you'd be better off spending some time at church, instead.'

At home, that night, I tell Neill about my curious day. 'I went to the Freud Museum,' I say, 'and I found these really interesting letters about how he half-believed in the occult, and then on my way back, I ended up outside the Jews for Jesus office. It was such a coincidence.'

'Why was it a coincidence?' says Neill.

'Well, because my grandfather joined the organization, and he was a spiritualist, too, and my father is always saying that his father should have read Freud, instead of wasting his time on all that rubbish.'

'And?' says Neill.

'That's all,' I say, trailing off.

'But I don't quite see the significance,' says Neill. 'You've lost me . . .'

I sigh. 'Well, it seems to mean something,' I say, 'but I'm not quite sure what, exactly.'

*The Skeptic's Dictionary*

**Apophenia**. There is currently a controversial debate concerning whether unusual experiences are symptoms of a mental disorder, if mental disorders are a consequence of such experiences, or if people with mental disorders are especially susceptible to or even looking for these experiences.

Apophenia is the spontaneous perception of connections and meaningfulness of unrelated phenomena . . . In statistics, apophenia is called a Type I error, seeing patterns where none, in fact, exist. It is highly probable that the apparent significance of many unusual experiences and phenomena are due to apophenia, e.g. EVP, numerology and a host of other paranormal and supernatural experiences. See related entry on **pareidolia**.

**Pareidolia** is a type of illusion or misperception involving a vague or obscure stimulus being perceived as something clear and distinct. For example, in the discolorations of a burnt tortilla one sees the face of Jesus Christ. Or one sees the image of Mother Theresa in a cinnamon bun or the face of a man in the moon.

Robert Todd Carroll, SkepDic.com

## SUNDAY 17 DECEMBER

ANOTHER EMAIL ARRIVES from my father. He seems happier communicating this way, which is fine by me: his voice on screen is calm, and there are no jagged edges in these conversations for us to cut each other to pieces with. (When someone dies in a family, the survivors rearrange themselves in unexpected places; find different ways of talking to each other; negotiate the spiked mantraps of grief. This struggle to make the separate pieces of a broken family fit together again is, possibly, as bewildering as anything one might encounter in a séance room.) My father writes:

> Justine:
> I am doing a talk on Jewish mysticism (Kabbalah) – a purely psychological approach – no magic, and I thought you might be interested.
>
> Hope you were inspired by Freud's evident link between archaeology and exploring the unconscious – the old Middle Eastern figurines in his place at Maresfield Gardens – analogous to symptoms (condensed, displaced, symbolically revised outcomes) of unconscious historical-religious conflicts and, in parallel, the history of our guilt-neurosis.
>
> Love,
> Dad

~

## TUESDAY 19 DECEMBER

> . . . even if all the parts of a problem seem to fit together like the pieces of a jigsaw puzzle, one must reflect that what is probable is not necessarily the truth and that the truth is not always probable.
>
> Sigmund Freud, *The Origins of Religion*

I'M TRYING TO get home before the children do, but I'm still sitting in the car, stuck in a Christmas shopping traffic jam on Upper Street, so I ring Neill to tell him that I'm going to be late. Before I can say anything, I hear him crying. 'Kirsty's dead,' he says. His sister is dead. 'She died in the water,' he continues, 'in the sea . . . She was killed in the sea.' His voice is breaking up on the phone, and I can hardly hear him. There must have been a mistake. This isn't possible. My sister is dead, not his. 'Neill?' I say. He's silent. 'Hold on,' I say, 'I'll be home soon. Just hang on . . .'

I arrive back just as the children are walking along our street from school with Cate. 'Kirsty's dead,' I say to Cate, under my breath. She looks shocked. I am blank-faced. I unlock the front door, and we go into the house. Neill is sitting at the kitchen table, a bottle of rum in front of him, hanging on . . . I hug him, this man who I love, my bedrock, and it feels as if he is crumbling in my arms. I steer him out of the kitchen, down the road, and into a nearby bar. I order him a black coffee. He asks for a whisky and some prawns.

'She was on holiday in Mexico,' he says. 'She was diving with her kids. A speed boat drove into her.' His face crumples. 'How unlikely is that? To be killed by a fucking boat . . .' He buries his head in his hands. At the next table, some people are having a Christmas party, and they look over in our direction. I want to stand up and say, briefly, My husband has just found out that his sister is dead, so please don't stare at him. But I'm hugging him, so I can't stand up.

He drinks the whisky and pushes the plate of prawns away. 'They make me feel sick,' he says. We walk home again, and the phone starts ringing and ringing and ringing. Kirsty is a semi-famous pop star, and the story of her death will be on the radio in an hour or less. A friend of mine calls from a newspaper and says to me, 'It's on the wires.' I imagine the wires stretching across the ocean from Mexico to London, taut and steely and cold, sharp enough to cut you, while words balance on them, like starlings.

I go upstairs to the attic, to answer calls and ring people to let them know what's happened, before they hear it on the news. At six o'clock, through a fog, I hear the phone ringing. I pick it up, and it is Laurie Campbell, the medium I emailed last month, thousands of miles away, where it is still morning in America (and if there is eight hours between London and California, I think briefly, what is the time difference between here and Mexico? How far back is the Mexican clock? Could Kirsty still be alive there? Could the accident be still waiting to happen?)

I pull myself together and tell Laurie that I won't be able to speak to her today. 'My sister-in-law is dead,' I say. 'She was killed this morning. By a boat. It hit her while she was in the water.'

'Oh my God, that is so terrible,' says Laurie. 'It must have happened very fast . . . instantly . . . a blow to the head—'

'How do you know that?' I say.

'I feel it,' says Laurie. 'I'm seeing her . . . . and the blood—'

'Oh fuck, I'm sorry I sent you that peculiar email about the blood,' I say. 'You must think I'm mad.'

'No, that was your sister-in-law's blood in the water,' says Laurie. 'It was precognitive.'

'My email was precognitive?' I say, confused. 'Look, I'm sorry, I've got to go now. I'll call you next week.'

I'm still confused when I go downstairs – not just about my conversation with Laurie, but about everything, *everything*, it's all a mess, I can't think straight, can't talk straight, can't find the words . . . Somehow, it is arranged that I will drive Neill down to South London, to his brother's house. Neill sits in the passenger seat, staring out of the window on to the streets, where other people are going home to live other lives. 'Every death reminds you of the last death,' he says. 'It's like falling in love. You don't know what it feels like until it happens to you for the first time. And then afterwards you think you've forgotten what it feels like, but it happens again. And again . . .'

As we cross Blackfriars Bridge, he says, 'Why do we always cross this bridge when someone has died?'

'Not always . . . just when Ruth died,' I say.

'My friend Tony walked into the river and drowned near here,' he says. 'From the south bank, between this bridge and Waterloo, I think . . . There should be a Blackfriars gatekeeper, like the ferryman for the River Styx.'

When we get to his brother Calum's house, their younger sister, Kitty, is already there, her pale face wet and swollen with tears, like a rain-soaked baby mushroom; and their mother, Peggy, who is not Kirsty's mother, has just arrived from America, where she lives. (Neill's family is complicated: his father, Ewan, who is dead, had three wives and five children. Neill and Kirsty were born seven months apart. They were close, and yet not close. They looked very alike, and sometimes sang together in clear, similar voices that wove in and out of each other. My children have inherited her red hair. She used to say they looked more like her than Neill.)

Everyone in this house has already drunk a lot of whisky, apart from me. They're all talking at the same time. Peggy's partner, Irene, who is Irish, is trying to tell me about her recent dream. 'I saw this boxer in my dream – and he was hit hard, really hard, and he fell to the floor – a white canvas floor – and then that famous boxer – what was his name? I've forgotten his name – the one who is in a coma, he's been in the newspapers – his accident happened after my dream, so why did I dream about him?'

'I don't know,' I say.

'But did the boxer – the real boxer – fall on to a white floor or a blue floor?' she says. 'I dreamt he fell on to white floor. But in the newspaper pictures, it looks blue. So was it a premonition of death or not?'

'I don't know, Irene,' I say. 'I'm sorry.'

Calum, who is four years younger than Neill, is talking quickly, describing the Sundays they spent as children at Kirsty's mother's house. 'Dad would be upstairs somewhere, and you and Kirsty always ran off into the woods together to play, and you left me behind,' he says, looking mournful.

'People always die south of the river,' says Neill, to no one in particular. 'Ruth, Tony . . . well, not Kirsty, though she died south across the water. And Dad's funeral . . . And Kimberley's funeral was on the south side of the river, in Mortlake, and so was Jon's. Bloody Mortlake crematorium . . . I hate that place.'

'Tony died *in* the river,' says Kitty, raising her head for a moment.

'I'll have to take you up on that point,' says Calum, who is beginning to slur his words. 'Ruth did *not* die south of the river.'

'She did,' I say. 'She died in Trinity Hospice in Clapham.'

'Oh,' he says. 'Sorry . . .'

'How did Kirsty die?' says Neill, kneading his grey face as if it was dough. 'Was there a lot of blood? Was she hit on the head? What happened to her head? I can't stop thinking about . . . I mean, no one seems to know what happened.'

I am silent. I do not think this is a good moment to offer up Laurie Campbell's version of events. It is late by now, and I drive Neill home. He does not want to talk. 'I just want to sleep,' he says, curled up against the window on his side of the car.

But now alas the tide has changed,
My love she has gone from me,
And winter's frost has touched my heart
And put a blight upon me.
Creeping fog is on the river,
Flow, sweet river, flow.
Sun and moon and stars gone with her.
Sweet Thames, flow softly . . .
Swift the Thames runs to the sea,
Flow sweet river, flow,
Bearing ships and part of me.
Sweet Thames, flow softly . . .

Ewan MacColl, 'Sweet Thames,
Flow Softly', 1965

## FRIDAY 22 DECEMBER

I FIND NEILL SITTING on the sofa, half-past ten at night, staring ahead into space. The children are asleep, so there is nothing to fill the silence. The school term ended today; the holiday is here. There is everything to do, and nothing to be done. 'What are you thinking about?' I ask.

'I feel like I'm in a very empty place,' he says.

I sigh, and sort today's cards into two piles (Christmas cards on the right, sympathy ones on the left). 'You've got to give yourself time,' I say, 'it's been less than four days since your sister died . . .'

He does not answer. 'We'll get through it,' I say, unable to meet his eyes. 'But I know it seems so hard . . . It's like . . . I don't know . . . it's like a curse.'

'There's no significance to any of this,' says Neill, angrily, 'no pattern. It just happened. These things happen. That's all there is. People die.'

I walk away from him, into the kitchen, where he and the children have been putting together a jigsaw puzzle that his mother gave them for Christmas. It is still unfinished, still full of gaping holes, so I compare it to the picture on the box. The puzzle is called 'I LOVE NEW YORK', and it is a tableaux of chaos: traffic jams, accidents, gridlock, potholes. A wide-eyed skeleton is driving an ambulance to Beth Israel Hospital, but the vehicle still has pieces missing. I can't see who might be inside. I start hunting for the bits of ambulance in the box, and Neill comes to help. Together, we try to finish the puzzle. 'Bereavement counselling?' he says, raising one eyebrow. We are, for now at least, on the same side again.

## Saturday 23 December

Our friend and neighbour, David Toop, comes round in the evening with Juliette for mince pies and ice cream. Later, when all the children are in bed, David (the keeper of many curious pieces of sonic history) plays us a recording that someone has sent him of Dr Konstantin Raudive, the former professor of psychology at the Universities of Uppsala and Riga, who believed that he could record the voices of the dead, either by leaving a tape recorder running in an empty room, or by attaching a microphone to a de-tuned radio. (Raudive's work continues to be admired by Judith Chisholm and Dale Palmer: a siren voice beyond the grave, that leads them deeper into their arcane studies of EVP). The recording that we are listening to tonight is in German, and as none of us can speak the language, it is incomprehensible; as are the voices of the dead, which sound on this tape as if they are random whispers picked up from distant radio stations on the other side of the world. As the tape continues, I become more and more aggressively sceptical. 'It's so *ridiculous*,' I say, 'how could anybody take this stuff seriously?'

'Well, of course I don't believe in it, but that's not the point – what's interesting is that these voices have significance to people who are looking for something,' says David, gently.

'But no sane person could find any significance in them,' I say.

'It's about magic,' says David.

'I found it more magical listening to Kirsty's voice singing on a CD this afternoon,' I say, and eat another mince pie.

When the Raudive recording comes to an end, Neill puts on the Grateful Dead instead, which makes me smile, but then before I've quite realized what's happening, we're having the same argument as last night, though I don't understand why. 'There is no pattern to Kirsty and Ruth's deaths,' he says, tersely, 'no symmetry, there's nothing unusual in it. For God's sake, there was a child in Tom's class who died of meningitis . . .'

'I'm *not* saying there's a pattern,' I reply, 'and of course lots of people die in horrible and unexpected ways, but it is unusual that we both have sisters who died young.'

'Every death is different,' says Neill.

'I *know* every death is different – you know I understand that – I'm not stupid,' I say, feeling fractured, and then grinding to a halt. There doesn't seem to be any point in finishing the conversation, so I go to bed, leaving Neill and David to whisky and lost voices, while wreathes of cigarette smoke creep upstairs, settling in the dusty corners of every room, an acrid late-night pall that will last until morning.

## SUNDAY 24 DECEMBER

> . . . two sorts of elements will be recognized in religious doctrines and rituals: on the one hand fixations to the ancient history of the family and survivals of it, and on the other hand revivals of the past and returns, after long intervals, of what has been forgotten . . .
>
> Sigmund Freud, *Moses, His People, and Monotheist Religion*

LOLA AND JOE come to visit this afternoon, and so does my brother-in-law, Matt, and my mother and father, in an unusual show of seasonal unity. We exchange presents and kisses and good wishes for the coming year. Lola, who is exceptionally articulate for a child of five, is worried that Neill is sad about his dead sister. 'Are you OK?' she says, anxiously, turning her small, serious face up to him. 'I'm OK,' he says, picking her up and holding her close. 'I'm very worried about the floods,' she says. 'There is so much flooding. The rivers are overflowing. If it carries on raining, our houses will be filled with water, and we'll have to live in the attic.'

'Don't worry, sweetheart,' I say. 'It's not raining very hard.'

'It is,' she says. 'It has rained more rain this winter than for the last three hundred years. The man told us on the radio. The sun has gone away.'

We eat crisps and sandwiches and cake, and then my father brings out his Menorah, which he brought with him to remind us that it is the fourth night of Hanukah, as well as Christmas Eve. Lola and Joe light a candle each, and so do Jamie and Tom. 'Four cousins lighting four candles,' says Lola, who likes counting her family members, to reassure herself, perhaps, that there is strength in numbers (or that no one else has disappeared).

'Let the light of God in,' says my father.

Afterwards, Matt takes Lola and Joe home to South London, and I make mushroom soup for the remainder of my family. It seems like a good thing to do. (When Ruth died, Neill filled the fridge with food, and cooked for me every day, slowly, laboriously. 'You need to keep your strength up,' he said. 'You need more vitamins.')

Over dinner, my father tells us about his blind dates – arranged through the *Guardian*'s 'Soulmates' page. He has had twenty-nine responses from potential girlfriends, he says, in reply to his recent advertisement. ('Moses supposes his toe-ses are roses; or: All About Eve. Radical Jewish man, ex-South African, was academic, playwright and actor, sixty-four, looks and feels fifty-ish, seeks good woman. Hope you, Eve, will contact me, Adam. This time God is on our side!') My mother sits silent at the other end of the table, raising her left eyebrow every so often, while my father describes his romantic adventures. ('We met for lunch in a vegetarian restaurant in Bath. But there was something strange about her teeth . . .')

My father is living by himself in a small house in Cardiff; he doesn't yet know many people in the city. He refrains from saying that he is lonely, but I think he must be, though he tells us that he is very busy, planting perennial shrubs in his new garden, and attending the local synagogue. (He had hoped, earlier this year, to train as a Rabbi, but these plans came to nothing.)

The candles on the Menorah have gone out by the time dinner is over, so I light them again. 'I said a prayer at Shul for Kirsty,' he says, and sighs. Then he starts singing Jewish hymns, quietly, but distinctly. 'They must have sung these hymns on the way to the gas chambers,' he says, mournfully. Neill has already retreated to the other room, with the children, to watch *The Wizard of Oz*. My father doesn't like Christmas, much in the same way that he hates Easter. When I was a child, he used to tell us that he was goaded into despair by this alien holiday that celebrated the birth of a Christian king, in whose name, as he so often reminded us, millions of Jews were slaughtered. This year, however, he adds a spin to the story. 'I hated Hanukah, too, when I was a child,' he says, 'because my mother was so right wing that she wouldn't let us celebrate that, either – at least, we weren't allowed presents, because she thought that would make it seem too much like Christmas. So I never had any presents . . .'

'But you like Hanukah now,' I say, trying to steer the conversation back to safer waters.

'Yes, I do,' he says, with another deep sigh. 'You know, I'm giving a lecture soon at the orthodox synagogue, on the Kabbalah. You should come.'

'I know,' I say, 'I got your email. It sounds interesting.' And then – but why do I do it, when I know the danger ahead? – I add, 'So, do you believe in God now?'

'You know I don't!' he explodes. 'Why don't you ever listen to me!'

'Well, it just seems strange not to believe in God,' I say, widening the rift between us, 'when you spend so much time at synagogue.'

'You don't have to believe in God to be a Jew,' he shouts. 'Only an idiot could believe in God. *An idiot!* Six million Jews died in the Holocaust – and there was no God to save them. Six million Jews!'

I start laughing, which is of course the wrong thing to do, a cruel and dangerous act of provocation, but I can't help myself, because suddenly everything seems so ridiculous. 'How can you laugh at the Jews' suffering!' says my father, outraged.

'Why can't you have a sense of humour?' I say.

'You can't have a sense of humour about the Holocaust!' he bellows.

'Oh please, no, not the Holocaust *again*, not tonight,' I say.

'That's right, avoid the subject of the Holocaust, as usual,' he says. 'You just switch off when I try to talk about it . . . You don't care, you never have done.'

Then I stand up and start shouting, too. 'How dare you come to this house, and start talking about death as if you own the subject, when Neill's sister has just died, how *dare* you! You can't bear not being the centre of attention! You are a horrible, selfish man!'

My father looks even angrier, though frail, too, as if I have hit him, so I march into the next room, where Neill and the boys are sitting on the sofa, and Judy Garland is still searching for the Wizard. Neill smiles with one corner of his mouth. Jamie and Tom are white-faced and solemn. 'I'm sorry,' I say to the boys. 'Anyway, it's nothing to worry about. Sometimes people get cross with each other at this time of year.'

'Ho, ho, ho,' says Neill.

My father walks upstairs, heavily, and goes to bed. My mother goes after him, and then comes back downstairs. 'He's saying his Jewish prayers,' she says.

'Good for him,' I say.

'He says he'd be better off dead,' she adds.

'I couldn't agree more,' I say, and she looks shocked. Then I start feeling guilty, and worry that I've gone too far. 'You don't think he's going to try to kill himself tonight, do you?'

'Oh no,' says my mother, 'he'll outlive us all.'

## MONDAY 25 DECEMBER

> And suddenly there was with the angel a multitude of the heavenly host praising God, and saying, Glory to God in the highest, and on earth peace, good will toward men.
>
> St. Luke, Chapter 2, verses 13–14

IN THE MORNING, after the children have opened their stockings, but before my father is up, I'm in the kitchen stuffing the turkey and talking to my mother. 'I'm not doing this again,' I say, shoving sausage meat into the dead bird, 'this stupid pretence that we're having a happy family Christmas. I mean, you and Dad are *divorced* for God's sake. Why do we have to spend it together? He's not your responsibility.'

'I feel guilty,' she says. 'Someone has got to look after him.'

'Why on earth do you feel guilty?' I say, crossly. 'What's the bloody point?'

'Maybe it's to do with my twin brother,' she says, thoughtfully. 'I never see him, so I feel responsible for Dad, instead. They're both as difficult as each other.'

'Well, why don't you give up trying to rescue your

ex-husband,' I say, even more unkindly. 'It's not fair inflicting this on Neill and the kids. It's hard enough already this year . . . Not that a ghastly Christmas is anything unusual. I mean, remember the one when Dad was in mental hospital, and you took me and Ruth there for Christmas Day, and we sat outside in the corridor while you spent the morning with him in some padded cell.'

'I would never leave you alone in a mental hospital!' she says. 'I think you must be imagining that I left you in the corridor.'

'You did,' I say, irritably, childishly (though as a child then, I remained silent and stoic). 'I was eight, I *remember* it . . .' (And I can remember it, I can. Ruth and I sat on a bench, very close together, and strange men with thin white faces and beards walked past. One of them stopped and told us that he was Jesus Christ. He had a crown of tinsel on his head. He looked like Jesus, I thought, except for the fact that he was wearing his pyjamas. It smelt of cabbage in the hospital. Even the Christmas tree in the corridor smelt of cabbage. There was a lopsided fairy on top, and her wand was pointing to the wall. 'Don't worry,' I said to Ruth, holding her hot little hand. 'We're going home soon . . .')

I pull myself together when my father comes downstairs. 'Happy Christmas,' we say to each other, with a tentative hug. 'Happy Christmas!' He gives me a present, a pot of 'Self-Heal skin cream'. It is made out of flower essences and herbal tinctures. After more exchanges of presents, I spend the morning cooking turkey, roast potatoes, sausages, bacon, parsnips, bread sauce, cranberry sauce, peas, sprouts and gravy. (There has to be some tradition here today, somewhere in the midst of this chaos.) For my father, I make two nut cutlets. 'Actually, I quite like bacon,' he says, mildly, 'even though I am Jewish.'

'This is the best Christmas ever!' says Tom, who has been given a Gameboy and a scooter.

'Thank you for your generosity and hospitality,' says my father, with strange formality, though no apparent trace of irony. 'Thank you, sweetest child . . .'

After lunch, we watch the Queen ('Now *she* really has got a dysfunctional family,' says my father, happily).

I go to bed early, at the same time as the children, with a sore throat. ('Your throat is sore because you don't say what you are really feeling,' says my imaginary therapist. 'Yes, I do,' I reply. 'In fact, my throat is probably sore because I shouted at my father. I shouldn't have shouted.')

When I wake up in the morning, my parents have already left. My father has left a note on the kitchen table. 'The best Christmas ever!' he has written. 'But also the saddest. See you at my talk on 10 January 2001.'

## SUNDAY 31 DECEMBER

> Children, it is the final hour.
>
> 1 John, Chapter 2, verse 18

I HATE NEW YEAR'S Eve. I hate the sense of expectation, when nothing will be different tomorrow. I hate the cold, the rain, the dark, the mud. I hate being depressed. Depressed – what a boring word; what a boring thing to be. My hands are dry and my fingernails broken. I eat and eat and eat, filling up on the Christmas cake my mother baked for us; filling up the gaps; building more flesh over the scratches inside me.

Neill drives us to Norfolk, to be with other people, other than each other. We are staying with friends, in the house I visited last August (the house where there was a handprint on the living-room window, though now the mark has gone). The children are excited; rosy cheeked, bright eyed, almost feverish. They will be up until after midnight, to see the new year arrive. Perhaps they think it will be clean and fresh and exciting, this unspoilt year, like the snow that fell yesterday. Two thousand and one: my first century uninhabited by Ruth. ('I don't think so,' says the voice in my head.)

I make a chocolate cake for the children and their friends to eat later. (Baking is good; it makes me feel like I'm getting somewhere, as the sponge rises). We go for a walk in the afternoon, across the frozen fields. It is so cold here that the mud has turned to ice, which is better than sodden, slushy London. Every time I slow down to talk to Neill, to walk alongside him, he speeds up. When I try to catch up with him, he falls behind. I cannot blame him for avoiding me. We remind each other of ourselves: pale surviving siblings; twins for a time.

## Tuesday 2 January 2001

I HAVE BEEN AT home all day, alone, except for the cat. I came back last night from Norfolk to do some work, and Neill stayed behind with the children (I'm sufficiently rattled to think he is still avoiding me). This is the first time I have been by myself in the house for quite so long, and the silence is disconcerting. I send an email to Dale Palmer in Indiana to wish him a happy New Year, and reply to one from Sarah Estep in Annapolis, my new computer correspondent. (Sarah never complains, even though she is old and often ill. She has sent messages to me every week, sometimes more often, ever since Dale introduced us via email after my trip to New York last October. I have asked her – in her capacity as the current world expert on EVP – to listen out for a message from my sister, and though she has not yet heard one, Sarah always encourages me not to give up my search for Ruth, to continue trying to contact her through the computer or via a tape recorder. 'Successful recorders must have an ocean of patience and perseverance,' she writes, 'but it's well worth it, when the other side starts to communicate.' She also suggests I should play my EVP tapes backwards. 'A number of voices appear on the reverse, or wrong side, of recording tapes. To me, the reverse voice is the best evidence we have that they are genuine. Your voice, asking short questions, will come out gibberish, but their voice can be as clear as crystal.' I don't have the heart to tell her that I've given up EVP taping, because the sound of my voice speaking to the unchanged silence was too disconcerting to live with.)

Afterwards, I feel quite strange and disconnected. I punctuate the day with food. Two bowls of cereal. Five chocolate biscuits. Scrambled eggs. Another cup of tea. Two ginger nuts. I rub the Self-Heal skin cream that my father gave me into my dry hands. My mother rings, but I don't seem to know how to talk.

'How was your New Year's Eve?' I say, though it feels like I'm speaking a foreign language.

'Oh, you know, fine,' she says. 'One always has the expectation that one will be spending it with one's loved ones, and the reality never lives up to those hopes.'

'Hmm,' I say. 'Oh well, I'd better go.'

'Yes,' she says, 'I have a patient coming to see me.'

'Bye,' I say.

'Goodbye,' she says.

I go to the chemist and buy some vitamin C. I come home and take a tablet, hoping to feel more normal. It doesn't quite seem to work. At four o'clock it is dark again. 'Why is it so dark?' I say to the cat. She doesn't reply.

At seven o'clock, I decide to do something to fill the space in the house. I am going to try Automatic Writing. I know the theory, at least, because Neill gave me a book for Christmas called 'How To Do Automatic Writing'. This may have been a joke, but I decide to take it seriously. The thing to do, apparently, is to light a candle in front of a mirror, and look into the mirror; eventually, the spirits will come through and guide your hand. So I turn off all the lights downstairs and light a candle. I look into a mirror in the kitchen, holding a pen in one hand and in the other a photocopy that I brought home from the Freud Museum last month – eighteen pages from Ernest Jones' *Sigmund Freud: Life and Work* (Chapter XIV, 'Occultism'). It seems like a good thing to write on, or at least, to write on the back of . . .

I look into the mirror, and I do not like what I see. Me. Not Ruth. Somewhat fatter than before Christmas. Pale pudding face. Dark circles under my eyes. I write the following lines (though I do not feel as if my hand is being guided from another world).

Who is in the glass?
I see myself.
I see Kimberley's dead body in her flat, in the shadows.
I am spooking myself. No, no, start again.
The house is alive.
I see the reflection of the kitchen window in the mirror. There is no one there. The back of my neck is cold.
Back, back, one cannot go back.

I stop writing. None of this seems to me to be very significant or meaningful. I try again, letting my hand drift across the page, as instructed in the book. This time, I have no sense of writing anything at all. Just squiggles. It is quite relaxing, this squiggling, the drifting through the dark . . . Afterwards, I read what I have written. It doesn't look like anything at all. There is a word on the first page that looks like 'jolly', or maybe 'jelly'. On the next page, the ghost words are incomprehensible ('slesssegsthaly Mslshnnn'). They make no more sense when I try to read them backwards. On the third, and final page, there is a word that looks a little bit like 'lunacy', then some more squiggles, and at the end, 'thennnnnnnnnn'.

I turn over the page, and read what Ernest Jones has to say instead. This seems rather more helpful:

> Freud had shown in his book *Totem and Taboo* that the animistic stage through which mankind must, however imperfectly, have passed in his early stages of development recurs in the mental life of the young child, and so has to be once more 'surmounted' before an adequate grasp of reality is achieved. This surmounting, however, is more often incomplete than is commonly thought, and there exists a tendency to revert to it in various circumstances. Situations which revive this mode of thought, with its accompanying belief in magical powers, arouse the feeling of uncanniness . . . The dread of something terrifyingly mysterious and malevolent proceeding from a demonic or supernatural agency, such as the appearance of a ghost at midnight, is always the result of projection into the outer world of unconscious repressed wishes . . .

The trouble is, I *want* to see a ghost. I do not dread being haunted. So where does that leave the Freudian theory of repressed wishes? Clearly, I need a therapist. I ring my mother. 'Mum,' I say, 'it's me. Has your patient gone?'

'Yes,' she says, 'some time ago. Are you still on your own?'

'Yes,' I say. 'Sorry I sounded so distracted earlier.'

'That's OK,' she says.

'Um, I've got a question,' I say.

'Yes?' she says.

'You know Ernest Jones says that Freud says that the dread of seeing a ghost at midnight is the result of projection of an unconscious repressed wish?'

'Yes,' she says. (This familiarity with obscure Freudian references is one of the many advantages of having a therapist for a mother). 'And . . .?'

'Well, what does it mean when you *want* to see a ghost? When you don't dread it?'

She pauses for a few seconds, as if choosing her words carefully. 'I think Freud would say that wanting to see a ghost is to do with unresolved grief, or unresolved loss. You might look up what he has to say about narcissism. Narcissism is not what you think it means – it's a developmental stage, a wanting to stay in a certain state of being – and being locked in it, and not moving on.'

'What else?' I say, trying to keep my voice level, because I don't want to alarm my mother unnecessarily by letting slip that yes, I am stuck, locked in and left behind, staring at myself in a mirror, in an attempt to reach my sister on the other side.

'It's when you want that world which can be magically controlled,' continues my mother, 'because it's more comforting, because reality is unbearable.'

'That sounds interesting,' I say.

'You might look up what Freud says on "phantasy" as well,' she adds.

'OK,' I say. 'I'll go and do some reading.'

I'm half-way through Freud's essay on 'Taboo and Emotional Ambivalence' ('to turn away from reality is at the same time to withdraw from the community of man') when the phone rings again.

'It's me,' says my mother. 'I've just had another thought. Why don't you read what Freud has to say on Thanatos – or the death wish – and Eros, the life force? You know, the Cartesian duality . . .'

'All right,' I say, though in fact I don't understand Cartesian duality at all.

'Are you still by yourself?' she says, sounding a bit worried.

'Yes,' I say, 'but I'm fine.'

'Take care,' she says.

'I will,' I say, and put the phone down.

I get rather lost with Freud on the subject of narcissism, especially the difficult stuff about 'libidinal hypercathexis' (more proof, as if I needed it, of my regressive – possibly retarded –

inability to move on); and then I grind to a complete halt at the footnote on the subject of 'intellectual narcissism and the omnipotence of thoughts'. (1. 'It is almost an axiom with writers on this subject, that a sort of Solipsism, or Berkeleianism (as Professor Sully terms it as he finds it in the Child), operates in the savage to make him refuse to recognize death as a fact.') By this time, I'm so tired that my eyes are swimming; I'm seeing double. But still, I know there is only me. 'And me,' says Ruth's voice in my head. 'Don't forget about me.'

'I won't,' I say. 'How could I ever forget you?' And I smile, a wide smile, for the first time in two weeks or more. Happy new year . . .

## Wednesday 3 January

I DREAM I AM at Kirsty's funeral. It's not a solemn affair: in fact, there's a lot of people standing in front of a stage, chatting, listening to music – listening to her sing, at one point. Then after the singing, a man starts reading a eulogy about her: at first I think he is her father, Ewan MacColl (a musician, too, like his children). But I'm confused, because I know that her father – who is also Neill's father – is dead (and anyway, what's Kirsty doing, singing at her own funeral?). The man is delivering his speech, reading from a text that he is clutching in his hands, but I can see that he has decided to leave certain words out – because they are words that must remain unsaid. Normally, in my dreams, I cannot read (the letters simply melt away), but tonight I see two words on the printed page that the man is holding: 'inner' and 'utter'. These are the words that cannot be spoken. When I wake up, I can still see the words, but they don't seem to make any sense: they're like the clues to a cryptic crossword (or maybe the answer, though I don't understand the puzzle).

I fall asleep again, and dream of my friend, Oscar Moore, who died of Aids in 1996: except in my dream, he isn't dead. And it's not like he's come back from the dead, either – it's as if he never went away. We go to a bar together, and then to a party (as we often used to), with him leading the way through streets that I don't quite recognize. It's reassuring to see him again, looking so well, so entirely real and wry and robust, after all this time. Oscar was always a great believer in the pleasures of this world, rather than the next. In my dream, I say to him, 'Some things never change, at least.'

In the morning, I realize that last night's party – the dream party – is the first social event I've attended for some time. Perhaps I need to address this issue: to get out more, given that I now seem to be spending most of my nights emailing elderly psychic researchers on the other side of the Atlantic; either that, or talking to the dead.

## Thursday 4 January

Jamie is sick. He has a high temperature, and aches all over, and shields his eyes from the light. 'What if I have meningitis?' he asks me, after vomiting into the kitchen sink.

'I'm sure you haven't,' I say.

'How do you know?' he says.

'I just know,' I reply, putting my arms around my shaking child; but at the same time a part of me is scared that maybe something terrible will happen again. (Death is all around us; it stalks us . . . so why not one more disappearing act?)

'Are we cursed?' says Jamie, as if he can read my mind.

'No, of course not,' I say, firmly. 'We're very lucky, in many ways.'

'What ways?' he says.

'Lots of ways,' I say. 'Now get some sleep, and everything will feel better in the morning, OK?'

## Friday 5 January

Kirsty's funeral. Before we go there, I take the dog for a walk, round the corner to our local park. It is drizzling and empty and silent; but then I see a robin, and the robin sees me, yet does not fly away; and as I listen to his voice, sweet enough to pierce the sky, it feels as if the whole park is suddenly filled with birdsong; and a strange, pure, miraculous joy rises from the muddy trodden grass, like steam, like someone else's breath. Life is fragile, impossible . . . and all we can do is to cherish it. I walk home, thinking that puddles are beautiful; and most people have good hearts, even the grumpy skinhead with the Alsatian dog on the other side of the football pitch; and then I go and find Neill. 'I just had a life-enhancing moment,' I tell him. 'In the park.'

'Oh, good,' he says, looking bleak. 'And why was that?'

'I saw a robin,' I reply, and then stop, realizing that I sound lame, like a manufactured motto in a limp greeting card. ('All things bright and beautiful, all creatures great and small . . .')

By the time we're driving across town, on our way to Mortlake Crematorium, my pocket of joy has filled up with dust and decay. The January city is grim; the sky hangs low over London. The people gathered outside the crematorium look shocked, and crippled, almost; bent over with grief and holding themselves as if they hurt; as if they might break into splintered pieces after unwrapping their arms from around themselves.

Inside the crematorium, Kirsty's coffin is covered with pink and orange tropical flowers; and fairy lights are woven around the frame that surrounds it, like a four-poster bed in a goodnight story. I think that she would have liked the flowers – tiger lilies, the colour of her hair – and all the little lights, but I can't feel her in this place, yet surely, she must be here. I stare up at the ceiling, but I still cannot see her; though across the aisle, she is partly mirrored in the faces of her children, who look surprised to find themselves here. At the end of the funeral her voice fills the room for a few minutes, when one of her last songs is played, and the sound of her warm breath laps about us, and then she is gone.

Afterwards, we walk around the garden, where previous mourners have hung Christmas cards and crystals in the bare winter trees. 'To Gran, RIP, Happy New Year,' says one of the messages, pinned to a branch alongside a rosary. Some of the cards have lost their colour, drained away in the rain. There are fading photographs, curling in the damp behind glass frames; and frail wreaths of flowers, too, placed on the bare earth of the crematorium borders, and wilted roses, still wrapped in cellophane, misted with condensation, like tears. In one corner, a small wet teddy bear is leaning against a little frosted plastic Christmas tree, as an offering to a dead child.

Neill and I wait for his younger brother and sister, Calum and Kitty, who have not been invited to the funeral, yet need to find something of her today. (What divides a family also ties it together in unyielding knots; I think we all know that.) The next funeral is already underway, and another hearse has just arrived, and there will be more before the day is out. (How many dead people pass through here every year, year after year, trailed by black cars and undertakers and more grief-stricken faces?) So we walk around the garden together again, searching for Kirsty, but nothing is left to see. Her flowers and fairy lights have gone.

There is no smoke, no fire, no ashes. (Sometimes the living feel colder than the dead.)

Eventually, we leave the crematorium, and go for a cup of tea nearby, in the upstairs room of a café overlooking the river. The tide is coming in fast, and the water rising. As it grows dark outside, an arrow of birds fly west along the river. 'When I was falling asleep last night, I dreamt of Kirsty,' says Calum. 'We didn't talk, we just sat close together. She felt so warm . . .' The walls of the café are auburn, like her hair, and when someone laughs, I think it is her.

Now it is late, and Jamie is sleeping, and I hope that Kirsty is peaceful; swooping up, up, up, to the place where her voice, her lovely voice, has pierced the sky.

> 'Oh, Aslan,' said Lucy. 'Will you tell us how to get into your country from our world?'
>
> 'I shall be telling you all the time,' said Aslan. 'But I will not tell you how long or short the way will be, only that it lies across a river. But do not fear that, for I am the great Bridge Builder. And now come; I will open the door in the sky and send you to your own land.'
>
> C.S. Lewis, Chapter 16, 'The Very End of the World', *The Voyage of the Dawn Treader*

## Saturday 6 January

OK, so I am going to go to a party. A real party. By myself, because Neill doesn't want to talk to anybody. But a party, nevertheless. On the way, walking through Soho, I'm almost too scared to go through with this plan (ghosts are so much quieter than real people); but I force myself along Dean Street. Inside the party, I don't seem to be able to speak: the words come out in the wrong order, or I can't think of anything to say. ('So, how are you?' 'Fine, I'm fine.' 'Good . . .' 'Yes . . .' 'Well, see you soon.') I try to have a conversation with a man who is an actor; he is playing the Scarecrow in a pantomime version of *The Wizard of Oz.* 'It's very simplified,' he says, 'but the kids love it.'

'Do you still have a Wicked Witch of the East and a Wicked Witch of the West?' I ask him.

'Yes,' he says.

'Does Dorothy go from east to west?' I say.

'I really don't know,' he says, before moving away to the far side of the room.

Towards the end of the evening, I start talking to someone about my trips to the Spiritualist Union of Great Britain, and she looks at me with concern. 'You don't really believe in any of that stuff, do you?' she says.

'Oh *no*, not at all,' I say, confidently, but feeling immediately guilty, as if I'm betraying Ruth. (And what if Ruth can hear me, denying her very existence? Of course she can hear me – she's inside my head . . . ) After the party, I walk back to the car, which I'd parked on a quiet, unlit side-street; a street which now looks sinister, at 1 o'clock in the morning. Three men are walking behind me, catching up, and paranoia is bubbling in my stomach. And then, instead of breaking into a run, I decide that I am safe: I have at least three ghosts accompanying me – the best protection you could ask for. 'Yea, though I walk through the valley of the shadow of death, I will fear no evil,' I say out loud, holding my keys between my clenched knuckles. The men behind slow down. Perhaps they're frightened of me.

(Back in the car, I decide that maybe we shouldn't rely on ghosts, after all. They seem so inconsistent in their actions: flibbertigibbet, fly-by-night spirits, flimflamming around the ether. Where were the friendly ghosts to help Kirsty, in her hour of need? Why didn't her dead father nudge the boat out of the way, five inches in another direction, to save her? Why this? Why her? Why not . . . )

## WEDNESDAY 17 JANUARY

MY HOUSE IS sad. Even the dog is sick, and will not move from our bed. My husband is grieving, and will not come out of the attic. My oldest son is ill, and will not stop coughing. My youngest son wants to be with his friends, to be anywhere but here. I move through the house like a ghost, making no impression, tidying things up to no effect at all. Piles of paper mount on the kitchen table. Dirty washing lies in a corner of the bathroom. I go upstairs to the attic to talk to Neill, and find him lying in a sleeping bag on the floor. 'Do you want to talk?' I say.

'No,' he replies, and turns his face to the wall.

'Do you think you should go and see a therapist?' I say.

'No,' he says, closing his eyes.

(The week before Ruth died, she came home from the hospice for a couple of days, and I went to visit her, to massage her, because she didn't want to talk by then. I stroked her poor, wasted arms, rubbed lavender oil into her hunched shoulders, and then she turned away from me, turning her face to the wall, closing her eyes, preoccupied, silent . . . )

I go back downstairs and cook lamb chops for dinner. Jamie is reading his book about air crashes. It lists the weather conditions at the time of each crash, the pilots' dialogue from recovered black boxes, and the names of the dead. 'Where did you get that book?' I say.

'Don't you remember, I got it when we were in Wales and it

was raining all the time?' he says. 'I just haven't wanted to finish reading it until now.'

'Isn't it a bit depressing?' I say.

He does not reply, absorbed in the statistics of loss. Afterwards, over his lamb chops, he says, 'I read a story in the newspaper about a girl who died of BSE. She got it from her baby food. Do you think I've got BSE?'

'No,' I say.

'I bet I have,' he says.

'I bet you haven't,' I say.

'How much do you bet?' he says. I do not reply, and he returns to his book. I go back upstairs to talk to Neill. 'I'm worried about Jamie,' I say. 'I think he's become very morbid.'

'Who can blame him?' says Neill, who has emerged from the sleeping bag by now, and is staring at the computer screen.

'Do you want to come down?' I say.

'No,' he says. 'I'm working.'

Later, when the children are in bed, and the only sound in the house is their breathing, I turn on my computer. I'm longing for some emails – from someone, anyone, I just need somebody to talk to. There is one message waiting. It is from my father, whose lecture I missed last week on the Kabbalah. It is addressed to 'Jay-Bird': the affectionate name given to me as a child, by my mother. No one has called me Jay-Bird for over twenty-five years. This is what he writes:

> At every point in Jewish history where suffering and exile afflicted the people there was an understandable retreat into mysticism and magic. Of course, too, there was a violent reaction towards militant nationalism eventually put down at the time, and only realized more fully in 1948 with the establishment of the Jewish state: hence the Hanukah story involving the Greek Syrian repression of the periodic success of the Hasmonean revolt. With this partial victory came the traditional belief in a miracle: the candelabra burning eight days of oil from one day's

> oil – the mystical act whereby God works through his sacred personages.
>
> The Book of Ezekiel involves the visions of that prophet written during the Babylonian repression of the eighth century BCE [BC]. The visions of the divine chariot which, so it was written, took the prophet Elijah to heaven in the era of the later Kings – post Solomon of the eleventh century BCE. Elijah, it is written, went to heaven without actually dying by means of the mystically-understood divine chariot. This became the foundation of what Jews later called the Kabbalah – the Tradition – in this case the mystical retreat into the Other World through meditation which transcended rabbinical legalism, a dry as dust Pharisaic activity, and which transcended the power-ploys of the wealthy aristocratic Sadducees of Jesus' time . . .

The text goes on in this vein for several more paragraphs, but though I read it and reread it five or six times, I still can't understand what he's saying. So I send him an email, asking when he first became interested in the Kabbalah. His reply arrives soon after:

> Justine,
> I first became interested in Kabbalah when I was living in Hillbrow in Johannesburg in the early nineties trying hard to understand my dad and his curiously female-dependent personality . . . I believe with Jung that religious archetypes underly the unconscious. The male-female division is arbitrary but he was dominated by a de-sexualised Tiferet and overwhelmed by his Shekhina – see his romantic poetry. My aunt Anne who died on Christmas eve told me scornfully that 'he had to marry a virgin . . .' (!)
>
> Dad
> DAFD

I still don't get the point (and I don't understand who DAFD is); but, nevertheless, the mere fact that we communicate with each other seems like a good thing. Maybe I need to read more carefully between the lines? Love, surely, is contained there.

## Friday 19 January

'Sir, did that youth confess he had cheated me,
I'd disbelieve him! He may cheat at times;
That's in the "medium"-nature, thus they're made,
Vain and vindictive, cowards, prone to scratch.
And so all cats are; still, a cat's the beast
You coax the strange electric sparks from out,
By rubbing back its fur . . .'

Robert Browning, 'Mr Sludge, The Medium'

I feel like I'm failing my husband; failing to come up with words of comfort (yet what can words do now?). Our friends are kind, but they, too, have little to say to Neill, to me. Their struggle mirrors mine; and it is as if we have moved beyond the realm of normal conversation (or maybe death seems infectious, in the darkest month, and we therefore find ourselves in an isolation zone; incommunicable). This is, in part, why I have enrolled at the Arthur Findlay College, in Essex, to join a training course in mediumship: extreme circumstances demand desperate measures. (And yes, I'm desperate, given the difficulties of talking to the living, let alone the increasing number of dead people in my life.) I realize that others might see this decision as bizarre, which is why I have not told anybody – apart from my silent husband –

about the plan. So I've been driving up the M11, and no one knows where I'm going, which is an unusually liberating experience.

My destination is near Stansted Airport, forty miles or so north of London, yet I might as well have driven a hundred years or more away. The college is a sprawling Gothic mansion, built on the remains of a fifteenth-century house, and the epicentre of the Spiritualists National Union: the place where mediums great and small flock to hone their art.

It is snowing, and the trees that line the long driveway leading to the college are white against the grey-dusk sky. The house lies far from the sight of the road, beyond a Victorian gatehouse, hidden from the airport and the motorway. I park my car underneath a tall fir tree, and walk inside. There is a cat with no tail in the front hall, and a man in black leather trousers and a long dark coat, sitting beside the unlit fireplace, filling in an entrance form. It is very cold, and a faint smell of wet cat food hangs in the still air. The man in black has an extraordinarily large crystal hanging around his neck, but I don't want to be caught out staring at him, so I concentrate on the cat instead, who returns my gaze, with yellow eyes that do not blink.

A business-like woman emerges from another door, and takes her place behind the reception desk. 'Is it still snowing outside?' she says to me.

'Yes,' I say.

'Good,' she says, with a smile, 'we'll all be snowed in here.' She hands me a printed form: there are questions to answer about whether I have any previous experience as a medium; about my spiritualist contacts; about what I hope to gain from the teachers on the course. I write that I am in search of my dead sister; that I wish to learn how to distinguish between real and imaginary voices in my head.

She leads me down a wood-panelled corridor, through two sets of double doors, into the lecture hall, a large room overlooking the pale frosted lawn. At least a hundred people are already seated in rows, though the platform before them is still empty. I sit down, surprised that I am one of so many, and look at the sombre oil paintings that hang on the walls: portraits of Arthur Findlay, the former owner of this house, and his family, I suppose (for it was Findlay – a successful Edwardian stockbroker turned writer and philosopher – who bequeathed the property to his fellow spiritualists as a centre for their endeavours).

The mediums-in-training around me are of all ages; though there are slightly more women than men. I had expected most of the audience to be grey-haired, but in fact, a sizeable number are my age or younger: people like me . . . At 4.30 p.m., our course leader strides into the room – Glyn Edwards – followed by eight tutors. He stands on the platform, wreathed in the scent of aftershave (or is it holiness?) while the tutors arrange themselves in a solemn semi-circle behind him. Five of the teachers are older women; three are younger men. One of the latter is thick-set and crew cut, with tattoos on his forearms, heavy-duty boots, and the nerveless look of an ex-soldier. The other two men are rather more diffident, while the women have a cosily theatrical air: draped in wispy chiffon scarves and conspiratorial stage whispers, gilt costume jewellery glinting in the badly lit room. As for their leader: Mr Edwards is wearing a gold tie, with a matching gold handkerchief tucked into the pocket of his tweed jacket. I find myself transfixed by his remarkable colour co-ordination: mustard-yellow shirt, immaculate brown trousers, dapper houndstooth waistcoat, fine tweed jacket and a pair of matching polished brown leather shoes. His blow-dried hair is carefully arranged, and his sizeable sideburns neat. 'Happy New Year!' he says to us all, baring his teeth in what I take to be a smile.

Our voices are not sufficiently confident for his liking, so he tells us to give a louder response. '*Happy New Year!*' we chorus, like an obedient pantomime audience. Mr Edward's first task is to put us into groups, but this takes some time, because he is deaf ('I do have a hearing aid, but it doesn't always work') and we do not speak loudly enough for him, and there is additional confusion because of misspelled names on the list that he holds before him. When he comes to my name, it bears no relation to reality, so as I spell the correct version out loud for him, he raises his eyes to the ceiling, in mock-despair. 'Is there anybody there?' he cries, to gales of laughter.

Afterwards, Mr Edwards lectures us on the importance of hard work and responsibility in our training. 'I'm clairvoyant, ladies and gentlemen, I see *everything*,' he says, by way of warning. 'We are going back to where we came from,' he continues, his voice filling the hall, as he glares at us with apparent dislike. 'Do you know your own spirit?' he says, to the now silent audience. '*Do you know your own spirit?*' Still, no one replies. '*Why in God's name don't you?*' he thunders. 'This weekend is going to be run the way I want,' he continues, with a faint air of belligerence, though no one is disagreeing with him, 'and the way the spirit world wants.' His voice softens – and I'm impressed by his powerful oratory technique, despite being faintly repelled – as he continues with this peculiar mixture of admonishment and inspiration. 'Tonight we are going to get you used to sitting in the stillness, to blend with the spirit world, to feel peaceful, calm, content, to let your spirit people link with you. You will be taught how to let them communicate with you, to become aware of how they are affecting you, and to begin to accept those experiences . . .

'You have to have your own experience,' he says, his voice even quieter than before, and suddenly, he's shouting again, so loudly that I jump, '*And that's what you're going to get this weekend!*' Then he's whispering, as faint as a bird in the attic. 'If we can do that, then the key is in the door . . .'

Mr Edwards screws up his face tightly, as he peers at his rapt audience. 'We're talking about a power from the spirit world, about a vibration, about an energy,' he says. 'It can only come about if you want to cooperate with it. I'm interested in you, I'm concerned about every single one of you, I'm sensing what's come with you – but I need you to trust me, the spirit people need you to trust them. We are opening doors – opening a window into your soul . . . Often, when things don't seem to be happening, something *is* happening in the background. You start to open up. Will you do that?' he asks us.

'Y*es!*' we chorus, as one.

After the lecture, we file into the dining room for dinner. I find myself a place at a table with six others: three improbably bright-faced, well-dressed twentysomethings from Devon (a nurse, a shop manager, and a taxi driver, who met each other at a local Spiritualist church); two Guernsey mediums, who have flown here for the occasion; and a twenty-eight-year-old woman in the light-haulage business. There is one empty space at the table. (I like to think that it might be occupied by Ruth, but the others have doubtless brought their own ghosts with them, too.)

My dinner companions are all very keen indeed on Mr Edwards, and are well ahead of me in their spiritualist training, so I keep quiet over the food (tureens of vegetable soup; large gammon steaks with mixed vegetables to follow; and plenty of weak tea all round). Half-way through the proceedings, Mr Edwards – who has changed into a crisp print shirt – rings a hand-bell, and the dining room falls silent. 'Your group work will begin at 7.45 p.m.,' he says. 'Do not be late under any circumstances . . .'

I have been assigned a tutor named Muriel Tennant. At 7.40 p.m. I gather, along with the rest of my group, in a room that is known by college regulars as 'The Large Lounge'. There are fourteen of us altogether, sitting on hard plastic chairs arranged in a circle in the middle of an enormous, high-ceilinged, pale pea-green parlour. Red-velvet chaise longues and plush upholstered armchairs have been pushed back beyond the circle. A small electric heater stands, switched off, in front of the empty marble fireplace. A decrepit television set, with gaffer tape stuck over the control panel, leans beside it. We do not talk, but our breath forms small, frail clouds in the chill.

When Muriel arrives, she sits facing us, almost part of the circle yet also at a slight distance. 'Keep your chairs on the carpet,' she instructs us, 'rather than the wooden floor.' For a moment, I imagine that the carpet will fly, taking us up and away into the night; though, as it turns out, Muriel is simply concerned that we do not scratch the parquet.

Muriel, like Mr Edwards, turns out to be slightly deaf; but she does not shout at us. She is a comforting and kindly teacher who speaks in a soothing voice, albeit with unusually perfect enunciation. I would guess she is in her sixties, but there is something ageless about her, too. She asks us to introduce ourselves, one by one, around the circle. Thus we all make each other's acquaintance: first Charles, a no-nonsense businessman with a side-line in spirit channelling who has come here from Florida; then Dee, a shy hippie from South London, who regards the rest of us from behind her curtain of dark hair; John, an elderly Spiritualist who is wearing his slippers and a yellow chenille jumper tucked into his track-suit bottoms; Joyce, a young Spiritualist in platform boots, who is buxom and pretty and nervous; Margaret, grey-haired and anxious and exceedingly polite; Yvonne, a trim-looking grandmother, here to advance her psychic and healing abilities; Bev, a Dorset Spiritualist who is about the same age as me; Daniel, a Taiwanese student now living in Amsterdam; Mark, from Dublin, who looks sixteen but says he is twenty-seven; Herbert from Sheffield, with an impressive grey beard that reaches his chest, and grey hair tied back in a ponytail; another, younger John (dubbed 'John 2' by Muriel) who is wearing a Hard Rock Café T-shirt; Virginia, a gentle Asian lady who lives in Oxfordshire; and Di, a healer from Reading, who has studied at the college several times before.

Our first exercise is to close our eyes and let the spirits join us. 'Many of you will be proficient at this,' says Muriel, 'but if you're finding it difficult, just imagine yourself surrounded by white light . . .' The circle is silent; the room is darkened. I am tired – the drive here, the lecture, these people are exhausting. I think of a white light. White heat, filling my head; white hot, in this cold place. In the darkness behind my eyes, the light melts the glass between Ruth and me. Ruth is in the dark woods, but alone no longer, and she takes my hand. She says nothing, but she smiles as I step into the forest with her. Then she disappears, and I am standing in the entrance of the house where Kimberley died six years ago. I am climbing the staircase, and I walk past her body. I carry on, up the final flight of stairs, to the little roof terrace at the top of her house. She is waiting for me there, bathed in sunshine, high in the sky, light on her face, glowing on the rooftops. I jump from the edge of the terrace, into the blue emptiness, and fall over the trees, over the straggly streets of North London, down to the river at Blackfriars Bridge. I stand on the north bank and look across the water. On the south side, I can see all my dead friends: Kimberley, Kirsty, Oscar, Adam, Beth, Jon, Simon. They do not speak to me, but they meet my eyes. Ruth is there too. She comes towards me, and the river has gone, and we are dancing together, dancing in the white light. To my left is a tunnel of white light; beneath my feet is a red void, going nowhere. Ruth has vanished again, but out of the tunnel, I see a figure: a plaster statue of Christ, holding a lamb. I touch the lamb. It is soft and warm and living.

'You can open your eyes now,' says Muriel. I open my eyes, and stare at the carpet, while sneaking a look at my watch. We have been sitting here for nearly an hour, and my feet are numb with cold. 'Would anybody like to share their experiences with the circle?' says Muriel. 'There seemed to be a lot of very powerful energy in the room.' I do not want to share my experiences (Christ – how embarrassing!) but I listen to the others talking about auras and spirit guides. (John 2 has a Red Indian who is always there for him.) Muriel is very pleased with us, and, eventually, the class comes to an end. Everyone else is staying here tonight, but I am driving back to London. 'I bet this place is full of ghosts,' says Tracey, who sat next to me at dinner, when I meet her in the hall on my way out. 'I'm not going to sleep a wink, I'm sure.'

'I'm glad I'm going home,' I say, which is the truth, and walk out of the front door, into the snow, into the darkness.

## SATURDAY 20 JANUARY

'MEDIUMSHIP REQUIRES DIGNITY,' says Mr Edwards, looking affronted. It is 9.45 a.m. and we are 'Sitting in the Power' in the Sanctuary, which is the Spiritualist chapel attached to the college. '"Sitting In The Power" allows you to develop self respect,' continues Mr Edwards. 'You cannot move forward until you respect your own spirit.' Mr Edwards is wearing a pale tangerine shirt this morning, with a burnt orange tie, and a matching sweater draped around his shoulders. He is very annoyed, because somebody – a nameless somebody, who is nevertheless in his bad books – has not turned up at the Sanctuary today. 'When people do not attend these sessions, it is an insult to me,' he shouts, his face purpling with rage, 'and it is an insult to spirit.'

And then his voice softens again. 'I don't want you looking for an experience, expecting an experience,' he says, jabbing his hands at the air. 'If an experience comes, you let it come, you let it go . . . You learn to let the power manipulate you . . . We need to find the way. Everything we have comes from a greater power.' Mr Edwards paces along the aisle that leads to the altar (or is a stage?). He is telling us about the magical power that has dusted the trees outside with snow; about the magic that is God, about the magic within us. 'I am not the manifestation of God, I *am* God,' he says, in a voice that reaches to the far corners of the Sanctuary.

Mr Edwards speaks to us for a very long time this morning, but finally we stop for a tea break, and Mr Edwards disappears for a cigarette in the medium's private sitting room. The pupils seem to be extremely uplifted by his lecture today, though there is some disappointment expressed about the lack of biscuits with the refreshments. ('Last year we had chocolate bourbons and ginger nuts,' says the lady behind me in the queue for the tea trolley. 'Cutbacks, I expect,' says her friend.)

At 11.30 a.m. we break up into our tutorial groups, so I'm back in the lounge with Muriel. The arrangement is the same as the night before – she's asked us to keep our original seats in the circle – but today there is an easel with a blank sheet of paper attached to it, standing in front of Muriel's chair. She draws a simple, stick figure on the paper, but with a large torso in the middle. Around the figure, she draws a line. 'This is the aura,' she says, pointing to the wavering line. 'What you were, what you are, what your hopes are – that's your everyday aura. We've grown with it, and it's grown with us.'

Then she draws a left-of-centre circle within the torso, where one might expect to find a heart. 'Something is stirring within you,' she says, pointing to the circle. 'It's your own spirit stirring within you. That is what has brought you to this place . . .' She draws some more wavy lines, emanating from the circle, towards the aura, and beyond it. 'These are the radiances of energy that start working through your everyday aura,' she explains. 'The Bright Ones – the spirit guides – start noticing those radiances of energy through your auric field. The Bright Ones say, "Aha! Isn't this wonderful!" So they start bringing energy and intermingling with the spirit power of each and every one of you.'

Muriel draws another line across the middle of the stick man's torso. Beneath this line, she explains, is the subconscious. 'This is the spiritual activator and the human computer,' she says. 'Everything is stored there in the subconscious, even if we haven't registered it in everyday consciousness.' In mediumship, she says, 'the subconscious has to come into play'.

My mind begins to drift, as I stare out of the windows of the large lounge, to the white lawns and snowy woods outside. Somewhere, nearby, church bells ring in an unseen tower. I count twelve rings, but the bells do not stop tolling. At the edge of the room, where it was too dark for me to see the night before, there is a large Victorian mahogany cabinet. Beyond the glass, where our breath trickles in condensed drops, the gardens and the Essex woods look like Narnia in the winter.

Muriel is telling us about her great mentor, a now-dead medium called Gordon Higginson. 'I've seen him go into a cabinet in that library,' she says, pointing to a door on the other side of the room, her eyes shining in her pale, powdered face. 'He went inside the cabinet in plain black trousers and a top, and he came out again in flowing, spirit robes.' His robes were made by the spirits, she says, and out of his mouth and nostrils came ectoplasm, which is the flesh and blood of the spirit world, the raw material of the other side. 'You could see the spirit faces in the ectoplasm,' she says. 'We all saw it, in that very room.'

'What is ectoplasm, exactly?' says Daniel, who is a stickler for detail.

'It's like smoke,' says Herbert.

'Or candyfloss,' says John 2.

'It's been analysed by a famous German scientist,' says Muriel, 'and it contains human flesh.'

Joyce wrinkles her pretty nose. 'The point,' says Muriel, 'is that mini miracles happen every day. You could be a mini miracle!' She pauses, and looks at each of us in the circle. 'I don't teach anyone who fails,' she says, 'I only see people who try.' Herbert nods, knowingly. 'Now,' says Muriel, 'I want you to split up into pairs, and each of you will read the other person in turn, using both psychic powers and your mediumistic abilities.'

Mark is not here this morning – apparently he was very sick in the night – so we are no longer an even number, and I end up in a group of three, with Yvonne and Bev. It is decided that I should go first, and begin with Bev. She is wearing embroidered jeans, so I guess that she must have a teenage daughter, who has encouraged her in such a purchase. I close my eyes, and try to imagine her life. 'You've got a teenage daughter,' I say. Bev nods. 'You're very close to her.' Bev nods again. 'You listen to pop music together, and read the same magazines.' Bev keeps nodding. 'You're very good at this, Justine,' says Yvonne, encouragingly. My right ear starts hurting. There is a faint buzz in my ear. 'I'm hearing an R,' I say. 'Does your daughter's name begin with R?'

'It does!' says Bev, though I don't feel I've done anything much at all.

'Switch over now, everyone,' says Muriel, so I turn to Yvonne. Yesterday, she mentioned a granddaughter, in passing. 'You have a little girl that you are very close to,' I say. 'Yes, yes I do!' she says, looking pleased. 'She's your granddaughter,' I say. 'Yes, yes she is!' says Yvonne. 'She loves you very much,' I say, 'and you love her. You have a special bond.' 'Oh yes, we certainly do,' says Yvonne. 'She's your son's daughter,' I say, guessing again. 'She is!' says Yvonne. 'You're very close to him, too,' I say. Yvonne looks even happier.

'Keep going,' says Muriel, so I look at Yvonne more closely. She is very neat, very tidy, very well put together. 'You have an exceptionally clean house,' I say. 'It's the kind of place where you could eat your dinner off the kitchen floor.' 'Well, I am *very* house-proud,' says Yvonne. 'You're spot on.'

Then Yvonne and Bev take over, and read me. 'You're a town person,' says Yvonne, looking at my clean trainers. 'You don't live in the country,' says Bev. 'Do you live on a main road?' says Yvonne. I say no, I don't, though yes, I do live in London. They don't get much further ('your husband is a professional man'; 'you have children?'); and then Muriel gathers us back into the circle and asks us about our progress as mediums.

'How do I know I'm not making it up?' says Joyce.

'Don't think of imagination as being negative,' says Muriel. 'Imagination is positive, imagination is creativity.'

'I felt like I was just guessing, just fishing,' says Joyce. 'I didn't see nothing.'

'Mediumship is often about *sensing*, rather than seeing,' says Muriel. 'To me, these things are mini miracles.'

We break for lunch (lasagne, apple pie, more tea), and gather again in the afternoon. 'Now, I want you to keep working very hard,' says Muriel, re-arranging her chiffon scarves. 'I want you all, in turn, to give me a reading. Stand up, speak clearly, and be confident. Off you go, then.'

Two of the trainee mediums see trees ('the tree of life?'). Muriel nods, encouragingly. One sees a church. More nods from Muriel. Daniel sees a hairdresser, who Muriel is close to. 'My granddaughter is a hairdresser,' says Muriel. 'Well done, Daniel.' John 2 sees his Red Indian guide with a peace pipe. 'I *do* have to make the peace, sometimes, in the spiritualist movement,' says Muriel. 'That *is* one of my roles.' Di scores very highly with her vision of Muriel's father, who is coming through from the other side. 'He's wearing worn corduory trousers,' says Di, 'and he's pointing to his feet. He's got these big bumps at the end of his shoes – I think his feet must have been troubling him.'

'Di, that's excellent,' says Muriel. 'My father had terrible problems with his feet before he passed into spirit.'

Then it's my turn. I take a deep breath, and stand up. Everyone is looking at me, expectantly. I close my eyes. I see Muriel dancing on a stage, twirling, smiling, beaming in the white light. 'You used to be a dancer,' I say to Muriel, my voice shaking slightly.

'That's right, I did!' says Muriel. 'I won many medals in my day, you know. I used to be on the stage.'

I close my eyes again. I see a young man in a wheelchair. He is bent and twisted, but his mind is still bright. There is a buzzing in my right ear again, an R, there's another name beginning with R . . . (This is ridiculous – I'm just trying to hear my silent Ruth.) The young man in the wheelchair is talking now; he's saying to Muriel, 'Dance with me, please.' I open my eyes again, blinking. 'I'm sorry, I hope this doesn't sound offensive,' I say, 'but I see a young man in a wheelchair, and he's asking you to dance. And I think his name begins with an R . . .'

'Ronnie!' says Muriel. 'He used to come to this college regularly, before he died, and he sat here in this very room with me, and I'd put music on to play on the record player, and we'd dance together, with me pushing his wheelchair around the room. Oh, I must tell his dear mother that he came through in spirit today.'

The circle around me is looking rather impressed. I sit down again. This is all nonsense, I think. Maybe Muriel is just telling me that she knew a boy in a wheelchair, in order to encourage me. But no, she's not acting, she believes in this stuff, I know she does. 'See, we've had a mini miracle today. Isn't that lovely?' She gets to her feet, and walks into the middle of the circle. 'Now, you have to know your stage craft, too,' she says. 'It's what carries your mediumship through. Say you're doing a dem – that's short for demonstration, as I'm sure you all know. You get the spirit message, and you point at someone in the audience . . .' She swivels her arm, dramatically, towards Yvonne. 'You give the message – ooh, I don't know, say, "Your granddaughter is very close to you" – and then you turn away, but *do* keep your arm still pointing towards Yvonne.' She turns away from us, gazing up at the ceiling, as if in search of more messages, and then turns back to Yvonne, fixing her with a piercing gaze. 'You see?' she says, letting her arm drop again to her side. 'You keep the dramatic tension with the pointing. And don't be hesitant – keep talking, even if you're getting things wrong. If you keep talking, you'll get something right, in the end. You don't need to interpret or explain. Always remember: the recipient is the analyst.'

Next on the timetable is trance mediumship. We take it in turns to enter the trance state – I close my eyes, and try to find the white light, but keep getting distracted by elderly John's snoring – while the others in the circle report back on the physical manifestations and auras that surround each of the aspiring trance mediums. Everyone else sees emerald green light and garlands of gold and blue flashes; I, on the other hand, see nothing, absolutely nothing, though I keep staring into the darkness, until my eyes are ready to weep.

'Did you hear anything, Joyce?' says Muriel. 'There was a lot of spirit power around you.'

'No,' says Joyce, stolidly.

'You didn't hear running water?' says Muriel.

'Oh yeah, yeah, I did,' says Joyce, 'blue water.'

'Well done,' says Muriel.

'I saw dwarves and chimney sweeps,' says John 2, who is wearing a different coloured Hard Rock Café T-shirt this evening. 'They were dancing around Justine's feet.'

'I think you should try to avoid such pictorial manifestations,' says Muriel, tactfully. 'Try to concentrate on the colour of the aura, instead.'

'I haven't had enough teaching,' says John 2, who is an eager yet sensitive soul.

'Don't despair, you have a great deal of potential,' says Muriel. 'I used to be a nervous young student, just like you. And then Gordon Higginson picked me out one day, while I was sitting here on a training course, and he said to me, he said, "Muriel, you will be a teacher in trance and physical mediumship."'

'I'll keep trying,' says John 2.

'Remember, there are no failures in my class,' says Muriel, 'only people who try.'

Outside, a fog has descended. It is impossible to see more than a few feet ahead. We are supposed to be 'Sitting in the Power' again with Mr Edwards tonight, which will keep me here until past 11 o'clock, and I can't do it, I know I can't. After dinner (pea soup, braised chicken, mashed potatoes, more tea) I search Muriel out in a corner. 'Muriel,' I say, 'I'm really sorry, but I think I need to leave early tonight. My oldest son hasn't been very well.'

'Of course, my dear,' says Muriel. 'You must leave now, and drive home *very* carefully indeed.' I wonder if she can forsee an accident ahead.

'I don't want to get into trouble with Mr Edwards,' I say. 'He was so cross this morning about the person who missed the "Sitting in the Power" session.'

'Don't worry,' says Muriel. 'I will explain everything to him. He'll just have to take my word for it.'

As I'm putting my coat on, I see Muriel talking to Mr Edwards, and maybe this is just my imagination, but I'm sure he's looking angry . . . Never mind, never mind, I'm free, on my way out of the front door, into the car, down the drive. I can't see a thing, but I'll get home somehow, soon. The road curves around to the left, but there are no lights outside, just the light from the car, just follow the light, get home, in the silence, let me sleep, let me sleep.

## Sunday 21 January

It is raining in London, and the snow has melted overnight. There is grit on the road, and it smears the windscreen of the car; but I keep driving, peering ahead, up the empty Sunday motorway, to reach the college in time for the first session of the day. By 9.30 a.m. I'm sitting in the Sanctuary, looking up into the stained-glass windows that are set high into the far wall. There are seven windows; simple shapes; simple block colours (red, yellow, blue). They remind me of the windows that signalled escape in the television programme – *Playschool* – that Ruth and I used to watch when we were little. (Would we go through the round window or the square window? You never knew until the last minute which one it was to be.)

This morning, Mr Edwards is wearing a beige shirt and a maroon jumper arranged around his shoulders. The rest of the tutors are sitting behind him, including the burly man with tattoos, who is in a shiny short-sleeved black shirt today. Everyone has their eyes closed, apart from the man in the black shirt, and – occasionally – me (when I open my eyes because I'm feeling spooked, I hope that he can't see me looking at him).

Mr Edwards is being visited by the spirits. He no longer sounds angry; he is almost soothing. The angels are with him, he says. 'We are more than your brothers and sisters, more than your fathers and mothers,' croons Mr Edwards, his voice rising and falling in waves. 'Let go of all your pain and suffering and loss – because God is within you.' The snow is falling again outside, soft and cold and silent; but inside the Sanctuary, it is warm, and even the fake flowers wilt in the airless room. My eyes droop, and I drift somewhere else, who knows where, through the round window, I'm not sure why . . .

After some time, the angels depart and so does Mr Edwards, for another cigarette break. Two ladies in the front row spring forward, taking the platform for a fundraising interlude. There is to be an auction – an auction for a song, sung by one of the tutors, a woman called Jill. The bidding goes to £60, and then the tutor steps forward. She leans on a walking stick, but her voice is powerful. 'Somewhere over the rainbow,' she sings, with no accompaniment aside from the smiles of the audience, 'way up high, there's a land I heard of, once in a lullaby. Somewhere over the rainbow, skies are blue, and those dreams that you dare to dream, really do come true . . .'

During the morning tea break (none for me, I'm drowning in weak tea), I wander up the big staircase in the main hall to the first floor, where a faded collection of spirit photography hangs on the walls. In one picture, a stolid-looking spirit in an Edwardian petticoat faces the camera, unabashed, centre-stage, with a chunky necklace around her neck denoting Orientalism. Elsewhere, ectoplasm is swathed around the mediums – like old muslin or cheesecloth; cobwebs or a smudge on the glass. There are black and white ghosts that could be double exposures; wraiths from the grave that are superimposed on to mourners' faces. Aside from the photographs, there is another memento on display: a crown of thorns, in a round glass case. It is not labelled. I cannot guess what has brought it here.

One more tutorial to go . . . Muriel teaches us her favourite mantra. 'I am good, I am God, I am all potential.' She tells us more about Gordon Higginson (he of the miraculous manifestations); and about Jesus, who Muriel believes to have been 'the greatest medium of them all' (greater even than Gordon himself).

One more lunch to go . . . Roast beef, Yorkshire pudding, mixed vegetables, and trifle for afters. ('More tea anyone?' 'Well, I don't mind if I do . . .') The girl sitting next to me tells me about her mother who killed herself twelve years ago ('it was her time to go'); and the woman opposite reveals that she had a baby who died, who is with her now, in spirit.

One more lecture to go . . . Mr Edwards will give us a demonstration of his astonishing mediumistic abilities. He talks very fast, with a great deal of detail that means nothing to me, about a garage and a set of traffic lights and a street that has disappeared; a place that has gone though the spirits remember it. A grey-haired woman nods: yes, she knows the place he speaks of. Mr Edwards weaves his spirit story, and then suddenly, he is angry again, he is bent over, as if in agony. 'How can you do this to me!' he shouts at the audience. Two people have just left the room, on their way to catch planes back home again. 'It is an insult to leave while I am still talking – I feel sick, *sick*,' he says, spitting out the words, like bile in his throat.

The audience is silent, on edge, uneasy. Will Mr Edwards vomit right here before us? No, Mr Edwards will not. He resumes his connection with the spirit people, though he is irritable, querulous, when the grey-haired woman does not follow him. The clock ticks; the audience shifts; no one must leave the room; Mr Edwards must not be angered again. At last, the day ends. I say goodbye to Muriel, and run to the car. By the time I've made it back to the motorway, the snow has disappeared; the white reflected light now faded into the January twilight.

> It's truth! I somehow vomit truth today.
> This trade of mine – I don't know, can't be sure
> But there was something in it, tricks and all!
> Really, I want to light up my own mind.

Robet Browning, 'Mr Sludge, The Medium'

## SUNDAY 28 JANUARY

EARLY THIS MORNING, I dream of Ruth. She has returned from America, at long last, and is living with Matt and the twins again. 'I'm a bit short of money,' she says. 'I haven't been able to work for a while.'

'Don't worry, I'll help you,' I reply. 'Do you have to return the money from Guys Hospital? The money for your death, now that you're back here?' (Some time after Ruth died, of a cancer that had gone undiagnosed until it was too late to treat, the hospital settled out of court for a reasonably substantial amount of money – not much for a life, but enough for the mortgage – which went to help Matt, Lola and Joe.)

'I've got to go on an IT course,' says Ruth. 'The court has ruled that the Guys money has got to be spent retraining me in computer technology.' We are speaking to each other in a minibus, which is driving eastwards. She is sitting alongside Matt and their children; I am with Neill and our children. I am very happy to see her, but confused, too, because Matt is married to Anna now; and I thought that Ruth was dead, but here she is again, alive and well: glowing with good health, in fact.

We are driving away from a house that we once lived in with our parents; an old farmhouse in Wales. We have all been back to this house in the dream – in fact, there has been some talk about us living there for good – but I do not feel comfortable in it. I was never happy in that house, and I am not happy in it now. 'I can't come back to the house,' I say to my mother in the dream. 'I don't want to go through all this again.'

We had moved to the farmhouse when I was a teenager. My parents had separated, and my father had left his job at Oxford University, and moved out to a rented room. But then they decided to live together again – in the Welsh farmhouse. We were going to be a happy family in the countryside. How quickly did things start to go wrong? I can't remember. My father was very depressed. We all were. He had a recording of Ted Hughes reading his 'Crow' poetry, and he used to play it very loud. It was about black times and death. Ruth found a record of Sylvia Plath's poetry, and started playing that, even louder, in her bedroom. That was pretty depressing, too. Sometimes she alternated it with her other favourite record, *Jesus Christ Superstar*. My father buried his head in his hands, and said he had gone back to living with three anti-semitic Catholic witches. My mother spent a lot of time growing flowers in the garden, and planting vegetables so that we could one day be self-sufficient. There was an old corrugated iron shed at the end of the garden, falling down piece by piece. One day, we found a nest of adders inside it, cradled in the brick foundations.

Our nearest neighbours were across the field: real farmers, in a new farmhouse. They had two huge sheds of battery chickens. I couldn't bear to walk past the chicken sheds. It looked like a concentration camp. Sometimes, if I caught a glimpse of the birds, you could see the bloody sores on their necks where the feathers had been pecked away. I didn't like the countryside. I hated it. I climbed into a tree in the field in front of the house – as far away from the chicken sheds as possible – and sat there, dreaming of escape. Ruth sat there with me, when she wasn't listening to Sylvia Plath and *Jesus Christ Superstar*. We had both become punk rockers by then, up there in the tree. She dyed her hair blue. Mine was bright orange. We had black plastic trousers and jumble sale jumpers. Every weekend, we walked a mile to the nearest village, and then caught the bus to Cardiff, to see punk groups play at Top Rank. We saw the Clash, the Jam, the Damned and the Sex Pistols. Then we caught the last bus back home again.

I was lucky. I got into Cambridge University when I was seventeen. But I felt guilty about leaving Ruth at home, up the tree alone. My parents had separated again. My father had a new girlfriend. My mother became an anti-nuclear protester at

Greenham Common. She lived in a tent. Ruth came to stay with me often; two years later, she got a place at the same university. That's how I remember it, anyway, but it probably wasn't in that order; and doubtless other people saw it differently. I still have Ruth's letters from then, and sometimes I re-read them, searching for clues. In October 1979, when I had just started my first term at Cambridge, she wrote to tell me that she had dyed her hair black and bought a new tartan dress to wear over her bondage trousers. Our mother was less depressed, said Ruth, and busy putting cork tiles on the bedroom ceiling. On 7 November, she sent me another letter, saying that she had dyed her hair green. 'Last Saturday I went second-hand shopping, looking for things for you,' she continued. 'I saw lots of nice stuff – lurex dresses, etc – but it was pretty expensive (i.e. 50p–60p) so I didn't buy anything as it was a lot to spend if I wasn't sure you'd like them. I *will* buy some things at the next jumble sale.' On 19 April 1980, she wrote to say that our father wanted to move back in, but 'everything will probably have blown over by tomorrow'. She had applied for a summer job at British Home Stores, and 'I bought some blue Crazy Colour hair dye and am going to streak/dye/lowlight my hair at some point. I was a bit naughty, and said I worked for a hairdresser, since this wholesaler sells only to hairdressers. I am feeling very paranoid about this, and am expecting the police to arrive with a warrant for my arrest any minute now.' On the back of the envelope, she drew a picture of herself in the sea, wearing a T-shirt with a heart on the front, surrounded by sharks. On 5 May, she wrote to say thank you for the earrings I had sent her for her sixteenth birthday. 'I had a tea-party with cakes, crisps and peanuts, to fit in with my sophisticated new image . . .' Our father had split up with his girlfriend, and Ruth had failed her Grade 7 piano exam. 'I couldn't believe it,' she said.

## Tuesday 30 January

An email arrives from Dale Palmer in Indiana. His long-awaited website is up and running, and he has invited selected friends, including Sarah Estep and me, to log on and test it to see if we can record the voices of discarnate beings, through the medium of white, pink or brown noise. I'm not quite clear about the meaning of the variously coloured noises, and Neill is no help either when I go down to the kitchen to ask him to explain, but nevertheless, I immediately run back upstairs to the attic to contact the discarnate beings *right now*. Unfortunately, I can't even gain access to the website, let alone download the noise files, because my London postcode is not the same as an American zipcode, and without a zipcode for registration purposes, I am somehow denied entry to what I now see as the field of dreams on the other side of my computer screen. I email Dale to explain my problems, and also for some advice on how to contact Ruth, and he emails back to say, 'I do expect everything we try to fail ninety-nine times but then the hundredth will work.' He adds, 'You want to get a message to Ruth? Simply say it out loud or even just think it and she will or at least can hear you. SC Beings in Higher Reality already can know, if they want to, what we are thinking and planning. It is nonlocal. The purpose of the site is so they can communicate to us; not us to them.'

Dale goes on to say that the last few weeks have been a trying time for him, as well. His new hearing aids, that cost $5000, disappeared just before the website was ready for testing, so he still cannot hear the discarnate voices (should they be received). On top of that, seventy-three computer viruses attached themselves to the downloaded files necessary for the tests. 'Some days I feel like Job,' he says. He may leave Indiana for a few days, and have a short holiday in Florida with his wife, Kay. But the research will still go on. With new software in place, the voices will be more easily understood in the future, thus ensuring that 'actual communications among dimensions of reality can indeed be readily comprehended by all'.

Miserable comforters are ye all.

Job, Chapter 16, verse 2

## TUESDAY 6 FEBRUARY

SIX YEARS AGO today, Kimberley died. Six years is a very long time, yet also, no time at all. Sometimes, it seems like yesterday; like today. When someone dies, they do not always disappear out of your life. You have a relationship with them: a relationship that changes, that begins to accommodate their silence. You move on, but they come with you. You do not leave each other behind.

At quarter to eight this morning, there is a flash of light in the sky, and a clap of thunder so loud that I thought a bomb must have exploded. Jamie and Tom are running into the room, eyes wide open. Outside, the car alarms are shrieking, and then the sirens start.

A second later, it's over. The world has not come to an end. Tuesday morning life goes on. Six years ago, it was a Monday morning. Tom had been ill – still a baby, feverish, pale, just out of hospital with suspected pneumonia that had turned out to be a bad dose of flu. I felt like I hadn't slept for weeks. I had stayed with him in hospital, half-dozing by his cot for nights that seemed to last for ever. (There were other problems, too. My mother had married a man – my stepfather the blood specialist – who had full-blown Aids. She was living with him in America, and I feared that she would be infected, in a throwback to her family's ancient Catholic martyrdom, which made me angry. She thought me superstitious. I thought her reckless. We did not seem to be able to talk to each other without shouting. As for my father: he had returned to his homeland, South Africa, where Ruth and I had visited him a few months before, taking Jamie and Tom with us for my maternal grandfather's ninetieth birthday party. Then my father seemed on the verge of another breakdown, grinding his teeth until I feared only brown stumps would be left; now, his life was even more fragmented, and his dental bills were soaring.)

I'm not trying to make excuses; or maybe I am, in a roundabout way, for my failure to stop Kimberley killing herself. Grief is not necessarily linear, and nor is the survivor's guilt. (After Ruth died, the bereavement counsellor told me that there are five steps on the road to recovery – numbness, denial, anger, grief, acceptance; the same steps taken by the terminally ill, if hospital pamphlets are to be believed – but it can't only be me who looks for short cuts, and ends up going the long way round? And surely there is more than one acceptable route; and any number of compelling detours?)

I had not spoken to Kimberley for several days. I did not know that her depression had turned into a black tidal wave of despair. I did know that she was unhappy – that she sought a way out of her unhappiness. She had taken to astrology, psychic healing, and to spiritualism. Once or twice a week, she went to a nearby spiritualist church. I don't know what she found there. I do know that she was looking for magic somewhere; for an escape route to another place. She had made friends with some people – one of them a fortune teller – who worked for an old-fashioned fair that came to our park every August. The fair filled the park with wooden horses that galloped on steam-driven roundabouts; with pink candyfloss and tiny aeroplanes that spun in circles and lifted up into the sky. Last summer, Kimberley had visited the fair in different parts of southern England. Death, however, did not seem like a place that she would choose to go.

Kimberley's little girl, Juliette, had blonde hair like hers, and blue eyes. She was very nearly five years old, just a few months younger than my first son, Jamie. On the day she was born, I had taken Jamie to visit this new baby in the hospital. (Was it my imagination, or did they look far into each other's calm blue eyes and see things we could not see?) They had grown up together: played together at nursery, learnt together in the same class at school. We lived next door but one from each other. Sometimes, when they had just learnt to run, in the second winter of their lives, Kimberley and I would take them to the cold park around the corner from our street. Often, we four were the only people in the park on those drizzly weekday mornings, when everyone else seemed to be at work, or at home, safe in the warmth. In the summer, Juliette had a pink tricycle, and Jamie had a blue one, and we had picnics in the park: apple juice and peanut butter sandwiches. Juliette and Jamie; Jamie and Juliette. Kimberley was an endlessly loving mother, willing to make cakes and paintings when I merely flopped beside the children on the sofa. Just after Tom was born, and Neill away working in America for weeks on end, and I was ragged-tired and grey-faced and dripping with milk and tears, Kimberley often stepped into the breach. When I heard she had killed herself, six years ago, I said, 'It can't be true. She picked up Jamie and Juliette from school last week . . . She loves her child.'

But now she had fallen into the breach. A chasm had opened and swallowed her up. Until that week before her death, we had talked most nights – exhausting conversations, that went round in circles, about her depression, and her confusion about where, exactly, she was supposed to be heading. 'Everyone feels this way, sometimes,' I said. 'But just take one day at a time.' Aside from platitudes, I had suggested therapy; she had tried it, to no avail. She told me that the first therapist she saw had made a circle of wool around her feet, which didn't seem to help. I told her that maybe she should change her therapist, and also go to her doctor, and she did. She started taking Prozac, as well as an array of homeopathic remedies. She had showed them to me, all her tablets lined up on her kitchen table: alongside a little bottle of something herbal called Rescue Remedy, and other secret formulas made of summer flowers and leaves.

'This is the hardest time of the year,' I said. 'But it will get better. After February, it will almost be spring. It will be light again. We'll be able to go for picnics in the park, like last year. Tom will be able to walk by then. Maybe we could have a holiday together in June? By the sea, somewhere?'

She smiled, and said that she was looking forward to that. Her birthday was the day before mine. Midsummer birthdays. 'We're both Geminis,' she used to say, 'schizophrenic twins. We think alike, you and me.' By now, she was separated from her husband, David. I couldn't understand why she had left him. 'He's so good for you,' I said. 'You only live once,' she replied.

Kimberley killed herself, sometime in the early hours that followed a long Sunday night, in the flat she had moved to on the other side of the park from here. Juliette wasn't there: she had spent the weekend with David. Kimberley left the door to her flat ajar; it did not therefore need to be broken into. Her body was there, waiting to be found in the silence. (When, exactly, did she decide to kill herself? I didn't understand. How had she thought of such a thing?) She had spent the evening before her suicide writing lists: long lists for Juliette's birthday party, that was to take place the following week; lists that went round in circles; knots of problems that would not come undone. She also left a note, saying that she had been in the darkness – a dark box – and was looking for the light. Death was just a bridge towards the light.

I never saw her body, which in some ways I now regret. I still see her, though, very occasionally, disappearing around the corner ahead of me, long blonde hair caught in a ray of light. Her funeral was at Mortlake Crematorium, on a cold weekday when we might otherwise have been trailing around the park. Afterwards, I walked out into the crematorium garden, and there I found Jamie and Juliette together, small faces looking up into the icy-clear sky.

'That's where Kimberley is,' said Jamie. 'She went up there, through the blue, to the stars. She can see us now.'

Often, I feel her standing behind me. If I turned fast enough, I think I might catch her, but I never do. I just feel her breath on the back of my neck. 'I know you're there,' I say. She never says a word.

## TUESDAY 13 FEBRUARY

TODAY IS JULIETTE's eleventh birthday. Jamie has an interview for a secondary school in the City. We get there early, and wait outside, beside the river. The sun is shining, and the tide low. He doesn't seem to want to talk to me; I suppose he is tired, and nervous.

'How did Kimberley die?' he says, out of the blue, staring away from me and down into the water.

'She killed herself,' I say.

'I know that,' he says, 'but how? How did she kill herself?'

I stall, trying to play for time. 'Does Juliette know?' I say.

'Yes,' he says.

'Well, maybe you should talk to her about it.'

'I don't want to ask her,' he says. 'I'm asking you.'

'I'm not sure,' I say, after a long pause. (Some secrets are not mine to share; some endings belong to other people; though I wish I could find the right answers for my children.)

'OK,' he says, still looking at the water.

Afterwards, while he is being interviewed, I walk over Blackfriars Bridge, to the south side of the river. There, on the gritty sand shore, is a bunch of yellow roses. They're still fresh, and neatly tied with a ribbon, as if they've been placed there as a token of love, or a wreath. But there's no note attached, nothing to identify where the flowers came from. I lean over the edge of the railings, to try and get a better look; but there's still no clues. I'm thinking of climbing over the railings that separate me from the water, when I remember Jamie, waiting for me on the other side of the river. I turn away from the roses, and set off back where I came from; back to my son.

That night, I dream of Kimberley. She is alive, and she hands me a note to read that she has written. I do not read it – I still cannot read in my dreams, however hard I try; the words simply melt into each other – but I take the note from her, because I know that it will prove, at last, that there is life after death. It is material evidence.

Then I start feeling confused. Maybe the note isn't evidence of anything. Maybe she never died at all. Was I mistaken? 'I went to your funeral at Mortlake Crematorium,' I say to Kimberley, hesitantly.

She simply smiles at me; an enigmatic, silent smile. 'Where have you been, all these years?' I ask her. 'What are you trying to tell me?'

She does not reply. I wake up, and the note has gone.

## Thursday 15 February

> Psychical research is an attempt to correlate and interpret what appear to be unusual facts. They may be facts which are unusual only in appearance, or they may not be facts at all.
>
> W.H. Salter, SPR President, 1947–8, *The Society for Psychical Research: An Outline of its History*

**6.30 p.m.** The Society for Psychical Research is holding its annual Gwen Tate Memorial Lecture in a hall at Kensington Central Library. This year the lecture is being delivered by Professor David Fontana, a psychologist at Cardiff University, former president of the Society, and currently a member of its council. His lecture title is 'New Light On Survival'. I know all this from my midnight surfing of the Net: when the children are asleep, and Neill is out, I often find myself searching for more information about how to contact the dead. One strange website leads to another; none of them lead to Ruth.

Nevertheless, the SPR (which has an entirely sober website) is a very august body indeed. It was founded in 1882 by a number of scientists, spiritualists, and classicists (though the spiritualists quickly withdrew, alienated by what they saw as the Society's overly academic approach, and set up what was to become the College of Psychic Studies). The first SPR president was Henry Sidgwick, professor of moral philosophy at Cambridge University; the founder members aimed 'to examine without prejudice . . . those faculties of man, real or supposed, which appear to be inexplicable in terms of any recognized hypothesis'. The society has numbered two British prime ministers amongst its members (Balfour and Gladstone), along with Freud, Jung, Sir Oliver Lodge, Sir Arthur Conan Doyle, and a host of other eminent Victorians and Edwardians. (The Gwen Tate commemorated in the lecture title was the daughter of Henry Tate – of Tate & Lyle Sugar – who left a generous legacy in his will to support the society's activities). The academic tradition has been continued today, with a multitude of professors involved in scientific debate about the paranormal and other occult affairs, though the society has a lower profile than it did in the devastating aftermath of the Great War. The comfortable world I lived in until recently – where people had birthday parties, not funerals – is not very interested in the activities of the SPR. But I find myself increasingly drawn to this side of life (the side that abuts death, where you can approach the edge, and look into the gap). So here

I am, sitting in a half-empty lecture hall, with fifty or so members of the generally aged audience, waiting for new revelations.

Much of what Professor Fontana has to say goes way above my head – the obsession with ether and ectoplasm that gripped his predecessors, the Victorian psychic researchers (an obsession that extended into the last century, too) seems to have been replaced by the language of quantum physics. Today, Professor Fontana is concentrating on 'the concept of non-locality' in an eloquent attempt to suggest, using the language of modern science, that consciousness may be separate from the body, and may therefore also survive death. Non-locality, he says, 'is the apparent ability to operate outside time and space. And if the human mind is non-local, you have a very powerful argument for the survival of life after death.' He bases his theory upon the fact that 'every atom in the human body is part of the quantum world', and that 'quantum mechanics indicate that within the atom itself, non-locality operates'. That far, I can follow – but when Professor Fontana moves on to the 'wave particles paradox' and 'the half life of random particles', I'm lost. I enjoy his lecture, nevertheless – there is a soothing poetry to be found in his interpretation of physics; in his tales of cloud chambers and deflected electrons. 'It is our act of observing that co-creates the world,' he says. 'What happens when we die? We are co-creators of whatever reality we experience after death.'

After the lecture there is tea and biscuits, and copies for sale of the Proceedings of the Society for Psychical Research. At one end of the room, several young physicists engage Fontana in esoteric quantum conversation; at the other end, the grey-haired majority of the audience swap anecdotes about poltergeists and hauntings. I feel stuck between the two sides – adrift in the middle, lost in the limbo. Instead, I wander over to the book stall beyond the tea-table, and buy 'Volume 58, Part 220 of the Proceedings: the Scole Report', by David Fontana, and two of his SPR colleagues, Montague Keen and Arthur Ellison. Ellison, a former professor of electrical engineering at City University, died last year, but Mr

Keen, a retired parliamentary correspondent, is here tonight. I have already heard of the Scole Report, which was published in November 1999 – again through the Net, whose furthest reaches are still buzzing with the rumours that this was at last the physical proof for life after death.

'You'll have to read the report before we talk further,' says Mr Keen, when I corner him after the lecture. 'And then I'll test you to see if you understand what we're saying.' I think he's joking – at least about the testing – but he seems to be a cautious, scholarly man nonetheless.

On 17 February 1911, Freud writes to Jung from Vienna:

> Dear friend,
> I see you don't believe me; you seem to think I have my cycles and that suddenly, at certain intervals, I feel the need of looking at the world through rose-coloured spectacles. I see I must give you further details . . .
>
> The Society for Psychical Research has asked me to present my candidacy as a corresponding member, which means, I presume, that I have been elected. The first sign of interest in dear old England. The list of members is most impressive . . .
>
> Yours ever,
> Freud

## Sunday 18 February

It has taken me several days to read my way through the 452 closely printed pages of the Scole Report (subtitled, 'An Account of an Investigation into the Genuineness of a range of Physical Phenomena associated with a Mediumistic Group in Norfolk, England'). Scole is the name of the village in Norfolk where four middle-aged people – Robin and Sandra Foy, and another couple named Diana and Alan Bennett – held a seance twice a week, starting in 1993, in the Foys' cellar. Robin Foy, an ex-RAF officer and manager in the paper trade, had taken a keen interest in the paranormal for over thirty years, a preoccupation shared by Sandra, his second wife. They were joined in their quest to seek physical evidence for life after death by Alan Bennett, a carpenter and medium; and his wife, Diana, a spiritual healer. The Scole group called themselves the New Spiritual Science Foundation, and after several months of effort, they claimed to be receiving both messages and physical objects from a team of 'spirit communicators'. The materialized objects – known in the world of psychical research as 'apports' – included a copy of the *Daily Mail* dated 1 April 1944, with a front-page report of the guilty verdict imposed on Helen Duncan, a medium who had been prosecuted under the eighteenth-century Witchcraft Act. The Scole group claimed that the spirit of Duncan had announced herself to them, and stated that her intention was to provide proof of her life after death. They also said that they had received messages from the other side that had been created on unexposed, unopened rolls of photographic film, and a recording on a tape recorder from which the microphone had been removed.

Their claims caused enormous excitement in the small, tightly bound world of spiritualism and psychic research, where everyone knows everyone else, and news soon spread to the SPR. For many years, 'physical' mediumship – the displays of table-lifting, spirit rapping, and ectoplasm that were so popular in the nineteenth and early twentieth centuries – had gone into decline. Several of its most famous practitioners had been exposed as frauds; and, as for the rest, their art seemed to die with them. But now the Scole group appeared to be offering something different – nothing to do with ether or ectoplasm (or regurgitated cheesecloth, for that matter, which is what Helen Duncan had been accused of using in her seances) – but a 'modern' form of spirit communication, using technology more appropriate to the present day.

In 1995, Arthur Ellison and Montague Keen were allowed to attend a Scole seance, as investigators and observers from the SPR. They were joined by David Fontana later that year, and it did not take long for the three men to become convinced of the authenticity of the communications with 'the Spirit Team'. They believed that the team was passing on the messages of dead scientists – including Thomas Edison and Oliver Lodge. In January 1997, an electrical diagram was said to have appeared, mysteriously, on a previously unopened photographic film, giving instructions for making a 'germanium device' that would allow the living to communicate directly with the dead, without the need for mediums. According to the Scole group, the diagram came courtesy of Edison himself – complete with his exact signature.

(Rumours about Edison's machine for talking to the dead have circulated for years, even since he gave an interview to the *Scientific American* in 1920, in which he said that he was working on apparatus which would give 'personalities in another existence or sphere . . . a better opportunity to express themselves than the tilting tables and raps and ouija boards and other crude methods now purported to be the only means of communication . . . This apparatus, let me explain, is in the nature of a valve, so to speak. That is to say, the slightest conceivable effort is made to exert many times its initial power for indicative purposes. It is similar to a modern power house, where man, with his relatively puny one-eighth horse-power, turns a valve which starts a 50,000-horse-power steam turbine. My apparatus is along those lines . . .'

Despite a number of searches after Edison's death in 1931, his apparatus has never been found. In the 1940s, an industrious researcher for General Electric tried to build the machine, following information said to have been passed on by Edison during a New York seance. It didn't work.)

There is more – much more – in the Scole Report, including the mysterious appearance on another photographic film of 'Ruth', a Wordsworth poem that allegedly contained minor changes made by the ghost of the poet himself in manuscript form. ('Sweet Ruth! With thee I know not how/ I feel my spirit burn . . .') But at the end of it all, the arguments still rage within the SPR – and beyond – as to whether the Scole group was a hoax or not. After much internal wrangling, the Scole Report itself was published with an appendix of several sceptical comments by SPR members less convinced of the evidence than the authors. According to one of the sceptics, 'the production of physical effects of the most mundane and banal nature – in near if not complete darkness – are certainly no "breakthrough" and nothing new.' As for the 'germanium device' – it never seemed to work properly, despite all hopes to the contrary, producing only a 'sea-like noise' in the presence of the investigators.

## Wednesday 21 February

**Tide cures:** 1887, 'Speranza' Wilde, *Superstitions of Ireland II.* To cure fever, place the patient on the sandy shore when the tide is coming in, and the retreating waves will carry away the disease and leave him well.

Iona Opie and Moira Tatem,
*A Dictionary of Superstitions*

WE HAVE COME to a warm island – Neill and I and the children – for a holiday; an escape from the grey silence at home, and the flu that spread from Jamie to Tom to Neill, leaving them all with a chorus of coughs and feverish night-time wheezes. We are by the sea, though we approach it with trepidation. No one says that they are frightened to go swimming, though Jamie speaks of sharks and eels. 'Is there anything dangerous in the water?' he says.

'No, not here,' I say.

'How do you know?' he says.

'Trust me,' I say, though I fear I might be tempting fate. (Our happiness is such a precious, precarious state; so delicately balanced, so close to the edge). After two days of skirting the ocean, we make a small venture into the water, still very near to the shore. It is shallow enough to keep our feet on the ground, but I try not to touch the sand and rocks below, in case something poisonous might be hiding there. The next day, we finally take a boat further out to sea, with masks and flippers, to snorkel as Kirsty did; as Kirsty so loved to do; as we once did, before she died. Neill jumps in first, with the children, holding their hands, and then I follow. I take a deep breath, and dive down below, beneath the sunlight on the surface. We now know that when she died, her blood filled the water around her, turning the sea red; and for a few seconds, I'm searching for the blood, searching for her, though I know I will not find her. There is only pink-tipped coral here today, lying like bones on the ocean floor. Little fish dart between the coral fingers, slipping through the water, disappearing out of sight.

> . . . by this time the Dawn Treader was gliding over a part of the sea which seemed to be uninhabited . . . they sailed in fairly shallow water and the bottom was weedy. Just before midday Lucy saw a large shoal of fishes grazing on the weed. They were all eating steadily and all moving in the same direction.

> 'Just like a flock of sheep,' thought Lucy. Suddenly she saw a little Sea Girl of about her own age . . . a quiet, lonely-looking girl . . . And just as the girl, gliding in the shallow water, and Lucy, leaning over the bulwark, came opposite to one another, the girl looked up and stared straight into Lucy's face. Neither could speak to the other and in a moment the Sea Girl dropped astern. But Lucy will never forget her face. It did not look frightened or angry like those of the other Sea People. Lucy had liked that girl and she felt certain the girl had liked her. In that one moment they had somehow become friends. There does not seem to be much chance of their meeting again in that world or any other. But if they ever do they will rush together with their hands held out . . .
>
> C.S. Lewis, Chapter 16, 'The Very End of the World', *The Voyage of the Dawn Treader*

## Friday 23 February

The last night of our holiday, and again, I visit the haunted house that I inhabit in my dreams. We had moved to this dream house because we needed more space, but now we are there, we do not venture beyond the ground and first floors. These rooms are safe, but the top floor – the attic – is filled with a strange wailing, the sound of lonely ghosts. 'I need to find an exorcist,' I say out loud, to the empty house. But I don't know where to find one. (Should I look under 'E' in the telephone directory?)

In the downstairs living room, at the front of the house, Neill has arranged lots of unfamiliar furniture: old mahogany pieces, rather like the ones I saw during my time at the Arthur Findlay College. 'I bought this furniture, because I thought it would fit in with the mood of the house,' he says. There are three tables, three sofas, and three sideboards. 'I think the room is getting crowded,' I say. 'Maybe we should move some of it to the attic upstairs?'

Outside, on the far side of the street, we have a view of the river. The river is rising, spilling its banks, coming in waves over the parked cars and towards our house. 'The cellar will be flooded,' I say.

Neill has gone, and I tell the children that we must go upstairs to the first floor, to escape the rising water. But even here, we're not safe. We have to go up another flight of stairs, to the attic floor. There are three rooms here: two bedrooms, still decorated with the faded rose-print wallpaper of another century; but the paper has split, torn apart by the cracks in the walls where the house has shifted over the years.

These rooms are eerie, but less frightening than the third room, which is up three more steps that lead to the final chamber in the house. The door has been opened to this room, even though I thought that it was locked. Inside, I see a shadow. Tom is walking towards the room, towards the shadow. 'No!' I scream, but no sound comes out.

~

## SUNDAY 25 FEBRUARY

WE LAND AT Gatwick Airport before dawn, but there is a soft pale light cast by the snow that lies on the ground. We drive across South London, heading home through the quiet

Sunday city, and find ourselves on the road that leads to Matt's house (Matt and Anna's home, in fact), just after six in the morning. There are no lights inside the house. 'I wonder if Lola and Joe are awake?' I say, looking up to the windows of the top floor, to their attic bedrooms; but I know they must still be sleeping.

And suddenly, I feel sure that Ruth's spirit is there with her children, in the pre-dawn sky, around and about and within the house – the new house, that they moved to after she died – and as we drive past, our hearts combine, briefly, fiercely, soundlessly. And then she's gone (or is it just the feeling – the faith – that disappears?) Not long before we went away on holiday, Lola said to me, 'How many people are in our family?' We started listing names together – and she wanted everyone to be included, Neill's brothers and sisters too – and finally we got to twenty-five. 'But how can Ruth be with twenty-five people, all at the same time, all over the place?' she said.

'Because she's inside us,' I said, providing the standard answer to Lola's good question, 'wherever we are.'

'Most of all with me and Joe and you,' she said, not giving up.

'Wherever you want her, whenever you want her, she'll be there,' I said.

Now, driving north again, over the river at Blackfriars Bridge, I take Neill's hand and say, 'Things are all right, aren't they?' He doesn't reply, just looks at me and smiles, but it wasn't a question. I know the answer. We have survived. We are getting there. (Where? It doesn't matter. All that matters is that we are still going.)

## TUESDAY 27 FEBRUARY, SHROVE TUESDAY

I WAKE JUST BEFORE 6 o'clock in the morning, jet-lagged, thinking about silence. It is not the same as absence, no, not at all. I know this, in part because Neill is always with me, even when he's not saying much, even when we're not together (even when I thought that he had gone). Silence is not a void. It can be full of many things.

Once upon a time, long ago and far away, where the years blur into a half-remembered story, I loved a man (no, not a man, a boy), and for a while, he loved me. One day, he stopped talking to me. We stopped seeing each other. I struggled against this – leaving messages, from time to time – but then I gave up, or gave in to the enforced silence. We still do not speak. But I do think about him, every so often, and I guess he sometimes thinks about me. Our relationship still exists, somewhere in our heads. I do not feel angry with him any more; or even rejected. It is rather peaceful this way. The silence is welcome. It washes over me.

Just before 7 o'clock, the children come into our bedroom. 'Pancake day!' they cry. The house fills with the sound of their waking. I mix up the eggs and the flour and the milk for the pancake batter. I cook the pancakes in the shape of little hearts (I bought a special heart-shaped frying pan for Neill on Valentine's Day). The hearts are so small, that they are gone in two mouthfuls.

## Friday 2 March

I meet Montague Keen, from the Society for Psychical Research, at a hotel restaurant overlooking Hyde Park. I've invited him out for lunch, after our brief meeting last month, in the hope that he can point me in the right direction. (What direction? Ruth's, as ever, because sometimes I forget to accept that the dead are allowed to be silent.)

Mr Keen is in his seventies; charming, funny, and unexpectedly ironic: a rare set of qualities in the world of psychical research; an appealing guide to the Other Side. (I seem to be developing a fixation on older men: first Dale, now Mr Keen. A grandfather complex, perhaps?) Anyway, Monty – as he is known to his circle of friends, which I hope to join some day – tells me an intriguing story about 'the spell-check ghost'. She appears through the computer of a Mr Smith – the administrator of a school in the north of England – and communicates by correcting his spelling in unexpected ways. For example, Mr Smith might misspell a word – let's say 'psychic', for the sake of argument – and the ghost comes back with a totally unrelated word through the spell-check programme of Mr Smith's computer, such as 'help'. Monty says that this laborious mode of communication from the other side is called 'anomalous word phenomena'. Apparently, Lady Prudentia – the name of the spell-check ghost – once lived in the mansion that now houses the school, and she is keen to set matters straight regarding the ill-deeds of a neighbouring family (rape, pillage and so on) that ultimately led to her death. Monty and his colleague, Professor David Fontana, were contacted by Mr Smith for advice, after Mr Smith's computer started channelling Lady Prudentia. Unfortunately, Lady Prudentia can only communicate in one word soundbites, due to the limitations of the spell-check mechanism. Nevertheless, Monty is convinced that she – and Mr Smith – are genuine; and therefore constitute the first known case of a new technology haunting. I try to persuade him to introduce me to Mr Smith, so that I could try out my laptop with Lady Prudentia, but he thinks that Mr Smith might be too shy for such a meeting to take place. 'Anyway,' he says, with a faintly gloomy air, 'my experience of psychic research is that something always goes wrong, just as you think you have found the final evidence to prove the survival of human consciousness.'

Still, we both have high hopes of the conference that is to be held at the University of Arizona next week, in which Professor Gary Schwartz, professor of psychology, medicine, neurology, psychiatry and surgery, and his wife and research partner, Dr Linda Russek, will be presenting their brand-new laboratory research into the accuracy of mediums. (Their experiments involved five mediums, who each gave readings to silent sitters that they had never met before, separated by a screen in the university laboratory, under constant video surveillance.) I'm already booked to go to the conference, and Monty thinks he might come along as well. 'Their work really is very exciting,' he says.

At home that night, I decide to conduct my own spell-check experiment, just in case there is a ghost on the other side of the screen who would like to have a chat. Monty says that you have to put in some intentional misspellings, to give them a chance to respond. So I type: 'Hellooo, is anybody there?' Then I click on spell-check, and this is what I get: 'Hello. Hellos. Helot. Hells.' By way of response, I type, 'What is your naame?' 'Name. Naomi,' says the spell-check. 'Who are yoou, Naomi?' I type. 'You,' she replies.

I decide to bring the spell-check experiment to a close.

## Sunday 4 March

A story about the University of Arizona research appears in the *Sunday Telegraph* newspaper today, under the headline: '*Spiritualists' Powers Turn Scientists into Believers*'. The piece has been written by Robert Matthews, the paper's science correspondent, and it seems very favourable. 'Until now, the whole issue of the "afterlife" has been dismissed by most mainstream scientists,' writes Matthews, 'with spiritual mediums being regarded as either self-deluded or charlatans. Now the first serious laboratory study of a group of mediums has found that they share an uncanny ability to state facts about the deceased relatives of people who come to them . . . The transcripts of each session showed that the mediums typically produced more than eighty pieces of information about the deceased relatives, ranging from their names and personal idiosyncrasies to the precise circumstances of their death. When analysed for factual accuracy, the mediums achieved a success rate of 83 per cent, with one achieving accuracy of 93 per cent.'

After reading the article, I begin to feel rather cheered – as if I am not alone. Aside from Monty and me, there are other people out there who are interested in this stuff: scientific people, people with laboratories and academic titles. Maybe I'm not mad, after all. ('Don't count on it,' says my imaginary therapist. 'Shut up!' I shout.) Maybe I'm heading to the right place. Arizona is a long way to go, I know, but after I've come back from there, after I've heard the evidence for myself, perhaps I can finally stop looking for proof, for Ruth . . .

## WEDNESDAY 7 MARCH

I'M ON MY way to the conference in Tucson, via Dallas. I get off the plane at Dallas to change flights, and pass through customs and immigration first; a typically long-winded procedure that is unusually fast today. 'Turn left, ma'am, for connecting flights,' says the customs officer. I turn left, alone, into a long corridor. One set of doors closes behind me, silently. At the far end of the corridor is another closed door. I walk towards it, expecting to have to push it; but it opens automatically, as if by magic. On the other side, I don't know why, I expect to see Ruth – real Ruth, arms wide open in welcome, waiting for me, after all this time. Instead – and I find myself surprised by her absence, and this inadequate replacement – there is a life-sized bas-relief of two figures; simple outlines, as if drawn by a child (or a computer?), saluting new arrivals to America.

By now it's late in London, but noon in Texas, and I'm beginning to feel confused, fuzzy, foggy, unclear. I make my way to the next flight; a smaller plane that seems to be filled with passengers returning home. As we come down to land in Tucson, on a high plateau surrounded by a ring of mountains, the man sitting next to me says, 'Look, there's a rainbow.' I peer outside, and yes, I see it, keeping pace with the plane, always ahead of us, however fast we fly.

The conference is being held at a local Holiday Inn. I take the shuttle bus from the airport to the hotel, and it starts raining hard, turning the streets grey. The cacti beside the road are dripping wet, and the desert looks muddy today. 'We've had a whole lot of rain this year,' says the bus driver, with grim satisfaction, 'more than I've ever seen here before. We may even have a flood in Tucson. A storm is coming this week, anyway.'

I check in to the hotel, and take the elevator to the fourth floor. I sit on the bed, and look out of the smeary window. The rainbow has disappeared. There is a six-lane highway right outside. All I can hear are the cars. I can't hear the spirits. The hotel is in the middle of an industrial area. There are pylons and dark parking lots, and a factory in the middle-distance pouring smoke into the yellowing sky. I don't seem to be able to turn on the heating in my room, or the television, so I go back down to the dimly lit lobby to find something to eat, but the restaurant is closed. There is a smell of bleach coming out of the fountain opposite the reception desk. It's rather cold – which is surprising, because I expected heat in the desert, and light. I'm not quite sure what I'm doing here, or why. Somehow, I've ended up in the wrong place – this can't be a place that Ruth would come to?

I go back up to my room, and watch the traffic outside. I keep my coat on, and don't unpack my bags. Then the phone rings, which is a relief, because I am beginning to wonder who I am.

'Hi, Justine, it's Laurie Campbell,' says a cheerful voice on the end of the phone. 'I've just arrived. It's hellish, isn't it? Why don't you come by and have some tea?' As Chairperson of the Mediumship Research Committee at Gary and Linda's laboratory – their main medium when it comes to scientific research – Laurie Campbell is here for the conference, too, to give demonstrations and lectures on her craft (or is it art? I don't know, but anyway, Gary has referred to her as 'the Michael Jordan of mediums'). Laurie is staying in room 364, and I'm in 402, so I tell her I'll be with her in a few seconds, but in fact I get lost, because her room is in another building: down the elevator, out the door, past the fountain, through another door, across the courtyard where three tattooed men sit, silently in a Jacuzzi, through an iron gate, and up three more flights of stairs. I knock on the door, and Laurie lets me in. We hug each other, because she already knows something about me from our emails and phone conversation (not to mention her parallel talks with Ruth, Kimberley and Kirsty, who speak to her in one ear, she says, while I'm coming down the line in the other). She looks about my age, my height, though larger – less faded, somehow – than me. I want to rest my head against her comfortable-looking shoulder, but it seems presumptuous, so I sit down instead. She is sweet-faced, dark-haired, and has rather beautiful eyes. She does not look spooky at all.

We talk about our children – she has a daughter of eleven, who survived cancer, and a sixteen-year-old diabetic son. She says her daughter seems to have inherited the same psychic gift, as has her younger sister. Laurie discovered her mediumistic ability on Thanksgiving Day, 1994. She looked into her bedroom mirror, and saw faces other than her own; and she knew that these were the faces of the spirits who were waiting for her. Now she channels a Victorian Cambridge scientist, who has told her that she must prove to the world that human consciousness survives death. She says that my English accent reminds her of his voice. When a psychiatrist (who is Laurie's client, rather than the other way round, because his son is dead) put her in touch with Gary and Linda, Laurie knew that she had come to the right place. 'It's part of the plan,' she says. She also thinks that I'm part of the plan. I went to university in Cambridge, after all, and I'm English, like the dead scientist. She can't tell me his name (he wants to remain anonymous), but she says he's pleased that I'm here.

She tells me that it was the famous psychic Sylvia Browne – who, like her, lives in California – that first told her that she, Laurie, would be an equally successful medium. 'She asked me if I'd felt weird tinglings in my hair – and I said yes, for years I've been imagining that I've got bugs in my hair. It's a tingling, like electricity. And Sylvia said that what I was sensing, without realizing, was my spirit guides trying to get through to me. Now I know they want to speak to me when I feel my crown opening up, and the electricity tingling in my scalp.' As she speaks, I feel my scalp tingling, too, and I wonder if it's coming from inside my head, or somewhere else.

By now, it's dark outside, and I'm feeling very sleepy, so I say I'm going to bed. 'OK,' she says, with her easy smile, 'let's meet tomorrow. I'll show you my transfiguration.'

'What's that?' I say.

'It's when my face changes shape into the spirit that is coming through me,' she says. 'I've just started being able to do it.'

'That's very unusual,' I say. 'Most mediums can't do that any more. It's a dying art.'

'Well, I can do it,' she says. 'I can feel hair growing out of my face, if I'm changing into a male spirit with a beard. But let's see if I can bring Ruth through for you tomorrow.'

'That would be unbelievable,' I say.

## Thursday 8 March

I wake up very, very early in the morning, just before daybreak. There is a mournful sound outside the window. I pull the curtains open, and realize it must be the wind, or a train on the railway line beyond the highway. I try to go back to sleep, but it still sounds like someone is sighing outside. (Where do the dead go? That's all I'm asking; that's not too much to ask, is it?)

I ring Neill in London. 'What have you been up to?' I say, and I can hear my voice echoing down the line, under the ocean (or do the wires run through the sky?).

'Nothing much,' he says. 'Working, you know . . .'

'What else?' I say, trying not to sound anxious.

'I've started swimming again,' he says. 'Oh, and I've gone for a couple of bike rides. I mended my bicycle. I thought it was about time . . .'

'Where have you been going?'

'Nowhere in particular,' he says. 'Back roads . . . There's a second-hand record shop in Palmers Green, run by a guy who thinks he looks like Elvis. Sometimes I cycle past there, and drop in to see if he's got any of my dad's old records. And Southgate. I went there today.'

'Why Southgate?'

'It's on the way out, rather than the way in . . .'

'Neill,' I say, 'do you ever wonder where Kirsty is?'

'It feels like she's disappeared,' he replies, slowly. 'But I can't believe she's gone, because I didn't see her go. When Dad died, we were with him in the hospital room, singing to him because the nurse said that even though he was unconscious, he could still hear us . . . And then I knew he was dead – it was as if his spirit left his body, and it was gone. But Kirsty . . .' The line crackles with static between us. 'Is someone else on the line?' he says.

'No,' I tell him, 'there's no one else. Are you still there? I can hardly hear you.'

'I'm here,' he says. 'I'm just thinking.'

'Take care of yourself, OK? And the children, give them a kiss from me. I love you, you know that, don't you?'

'I know,' he says. 'Come home soon.'

I don't want to say goodbye to him (it's hard to find the right words, to cross the wire); but I have to, it's my own fault, I came here . . .

I've arranged to have breakfast with a friend of Dale Palmer's, a medium named Lynn Gardner. Dale first told me about Lynn in one of his regular emails from Indiana: she left Indiana last year to come to Tucson, to work with Gary and Linda on a future research project. Then Lynn and I embarked upon an email correspondence (this is how the psychic world works – threads joining up across the Internet; arms open wide to embrace all the lost souls). Lynn also contacted my dead grandfather the spiritualist ('he's a hoot!' she said); though unfortunately, not on the Net.

Lately, she has been encouraging me to try some more automatic writing, after my failure at the beginning of the year. And now she has very kindly offered to come and pick me up from the hotel today. 'You'll know who I am,' she says on the phone. 'I'm the blonde wearing shorts.' Lynn is sixty-three years old, but truly, she looks twenty years younger: which is a good advertisement for having a direct line to Divine Love, as Lynn has done, ever since her youngest son died of heart trouble when he was eight years old, on Thanksgiving Day in 1977. She tells me about all this in a great whoooosh, in the car on the way from the hotel to her house, with a tape of tinkly New Age angel music as a background to our conversation. 'When my son died, I left my body,' she says, 'and I moved towards the white light. I could see God, I could feel God, I knew God. But I just thought I was psychotic.' Eventually, she says, the spirit of her son returned to show her that she was meant to use her mediumistic gifts to help other people. 'I saw this wonderful apparition of him as a man, and he said to me, "There is no such thing as a beginning or an end. I am your son David, and the Divine allows me to create vibrations in any form I want to create. I can create the voice vibration, so that you can hear me, but we in spirit are none of that – we are energy." Since then, Lynn has learnt to hear and see other spirits, both for personal clients, and on American television programmes. 'I've brought through Tennessee Williams,' she says, 'and JFK, who said, "Tell Jackie I'm sorry". That was a very moving experience. And I brought through Judy Garland for a friend of hers. Judy wanted to sing for her friend, but I felt that my voice wasn't up to it.'

Lynn has also had some experience of EVP, because she has led a group of EVP researchers, which included Dale's friend Sarah Estep, to Egypt, where they recorded the ancient voices of the dead in the tombs and beside the Sphinx. Lynn is very connected to Egypt, she says, through her past lives. So now she has three camels in her garden, to remind her of her special Egyptian connection. We stop at a big supermarket near her house, to buy some carrots for the camels. The carrots are on special offer, so we get 25lbs. The camels eat a lot of carrots, she says.

As we turn into the driveway that leads up to her house, in the foothills of the mountains, she stops the car so that I can meet the camels. There are three of them: two females and a baby. Even the baby is enormous – towering over my head, as they lurch towards us in search of snacks. 'Give them a carrot, and they'll give you a kiss,' she says. I'm not too sure about the benefits of being kissed by a camel – their breath smells, for a start, and they have enormous yellow teeth – but I don't want to seem impolite, so I offer up my cheek for a brief nuzzle.

Then we go into her house for breakfast, and Lynn introduces me to a friend of hers from Chicago, a nun named Blanche, who is staying with her in Tucson for a few days. Blanche asks me about my life, and I find myself telling her about Ruth's death. It's rather soothing, though my rambling account seems somehow disconnected to me; as if my voice is coming from somewhere else, while I sit quietly, silently, admiring the mountain scenery outside. Lynn shows me around her home – it's kind of ranch-style, with Egyptian touches. (My favourite detail is a sign pinned to the wall of her study that says: 'Reality is only for those who lack imagination.') Then Lynn cooks us eggs Benedict and, as we sit down at her big table to eat, she and Blanche join hands, and take mine too. They close their eyes, and I can see that there is to be a blessing. Lynn goes first, and Blanche follows with another prayer, and then I guess that I'm expected to say something. I'm frightened of looking like I've got a smirk on my face, so I bite my lip instead, and say, 'Thank you for having me, I mean, thank you for allowing me to be here with you, and share this wonderful breakfast . . . ummm . . . Amen.'

I'm quite keen to ask Lynn to channel Ruth for me, but this doesn't seem to be the right moment, and anyway, she has to take me back to the hotel before the conference starts. I tell her that I like her car bumper sticker very much. It says, 'The Goddess is alive and well and magic is afoot.'

'Can you get those in England?' she says.

'No, I don't think so,' I say, 'which is a pity . . .'

Back at the Holiday Inn, Laurie has just enough time to do the transfiguration session. I go straight to her room, and she draws the curtains and lights six small candles that she arranges on the coffee table. 'I wanted to light some incense,' she says, 'because the energy doesn't feel good in this place, but then I saw the smoke alarm in the room, so we'll have to do without.'

She sits down on a chair opposite mine, closes her eyes, and places her hands on her knees, palms facing upwards, as if in meditation. I study her face, which is shadowy in the candlelight. Nothing seems to be happening. I keep staring, though my eyes are beginning to hurt. After ten minutes or so, she says, 'Can you see anything?'

'No, not really,' I say, though I really wish I could, because I don't want to hurt her feelings, and she's gone to all this trouble for me.

'Maybe there's too much light in the room,' she says, and gets up and draws the curtains more tightly, so that the remaining chink of daylight is removed. She sits down again, and resumes her meditation. This time, I find that if I close my eyes slightly – half screwing them up, as if against bright sunshine – her face blurs. I'm trying to keep concentrating on the transfiguration, but I've got a pounding headache, and my head is swimming; I'm jetlagged, and desperate for some sleep. After another ten minutes or so, she says, 'Can you see Ruth yet?'

'No, I can't,' I say, 'but you seem to be looking rather more shadowy around the lips and chin. Like you've got a moustache and stubble . . . Actually, your face looks rather like Elvis.'

'Well, that's interesting,' says Laurie. 'I *do* get an English musician who comes through a lot in spirit. He could be here for you, instead of Ruth. See if you can recognize him.'

I stare at her some more. More blurred shadows. There's a buzzing in my right ear (the after-effects of flying, probably, though I would like to believe otherwise). I pull at my ear, hard, but nothing happens. Laurie said the spirit is an Englishman, so it can't be the ghost of Elvis, but he's got to be a pop star (I can't see Laurie as a classical music sort of girl). 'John Lennon?' I say, hesitantly. She shakes her head. 'Marc Bolan?' She shakes her head again. My mind has gone blank – apart from the dull ache inside

– and I can't think of any other dead English musicians in what seems to have turned into a surreal version of Twenty Questions.

'OK,' says Laurie, with apparently undiminished enthusiasm, 'let's try the mirror technique.' So we move away from the coffee table, and sit on the end of her bed instead, facing a large mirror, in the still-darkened room. We are sitting so close that we are touching, and I'm half expecting to feel the electricity that Laurie feels, but still, there's nothing; just the reflection of her face, calm as ever, and mine, anxious and tired and foolish-looking.

Several minutes pass. 'My face has disappeared,' says Laurie. 'That's when the spirits start coming through, so I can see their faces instead of mine.' I screw up my eyes again, and let the reflection blur, and then my face disappears as well, into a black hole inside the mirror. 'Are you meant to half-close your eyes?' I ask. 'Yes, that's fine,' says Laurie. 'That's how I first started seeing spirits in the mirror.' We sit there for another ten minutes or so, but still, no spirits turn up.

'Laurie,' I say, eventually, 'I'm terribly sorry, but I think I need to stop now. I've got a really bad headache, and my ear is buzzing.'

'That's the spirits coming through, because you have psychic abilities, too, I'm sure of it,' she says. 'For the first two weeks after I started with the mirror work, I felt as if I had a tight band around my forehead.' She turns towards me, looking concerned. 'Here, let me give you some healing. You need to be opened up more.'

'You can do healing, as well?' I say.

Laurie puts her hands over my head, not touching it, just resting her palms an inch or so above me. I feel the warmth of her hands; as if her blood is hotter than mine. She starts flicking her fingers, like she's flicking something away (the bugs in my hair, or my scepticism?). After a minute or so, she stops. 'That should help,' she says.

'Thank you,' I say. 'Thank you very much, for everything.'

'You're welcome,' she says, and smiles. As I stand up to leave, I see a CD on her side table. It has a picture of Freddie Mercury, the lead singer of Queen, on the front, and then suddenly, I've guessed right. 'It's him, isn't it?' I say, triumphantly. 'The dead musician! With the moustache!'

'You got it,' says Laurie, looking pleased, though also slightly worried. 'Just don't talk about it at the conference, OK? I don't think people will take me seriously if they know I'm channelling Freddie Mercury.'

'Do Gary and Linda know?' I ask.

'Yes, yes they do,' she says.

'And what do they think?'

'Well, they're amazed, of course,' she says. 'You know, he's always around me. When I'm about to appear on TV, I hear him say, "show time!" And once, when I went astral travelling, I saw him kind of fly past me, in a silver cat suit. I said, "Is that you?" And he said, "Of course it is! Who else did you think it was going to be?"'

'So were you a fan of his?' I say.

'I used to work in a record shop,' she says, 'and I knew his music, but no, I wouldn't say I was a huge fan, though I did feel very sorry when I read his obituary.'

'Does anybody else know about all this?' I ask.

'Well, my family, of course,' says Laurie. 'My husband is very supportive. And I did get in touch with someone in Europe who knew Freddie quite well, to say that I was receiving regular communications from his spirit. But I think this person was freaked out by it. So I didn't pursue it, because I don't want people to think I'm crazy. I mean, I'm just a normal ordinary mom from California.'

Today is turning into a very long day. We go down to the lobby, where the rest of the conference delegates have gathered – a hundred and fifty, at least – and climb into the buses that are taking us to the University of Arizona campus for 'The Great Debate'. Taking part in the debate tonight will be Gary Schwartz; Laurie Campbell; and 'leading skeptic' Ray Hyman, Professor Emeritus of Psychology at the University of Oregon, who is currently working on his forthcoming book, 'How Smart People Go Wrong'.

The only problem is, Professor Hyman has got lost somewhere between the Holiday Inn and the campus, which means that we're a bit short on sceptics here tonight. In fact, I think it is safe to say that Professor Schwartz is preaching to the converted. He takes to the stage first, looking professorial in a dark suit, white shirt and tie; neatly clipped beard, grey-flecked hair and wire-rimmed glasses. It quickly becomes clear that Professor Schwartz is a very good teacher: even I (still jet-lagged, by now very sleepy) can follow his explanations, sign-posted with handy graphics and sound bites projected on to a screen behind him. In his introduction to the debate, he says that Laurie is 'the believer'. She 'lives the process'. Ray is 'the disbeliever'. He 'searches for flaws'. Gary is 'the explorer'. He 'follows the data'. Linda, who is standing beside the stage looking like one of Charlie's Angels in a violet shot-silk suit, big black hair and killer heels, is 'the motivator'. She 'inspires loving science'.

After Gary comes Laurie, who tells the story she has already told me, about looking into the mirror on Thanksgiving Day and seeing her first spirits. She also says that she takes dictation from the spirits. 'I refer to myself as a secretary to the other side,' she says, which gets a ripple of laughter from the appreciative crowd (there are a lot of kaftans here tonight, and not many suits). 'I hear their voices in my head, though sometimes I hear them as my voice, as if I was reading a book.'

By this time, Professor Hyman has made it to the debate. 'I'm the bad guy,' he says, showing he has the measure of this audience. 'But not to worry – I'm outnumbered.' Professor Hyman is seventy-two years old – so naturally, I immediately fall in love with him – and describes learning magic tricks from his father when he was a child. By the time he was a teenager, he was able to do 'pseudo-mind-reading, and palmistry, and even spiritualism. I didn't believe in it – but I was able to convince people sufficiently for them to believe in me'. Since then, Professor Hyman has never been convinced by the truth of any medium; and he is certainly not about to buy into Gary and Linda's experiments. 'They have yet to produce solid gold evidence,' he says. I have to admit, while Professor Hyman is talking, I am completely swayed by his arguments; he seems like an entirely reasonable man. (And anyway, here am I, the cautionary tale of what happens when you start believing in magic and take a wrong turning: I've ended up sitting on a hard chair, thousands of miles away from my children and my husband, when I could be safe at home with them.)

Then Gary comes back on stage, and presents his evidence, and I'm soon back on his side again. He says that the probability is less than 2.6 trillion to one that all the facts gathered by the mediums in his laboratory research would be correct: so surely, that rules out clever guesswork? He also says that the argument that mediums are simply telepathic doesn't work here: because in his experiments, the mediums have come up with pieces of information that the sitters themselves did not know, until afterwards.

But then Gary blows it, for me, by saying, 'All of this relates to love.' I don't want love (I've got plenty of that at home). I came all the way here for science, and now he's projecting photographs of dogs on to the screen behind him: his lovely wife Linda with their lovely dog, Freudy; and a recently deceased medium called Susy Smith with her dog; and then Linda and Susy together with more fluffy dogs. 'Enough, already!' I want to shriek; surely this will not do the cause of psychic research very much good? Afterwards, Monty finds me and asks if I enjoyed the debate. 'Too many dogs,' I snarl. Outside, it is still raining.

> Then shall . . . the tongue of the dumb sing: for in the wilderness shall waters break out, and streams in the desert.
>
> Isaiah, Chapter 35, verse 6

## FRIDAY 9 MARCH

'WE WANT TO have some fun today!' says Professor Schwartz to the assembled conference, here in a ground-floor meeting hall at the Holiday Inn, just beyond the fountain that still smells of bleach. The audience whoops, but I stare down at the swirling carpet (whirls of pea green, custard, maroon and puce), feeling prim and English and insufficiently loving, which is not the right attitude for today's agenda: 'Celebrating the Living Soul'.

Apparently, Professor Schwartz's idea of fun is quantum physics. 'Energy is primary, and matter is organized energy,' he says. 'There is more to the universe than we see with the naked eye . . . Did I ever see an atom of hydrogen in college? No! I took my professor's word for it that it was there.' But Professor Schwartz isn't expecting us to simply take his word for it that the soul lives on: here stands a man with a mission to explain his 'Living Energy Universe Hypothesis', an original theory which underpins the research he has undertaken with Linda and Laurie. I think the hypothesis basically boils down to this favourite phrase of his: 'What goes around, and stays around, evolves around.' With lots more diagrams, Professor Schwartz goes on to demonstrate that if 'information and energy can be stored in atoms', then water has memory; a heart has memory; and if 'pure energy systems have memory', then maybe a soul can live for ever. Yes, I know it's a leap of faith – but the people in this hall seem ready to take that leap with him.

Then it gets weirder. This whole enterprise started in 1993, he says, when 'Linda Russek asked me a question. She said, "Do you think it is possible that my father is still here?"' Linda's father Henry, a distinguished cardiologist, had died in 1990. Linda, an equally distinguished clinician, wanted Gary, a tremendously distinguished scientist whom she had recently met, to prove that her father's life had survived death. 'I had fallen in love with her love for her father,' says Gary; and thus the experiments began.

But the story becomes even more peculiar. Linda and Gary set up house together in Tucson, and there they met a writer named Susy Smith, who lived alone with her miniature dachshund. Some years earlier, Susy Smith had become convinced that the dead live on, after the death of her own mother, with whom she believed herself to be in constant contact. Susy – a prolific author of twenty-seven popular books, including *The Book of James*, which she claimed was a team effort with the dead psychologist and philosopher, Dr William James – said that she was also able to contact Henry Russek, and Gary's dead father, as well.

Unfortunately, Susy Smith – who was supposed to be at the conference, to receive a special award for her services to this field of research – died last month, on 11 February, of an unforeseen heart attack. However, Gary explains to the audience – which includes a number of people who believe themselves to have psychic powers – that Susy has left behind a $10,000 prize for the first person who can successfully receive her secret code-phrase that she hopes to communicate from the other side. Gary also tells us that the instructions for testing whether the code is correct can be found on the Internet, at www.afterlifecodes.com.

By now, the audience is reeling from all this information, and Gary decides we need a break, though he has one more message for us this morning: it's the love thing again, and he's not going to let it slip away. 'What's love got to do with it?' declaims Gary from the stage, well into his stride by now. 'Everything! . . . Love is the connector.'

('How's it going?' says Neill, when I ring him from a payphone in the lobby. 'Not good,' I whisper, in case any of the delegates are listening, 'it's not working.' 'Maybe it's just the attempt that matters,' he says.)

Lunch beside the indoor fountain of disinfectant. I've ended up next to a past-life therapist called Barbara, who is holding the rest of the table rapt with her description of how death is all to do with 'unresolved issues'.

'So you're telling me that my sister died of breast cancer at the age of thirty-three because she had unresolved issues from her past lives?' I say.

'Yes,' says Barbara. 'She had to come back for this life because of traumas that were still within her. It must have been an unresolved trauma in her heart that caused her breast cancer. What a shame that I couldn't have worked with her to resolve those issues.'

'And what could you have done to save her?' I ask.

'Well, say she was Jewish, and in her past life, a German soldier came in and stamped on her children's heads, and then she died in the gas chamber . . .'

'Yes?' I say, trying not to choke on my potato salad.

'We would then go back in time,' says Barbara, airily, 'through four or five of her past lives, to see how many times that man had done this to her; and whether the person she was married to in this life could have re-ignited the programme.'

'Then what?' I ask.

'Then we would go up into heaven and bathe in the river of life,' continues Barbara.

'I don't quite follow you,' I say.

'It's all to do with thought form removal,' says Barbara. 'Let's go back thirty thousand years. Say your sister was a slave to this person. Somehow he feels like he owns her. He wants vengeance – and the memory goes into a file, like in a computer. Then two thousand years later, perhaps she's in a slave situation again, and it goes right back to the data file.'

'So how do you deal with that?' I ask.

'We go to the Temple for Thought Form Removal,' says Barbara, patiently.

'Where's that?' I say.

'In heaven,' says Barbara. 'I have created a huge glass ball there – and you're standing there, on this glass dome – and we ask for all the memories, all the tortures, all the traumas to pass into the glass dome, where they are caught. Then you ask God to disintegrate it, and He does. Then we bathe in a pool of perfect divine energy, and walk out into the Temple of Being—'

'We're still in heaven?' I say.

'Yes,' says Barbara. 'Then you take Excalibur—'

'Excalibur is in heaven?' I interrupt.

'Yes,' says Barbara, '. . . and you've removed the programme for ever.'

'How do you know all this?' I say.

'This is original Christianity,' says Barbara. 'I've been working with it for thirty years. It's mystical Knights Templar data. That's how I discovered this information – it was in a code. All religious material is written in a code.'

'Where did you find the information?' I say.

'In a US library,' says Barbara. 'Anyway, your sister will be reborn in about twenty years, and she'll have to go through all this again.'

'Oh dear,' I say, 'that's not very good news.'

'Yes,' says Barbara, 'but maybe I could work with you? I think you need to work on your unresolved issues. Did you dream of concentration camps as a child?'

'I did, actually,' I say. 'But that was probably because my father talked about them a lot, because he is Jewish and some of his relatives died in the camps.'

Barbara shakes her head, gloomily. 'No, you were *there* in the concentration camp, too,' she says, 'in a past life. That's why you need to work with me as soon as possible.'

'Unfortunately, I live in London,' I say.

'Well, we'll have to do it this weekend,' says Barbara.

'I don't think I've got time,' I say. 'The conference schedule looks rather tight.'

Barbara shakes her head again. 'I just hope and pray the Nazis shot you, and didn't gas you,' she says. By now, I have lost my appetite for the potato salad and ham. I would quite like a cup of sweet tea, to steady my nerves, but the afternoon session of the conference is about to begin. Barbara gets up to leave the table, still looking concerned. I'm feeling rather queasy, but I take a deep breath and go back into the hall. I wish there were some windows to the outside world. There's no fresh air in here; just a chemical sweetness that floats over the rows of chairs.

The next session is billed as: 'Crossing Over with Laurie Campbell: A Group Experience'. Laurie is going to try to contact the dead people that surround us in the hall today. This promise, I guess, is the thing that has brought some of the audience here to the conference. Expectation fills the room; old hopes and lost children; lovers and secrets waiting to be shared. 'A lot of times, I see something out of the corner of my eyes,' says Laurie, and my neck stiffens as I resist the urge to glance behind me and look for Ruth, whose silence at these proceedings is unnerving me. ('I wouldn't be caught dead in a place like this,' says a voice in my head.)

'I feel that a room opens up behind me,' continues Laurie, 'and the room is full of spirits. Usually the ones that have killed themselves are hanging back – but the more dominant ones throw the doors open.'

The doors to the hall are closed. The room is silent. We are waiting. 'I hear the spirits talking as if it's my own voice in my head,' says Laurie. 'People often don't realize that just because you're hearing your own voice, doesn't mean that it's not spirit speaking to you . . .'

Laurie starts talking about a dead child. Two women in the audience immediately respond to this. Both want the spirit child that Laurie is describing to be theirs: their story; their family; their lost baby. 'I'm getting the initial J,' says Laurie, 'and an M and a C.' Both women can find people in their lives with those initials. I'm still not clear whose baby we're talking about.

Then Laurie moves on, to describe a small man who loved old cars. 'I'm getting the initial V,' she says. Four more people put their hands up, to claim the spirit as their own. One woman is weeping. 'My grandfather's name was Victor,' she says. 'He loved old cars. It must be him.' Another woman on the other side of the room is also sobbing. 'I think it relates to me,' she says. 'He loved Volvos. That must be the V . . .'

'Let's all remember to breathe, to relax,' says Linda, reassuringly, taking over the microphone for a moment. But tension is stretched tight around the audience, and you can smell the anxiety mixed in with the air-freshener. 'There are a lot of unseen individuals in this room,' says Gary. 'They're all saying "me, me, me!" '

'I think we may be experiencing "bleed-through",' says Laurie, 'when information is being transferred from one medium to another – because I know there are other mediums in this room today – or from one sitter to another.' A woman sitting near me, who has been gnawing at her raw-bitten fingers, is muttering about foul play and electronic distraction by subversives – or 'plants' – in the audience (by which she means, I think, the living, rather than the dead).

Gary and Linda decide that maybe the group approach isn't working. So they ask Laurie to do what they call a 'blind reading' instead. She sits on the stage, facing away from the audience, hand over her eyes. Then Gary says he will pick a member of the audience to come up on the stage, for Laurie to read, without her seeing. You can feel the room hum with silent, desperate requests to be picked ('me, me, me!'). I'm willing Gary to pick a grey-haired, white-faced woman with dark shadows beneath her eyes; one of the women who responded to Laurie's mention of a dead child (a woman who seems to need some urgent answers). But he doesn't – he picks Monty, who walks up to the stage, and sits there, looking rather like Sherlock Holmes. I wonder what spirits Monty brings with him here, all the way to America.

I think that Laurie does reasonably well with him; he answers only yes or no to her statements and questions (albeit in an English accent, which is rare at this conference); she says she 'keeps getting an M name, a funny name that I don't recognize'.

After a few false starts, like a tentative conjuror, she comes up with Bess (his mother's name) and John (his father's name). Laurie also says that his father was killed by a bomb in the Second World War, which Monty confirms is correct. She adds that the circumstances before this death were very traumatic for Monty, because they had involved separation. When the reading has finished, he tells us that yes, before the bombing, he had been evacuated 250 miles away from his family. She scores another hit by describing him as having heart problems: he says that he has, in fact, had several heart attacks. She also insists that the spirits are referring to tomatoes. Later, Monty admits that he was, many years ago, 'the editor of a journal concerned with tomatoes'.

However, Ray the sceptic is unimpressed. We've seen nothing more – or less – than a clever cold reading, he says, when I corner him for his expert opinion. Laurie could have picked up Monty's age from his voice; and then it's hardly difficult to guess that an Englishman in his seventies may have had a father who died in the war. I find Ray's refusal to believe reassuring – his is, after all, the familiar culture that I was raised in – and yet also somehow unconvincing (or maybe my need to believe is greater than his). 'What about the tomatoes?' I ask. He simply shakes his head.

**7.30 p.m.** Gary and Linda are hosting an 'Evening Extravaganza' at their laboratory for everyone who has attended the conference. There are so many people here, that most of the party takes place outside in the garden, beneath the light of a full moon and the fairy lights that have been draped around the trees. A friend of Gary and Linda's – a former Catholic priest who is now married – gives a speech. 'I'm very romantic,' he says. 'When I watched Laurie this afternoon, I wanted everything to be hits, and for there to be no misses. But then I thought, that's not the world we live in, that's not reality.'

Later, I eat chocolate brownies and talk to a man called George, who looks like a clean-cut Hollywood actor (you could see him as a minor yet caring character in *ER*); but he turns out to be a psychiatric social worker from California who also works as a medium. 'How do you know the difference between the voices you hear in your head,' I ask, trying not to sound rude, 'and the voices that the mad people you work with hear in their heads?'

'That's a good question,' says George, evenly, as if dealing with a difficult client. 'Mediums such as myself are not mad, because we help people. Mad people damage their lives, and others. Mediums don't damage anyone.'

After my conversation with George, I wander around the laboratory by myself, aimlessly, and end up in a darkened, mirrored room with two of Gary's fresh-faced graduate students. One of them, Dan, says that I could take a look at my aura on the computer, if I'd like, by using a new machine in this room, called a 'GDV', which stands for Gas Discharge Visualization. 'OK,' I say, and he puts my right hand into a strange glove-like contraption, which is linked to the computer. The other graduate student, a young woman named Sabrina, starts tapping the keyboard, and then suddenly, I get an electric shock, and squeak in surprise. 'Is that supposed to happen?' I ask.

'No,' she says. 'Maybe you've got too much static electricity around you.' Anyway, it turns out that she can't read my aura on the computer; but Dan, who has a hearing aid, says that he can see people's auras without the aid of the GDV. 'I thought auras had gone out of fashion,' I say, 'like ectoplasm?'

'Well, I've always been able to see them,' he says, 'ever since I was a kid. Yours is blue, but it breaks up a bit, so that I can see you have some pain around your right shoulder and neck.'

I do, in fact, have a very stiff neck – possibly from the stress of being unusually nice all day, because everyone here is so nice to me, and to each other. The constant pleasantries are making me tense. I decide to go and find Ray the sceptic in the far corner of the garden. He appears to be hiding behind a tree. 'How are you enjoying the party?' I say.

'It's a whole other world,' he says.

'You know, these people really believe in what they're doing,' I say. 'Laurie is completely genuine.'

'I'm sure you're right,' he says. 'In my experience, 98 per cent of mediums are genuine, in that they believe in what they're doing – but that doesn't mean that they are speaking to the dead.'

By now, it's getting late, and on the bus back to the Holiday Inn, I find myself sitting next to Carrie, a massage therapist and former ballroom dancer from Boca Raton. 'You look like your neck is troubling you,' she says.

'It is,' I say, and then I find myself telling her about the rest of my troubles: Ruth's death; and all the other deaths, too. She just listens, and nods. By the time we get back to the hotel, I've given up with the story – it's hard to explain, and anyway, everybody dies – but she offers to give me a neck massage in her room. So we go there, and it's 11 p.m., and I lie on the carpeted floor, and stare at the beige flecked ceiling, and finally I close my eyes while she kneads my neck, and I'm slipping into the dark, towards the place where dreams are, quiescent at last.

Afterwards, I sit up and thank her. 'You're welcome,' she says. Then, as I'm about to say goodnight, she says, 'You know, you can't bring back the dead, but you can make your children happy.' This seems to me like the best advice I've heard for some time. I wish I could fly home to them now, and my husband, but I can't, and they will be sleeping, so I can't even ring them, but I think of them, warm heads on their pillows, breathing steadily, as dawn breaks in England.

## Saturday 10 March

At 9 o'clock this morning, a medium called Traci Linn Bray from Macomb, Illinois, gives me an impromptu reading. Stuff like this is happening all over the place at the conference now, as it enters its final day: little psychic huddles in corners of the Holiday Inn; confidences swapped and paranormal experiments undertaken. Traci says to me that she sees a small bird that is somehow connected to Ruth and I. She also says that she sees my sister riding a bicycle. 'And she has a pale white linen shirt wrapped around her waist. Does that mean anything to you?'

'Her favourite top was a white linen shirt from a designer called Ghost,' I say. 'And yes, the bicycle means a lot to me.'

'I see your sister on one side of a sheet of glass,' says Traci Linn. 'You're standing on the other side. Your hands are pressed against each other's, but you can't speak. Does that mean something to you?'

'Yes,' I say, beginning to cry, even though I don't want to, 'it does.'

'She wants you to know that you will be able to hear each other one day,' says Traci. 'And she wants you to do something for her now. She says, will you read "The Cow Jumped Over The Moon" to her children?'

'OK,' I say. 'She used to sing that nursery rhyme to my children when they were little. I'll do that for her.'

'Now she's handing you flowers,' says Traci, 'a bunch of wild flowers. You always give each other flowers.'

Afterwards, I rub my eyes, but Traci doesn't disappear. She used to work in law-enforcement, she tells me, but she couldn't ignore her gift for mediumship. It wouldn't go away. So now she's here at the conference, searching for a way forward, like the rest of us. We shake hands, and then I take my place inside the hall, though I feel like I'm sleep-walking. Professor Schwartz is talking about physics again. 'In quantum physics, there are ideas that are non-visualizable,' he says. A list flashes up on the screen behind him. It says: 1. Formism. 2. Mechanism. 3. Contextual. 4. System. 5. Implicit Process. 6. Circular Causality. 7. Creative Unfolding. 8. Integrative Diversity.

I don't understand what he is talking about. His lecture reminds me of my father's emails and Kabbalah diagrams. 'There are some things that are beyond words, yet you still know they're true,' says Professor Schwartz. 'That's part of the problem with this kind of research. We see the data – but on some level it doesn't compute – and maybe it will never compute. Maybe we just have to be peaceful about this.'

I decide I have to get some fresh air. I creep out of the hall, and go to sit in the courtyard outside. Professor Ray is there, as well, on his way to the gym for some exercise. 'How does all this stuff work?' I say.

'People make things fit,' he says, 'and people who have a deep sense of loss – the bereaved – are the quickest to make generalities seem relevant. You know, everyone can find a significant name beginning with "M" in their life.'

I ask him to give me a 'cold reading', to prove that he can be as apparently insightful as a medium. He takes my hand, and looks at the lines on my palm, as if they mattered, as if they meant something. 'You had at least two mentors in your life,' he says, 'and, um, a big change around the age of thirty.'

'How many children have I got?'

'Four,' he says, 'maybe five.'

'Not very good,' I say, with a sceptical smile. 'I've got two kids, and the rest of what you said was far too general.'

'Mediums deal in generalities,' he says.

'A medium this morning told me that my dead sister was riding a bicycle!' I say. 'That's a specific detail.'

'Lots of people ride bicycles,' he says.

'Yes, but it meant something important to me,' I say.

'You can always make generalities seem important, if you need to,' he says.

'I know,' I say. 'I know all about clutching at straws.'

Back in the hall, Gary is reminding us, again, that this conference – this entire process – is all about love; and I slump down in my seat. Maybe my disaffection is evident, because Gary seems to turn in my direction when he says, 'Here is a simple way to remember what love means: L stands for listen – because when you love someone, the first thing you do is to listen to them – with your ears, your eyes, your heart, your whole being. O stands for observe – because when we love someone, we observe them, and we celebrate them. V stands for valuing – because when we love someone, they matter to us, and so do their feelings, their goals, and their dreams. And E stands for empower – because when we love someone, we empower them. L.O.V.E. You can always remember that.'

Gary gazes lovingly at Linda, and Linda looks thoughtfully back at Gary, and everyone in the audience nods in agreement, except for me, and possibly Monty, who seems to be staring at the floor. (Ray, meanwhile, has completely disappeared.) I decide that Gary has been spending too much time with mediums – all these initials have finally got to him (and me, too, because I can write my own lists: if L is for love and Linda and life after death; then J is for Justine and Judas and jeering).

The conference is drawing to a close, wreathed in smiles. Linda talks about her plans for 'soul family therapy', whereby dysfunctional families can resolve their differences through the help of a medium, who will engage with the problems that still exist between the living and the dead. (This sounds like a good plan for my grandfather the dead spiritualist, and my father and me . . . Maybe I should sign us up?) When Gary says that Linda thinks it would be a good idea to do soul family therapy with Hitler, I'm not sure if he's joking. The audience applauds when Linda declares that she's 'a rainbow spiritualist', and then Gary says that he is going to sing to us as a final gesture of love, before we go our separate ways.

Gary sings several songs by James Taylor, karaoke-style. 'There's a river running under your feet,' he croons into his microphone, loosening his tie, swaying gently on stage. He tells us how much he loves James Taylor's work, particularly the ballad 'Wake up Susy', which he dedicates to Susy Smith. 'Maybe one of you will get Susy's afterlife code and win the prize!' he says, as encouraging as ever.

'Bless you all on your journeys as you leave this hotel,' says Linda.

'Bless you,' says Gary.

'Bless you,' says the lady sitting next to me.

But it's not over yet. I'm going out for a farewell dinner with Gary, Linda, Laurie, and Monty. Gary drives us to a Chinese restaurant in his enormous RV; a vehicle known to him and his admirers as 'the Spiritmobile'. Inside, there hangs a large picture of Linda's father, Henry Russek. Gary tells us that he has worn a different one of Henry's ties for each day of the conference. 'Linda gave me her father's ties,' he explains, 'which was such an honour.'

'They're very lovely,' I say.

'Yes, they are,' says Gary, stroking today's red tie, like a baby.

At dinner, I talk to Linda about dogs (she sleeps with hers, though Gary is sometimes banished next door for snoring); and then I turn to Laurie and we discuss the dead scientists in her life. 'They come through me, directly,' she says, 'people I've never heard of before – a physicist named Sir John Eccles, for example.' Monty looks intrigued, and starts telling Laurie about the practice of physical mediumship, which is almost unheard of these days. 'I can do that,' says Laurie. 'Justine has seen my transfigurations, when my face changes.'

On the way home, Gary sings some more James Taylor songs. 'I find them very moving,' he says, though Linda looks slightly tetchy. I realize that I do not yet understand Gary; or his relationship with Linda (how do they share a house with her dead father and their bed with a dog called Freud?); or their mysterious brand of loving research – but I'm glad that our paths have crossed. ('You can count me out,' sighs Ruth's voice in my head, 'if you think we're coming back to a place like this again.' 'I came here looking for you,' I say, 'and then you didn't turn up!' 'What do you expect?' she snaps. 'I couldn't get a word in edgeways, these people talk so much.' 'OK,' I tell her, '*fine*, but I was looking to prove something, that's all.'). After Gary has dropped us back at the hotel, I watch him disappear into the night in his Spiritmobile, straight down the highway into the darkness; and as he turns the corner, heading back to his house in the mountains, I like to think that he is still singing.

## Sunday 11 March

I leave Tucson first thing in the morning, on a flight to Dallas. I look out of the window, and imagine Ruth just out of sight, riding her bicycle beyond the plane, up into the pale sky, her dark hair streaming behind her, her Ghost shirt flying in the wind.

Halfway there, we hit a storm. Lightning flashes around the plane, and we dip and roll and plummet through the clouds. I close my eyes and think of Ruth – no longer on her bicycle outside, but inside here, crouching next to me in the aisle because the plane is packed full, holding my hand. I clasp my hands together. 'Dallas Airport is closed because of the storm,' says the pilot, crackling over the intercom, 'but don't worry, we should have enough gas to stay up here for a while.' The passengers are silent, though a woman behind me is praying, quietly. I do not want this plane to crash, to fall through a hole in the sky. I want to be with Neill again; to find the place where my head rests on his shoulder, where my lips meet his warm skin; and there is still so much left to say; so much I do not want left unsaid . . . How could I go anywhere but home again: to hold my sons, to see the curves of their mouths as they smile; and Juliette, who is waiting for me to teach her how to flip pancakes high in the air, like magic; and Lola and Joe, curled up with laughter between Neill and I on the sofa; this tangle of children in my life, who weave the broken bits together. I want to go home. I will get there . . .

After another hour of buffeting, it feels like we're travelling round in circles; and my stomach is somersaulting. Half an hour later, the plane lands, and the woman behind me praises the merciful Lord for his kindness. I thank Ruth, instead, but not out loud. We appear to have come to a halt in the middle of a field, as the lightning cracks and the sky opens. 'The airport is still closed, due to the electrical storm,' says the pilot, 'so I'm sorry, but we'll be sitting out here for some time.' I don't care: at least we're safe on solid ground – though it seems strange to be stuck in limbo, while the arrival gates are shut against our entry.

Eventually, the plane starts to move again, towards the airport (and I remember my mother's recurring dream, of cycling up a hill but never reaching the top of it, carrying her entire family on her wobbly bicycle, trying to balance the whole damn lot of us). By the time we reach the gate, I'm worried about missing my connecting flight to London, even though the whole airport must have come to a halt. The terminal is in chaos. I start walking away from the gate, looking to find someone who can tell me where I should be going. Eventually, a man stops with a golf cart, and gestures to me to climb on. An elderly couple are already sitting behind him, clutching their suitcases, which are in a precarious, top-heavy pile. 'Where are we going?' says the woman to her husband. 'Who knows?' he replies. 'The storm has closed everything down.'

The golf cart deposits us at a waiting place for an electric train that will take us to another terminal. The three of us – the elderly couple and me and their suitcases – get on to the electric train.

Dallas is a hub airport, and the train travels in an endless loop. We come out of the first terminal, past five concentric freeways and flyovers, and then grind to a standstill in the pouring rain. 'The sixth circle of hell,' says the elderly gentleman, tapping his fingers on his knees. 'Did you know that there is no driver on this train?' he adds. 'It moves in mysterious ways.' I wonder what happens to electrical trains in a storm. There is so much that I don't understand. Then the train starts moving again, and deposits us at another terminal. I get off the train, and start walking to my gate. I am on my way home.

Day turns into night, but not for long on the plane that is taking me to London. Dawn breaks in London just after the sun sets in Dallas. I don't sleep but it doesn't matter. The journey is smooth, once we leave the big Texan thunder behind. At Gatwick airport, I take another train into London, and then go down into the underground, into the thick of the rush hour, for the final stage of this long journey. I sit down, and there is a Henry Vaughan poem above the opposite window, printed there to inspire tired commuters, I suppose. It is called 'The World', and I half-remember it from long ago (was it Mr Hood that read it to us in junior school, after we had built the Roman villas, and before we moved on to 'The Last Battle'?). I read it over and over again, trying to fix it in my head before I leave this carriage.

I saw Eternity the other night
Like a great Ring of pure and endless light,
All calm, as it was bright,
And round beneath it, Time in hours, days, years
Driv'n by the spheres
Like a vast shadow mov'd, in which the world
And all her train were hurl'd . . .

## SUNDAY 18 MARCH

I HAVE ONE MORE place I have to go. There is one more woman I have to see: a woman named Tina Laurent, who comes highly recommended by people who know about these things; people who know about how to contact the dead through tape recorders. ('Do you have to go out on a Sunday evening?' says Neill, after we've put the children to bed. 'Do you have to do this at all?' 'I won't be gone for long,' I say, 'I'll be back before you're asleep.' 'Don't you think you're ready to stop now?' he says. 'You don't need these people to tell you what you believe.' 'You're right . . .' I say, my voice trailing away. 'I'm sorry, it's just I've already made the appointment to see Tina . . .' 'You don't have to say sorry,' he says.)

I could have gone back to Judith Chisholm, but maybe this new medium will take me forward to somewhere else. (Surely it's worth one last try, at least?) Tina Laurent lives in South Wales, but she comes to London for two weeks every month to look after an old lady in Barnet. Today, she says that we can meet at the flat where she works, because she stays there, when she is on duty.

It's not too far away from my house – five or six miles, straight up the Great North Road, through the outer suburbs of London. I've never been this way before, but I find the old lady's road, and park outside her block of flats. Upstairs, on the top floor, Tina is waiting for me. She has pale-strawberry blonde hair; and a smooth, ageless face, though I guess she must be in her fifties. She is wearing purple, lots of purple; she looks very strong, very capable. First of all, she introduces me to the old lady, who is in bed for the night (I'm not sure how to explain myself – 'Hello, my name's Justine, I've come to speak to ghosts' – no, I don't think so; so we just shake hands instead). Then Tina shows me into the front room, which is decorated with photographs of the old lady's relatives. Tina has prepared a list for me of all the names that she has received on her tape recorder since we spoke on the phone a couple of weeks ago. The list is three pages long, but none of the names are familiar, though 'Tommy' appears several times. 'And I keep hearing "Pip" or "Pipkin",' says Tina, 'ever since I started mentioning you on the tapes.' She has also written down the phrases 'deep freeze sister' and 'tea-cola' on the list: these messages came through loud and clear the other day, apparently.

She explains that she used to live in America, where her first husband was a doctor. There, she became convinced of her psychic powers, after she dreamt one night of a ball of orange fire with the number six inside. The next morning, she discovered that at the very moment of her dream, her husband the doctor had been called to an explosion where six bodies were found. Unfortunately, he was not happy with her new-found interest in the paranormal, and they separated soon after. Tina, however, stayed true to her quest, and when she came across Sarah Estep in Annapolis she knew that she had found the gate to the other side. Sarah taught her about how to get the best results from tape recorders, and about the importance of perseverance: of listening to the tapes over and over again, until the messages became clear. Like Judith Chisholm, she does not hear the discarnate voices at the time of recording: she has to wait until she plays back the tape, and often she will have to adjust the speed control on her machine, to slow the voices down in order to understand them. 'We have to assume that their vibratory level is higher than ours,' says Tina. 'They say things like, "we come down" or "Tina, look up".'

She plays me some of her tapes now. 'Listen,' she says, 'this is when I was trying to contact Ruth for you last week.' There is a hiss on the machine. 'Did you hear that?' she says.

'I heard something,' I say.

'Kid,' says Tina. 'The voice is saying, "kid". Did you call Ruth your kid sister?'

'No,' I say, truthfully.

Tina shrugs her shoulders. 'Oh, well,' she says, and we listen to some more murmurs on the tape. 'I heard from my third husband, Carl, after he passed on. It was his voice, as plain as plain could be.'

'Was he the doctor?' I say.

'No, that was my first husband,' she says. 'My second husband was a Jewish professor. And Carl and I used to be entertainers. He played the banjo, I played the keyboards. He sang one hundred and twenty songs non-stop, for over two hours at a time.'

'On your tape recorder, after he was dead?' I say, getting confused.

'Oh no,' says Tina, 'when we were on stage. I only get a few words from him now. It's very hard for them to communicate from the other side. But I've learnt that I get my best messages through the sound of running water.' That's why she walks around the flat with a tape recorder attached to her neck with a length of elastic, ready to be activated when she turns on taps and flushes the lavatory. She goes into the bathroom now and switches on the tape recorder, by way of demonstration, as well as her little hand-held radio, which is tuned so that it drifts in and out of faraway, muttering stations. The ghosts find it easier to speak through the sound of other voices, she explains, as well as water.

My stomach is beginning to churn, and I shift in the old lady's armchair, trying to find a way to sit comfortably. 'Hello, hello, who is on the line tonight?' says Tina, who has returned to the front room. 'Radio Tina is here, calling, calling.'

Much to my surprise, I think I hear a voice answering Tina, and then I realize it's not coming from the radio or the tape recorder, but from down the hall, where the old lady is in her bedroom. 'Hang on a moment,' says Tina, and goes to attend to her duties. By the time she's come back, I need to go to the bathroom, because I feel like I'm about to be sick. 'Here, take the tape recorder with you,' says Tina. 'Keep the record button on, and we'll see what happens when you flush the toilet.'

I take the tape recorder into the bathroom. I start retching, which is embarrassing because I don't want to wake up the old lady who is still trying to go to sleep next door; plus I'm being taped, which is disconcerting. I turn off the tape recorder, and sit on the floor for a few moments, moaning to myself, and rocking. I want to go home, but I'm not sure how I'm going to get there. I switch the tape recorder on again, flush the lavatory, wash my hands, and say, out loud, 'Ruth, are you there?' I go back to the front room, and give Tina her tape recorder. 'I'm really sorry,' I say, 'but I'm going to have to leave, right now. I don't think I'm very well.'

Tina peers at me, and shakes her head. 'You do look a bit pale,' she says. 'Are you going to be all right to drive?'

'I think so,' I reply, and we shake hands and say goodbye. I'm shivering as I turn back on to the main road, and the lights from passing cars are blurring double, but at least I'm headed in the right direction, with no need for map reading. When I reach the house, I rush upstairs and throw up in my own lavatory, in blessed privacy. Then I brush my teeth, take off my clothes, climb into bed, and curl up tightly, with a pillow over my head. I don't want to go out ever again. The next morning, I tell Neill that I can't get up. 'I'm feeling sick,' I say, from under the duvet. I stay there for the rest of the day, with the dog by my side. I don't want to talk just yet. I want to lie here in the silence.

## Saturday 24 March

Neill comes home with a video for us to watch: *Frequency*, the film I wanted to see on the plane to New York last October, about a son who speaks to his dead father via a ham radio.

I find myself completely absorbed in the plot (unsurprisingly). The son – who is a handsome thirty-six-year-old policeman – is still living in his parents' house, alone, because his girlfriend has left him and his mother has moved out to an apartment somewhere else; and, one day, he unearths his father's dusty radio from under the stairs. It's still working and, guess what, he's soon talking to his fireman father – but the father is alive, and the son (or at least, the boy he once was) is only six years old, and fast asleep in an upstairs bedroom. The connection has been made through time and space, in a Hollywood version of mystic physics (time is a circle, the universe moves in mysterious ways, and so on and so forth). Fortunately, the son seizes the magical moment – on a night lit up by the Aurora Borealis, in a sky where you can almost see for ever – and he tells his father how to avoid being burnt to death; because on his father's side of the radio, it's thirty years ago – the evening before the fateful fire that killed him.

So the fireman survives, with the help of his son, and then the plot gets even more complicated (the mother dies, because time has been tinkered with, but then she's saved again). In the end, everyone lives happily ever after, and they all play baseball together in the park. But this film has got me thinking. Could I have warned Ruth not to believe the doctors when they said the lump in her breast wasn't cancerous? Why can't I radio her back in time, to rework our history? Or how about an email: just one short email, flashing through space? That's all it would take: a little shift, a slip in the sky, a reshuffle of past blunders, a mending of mistakes. We would still be able to do ordinary stuff together – the small things that braid lives into a satisfying plait; the easy conversations that form the language of love. (What did we talk about before she got ill? Hair, husbands, parents, shoes; how to grow lavender, whether chocolate gave you spots.)

I can't stop thinking about the two-way radio communication, and even though it's late by the time the film finishes, I keep trying to talk to Neill about the mechanics of how it might work. 'It's just a story,' he says, when I ask him to explain some inexplicable blind alley in the plot. 'It's not real, it's make-believe. It doesn't have to make sense.'

## Wednesday 28 March

I dream that Neill and I are getting married again. I feel rather confused – I'm wearing the same white linen dress that I wore to our real-life wedding (a dress designed by Ghost, as it happens), but the details of this dream wedding are different. I have on thick black tights, for a start, and I can't see Ruth anywhere, even though she sat next to me during our real wedding, and handed Neill the ring, and made a funny, clever speech at the party afterwards. She bought flowers for our wedding: hundreds of flowers, for the registry office and the party, and a wild garland for my hair and some more for me to carry that day. It was her gift to us.

When I wake up afterwards, I'm still not quite all there. I go over the dream, trying to find a way back into it again, searching for clues. These are the things I remember. My mother is in my dream, but Ruth is just out of sight. I don't know where my father is – still in South Africa, I think, as he was for our real-life wedding. There are no flowers in my dream; and we are in a church that I don't recognize, halfway up a steep hill.

The dream reminds me that we have a video of the wedding party – which includes Ruth, of course – but I can't bear to watch it now. We were married in May 1993, which means that she probably had the early stages of undiagnosed cancer by then. If I could rewind time – watch the video and speak to that blithe, laughing Ruth on the other side of the television screen – then I could warn her; save her life. But I can't.

Ruth married Matt the following year: August 1994. This time, she wore a white linen Ghost dress, and I stood next to her, holding the rings. It was a sunny day, and she had white roses in her long dark hair. The party was at Matt's parents' house, in the countryside on the edge of the South Downs. We drank champagne in their garden, and ate slices of cake, sprawled on the lawn in the sunshine. Tom took his first steps that day, staggering across the grass, elated, triumphant. By then, the cancer cells must have been spreading, but we knew nothing. The following year, August 1995, the twins were born. A year later, we celebrated their first birthday with another sunny party in the same Sussex garden. We were still blind to Ruth's cancer, though the lump in her breast was as big as a clenched fist. ('Totally benign,' the doctors had said.) The year after that, August 1997, we came back to the garden for their second birthday. By then, we all knew that Ruth was going to die. She had spent the preceding weeks in Trinity Hospice, in South London, overlooking dusty Clapham Common. The tumours had spread through her blood to her bones, her liver, her lungs, her brain. She was no longer the same Ruth, and yet she was. It was confusing, and she was very confused. In the garden outside her room – a rambling, unexpectedly secret place to find in the city – we sat in the sun. She rested her head in my lap. 'What am I doing here?' she said. I stroked her hair – her shorn hair, like a lamb – and tried to find the words, but nothing would come. Next to us, a mulberry tree dropped its ripe fleshy fruit on the path. 'Like blood,' said Ruth, looking at the dark red stains. 'What a waste . . .' Ahead, the planes flew to and fro in the late summer sky, on their way to places she would now never see. There was a pond in the garden, with a sculpture in the middle that seemed to be some sort of sundial. When she felt strong enough, we walked in slow circles around the water, and then sat beside the mulberry tree again. The afternoons ticked away in Trinity Hospice – inch by inch, until I felt we were crawling towards nightfall, as I tried to piece together a story that she would understand of what had become of our lives. 'What year is it?' said Ruth.

'It is 1997,' I said.

'How time flies,' she said, with that familiar, quizzical arch of her eyebrow, 'when you're having fun . . .'

After the twin's birthday party, she went home with them and Matt, and though she slept most of the time, she managed to send some emails to friends. She did not speak much, but she liked it when I massaged her back with lavender oil. I bought bunches of sweet peas to put beside her bed, though the petals soon drooped in the hot, upstairs room. The days drifted past, in an Indian summer. She could not walk by now, but she came to Jamie's birthday picnic in Regent's Park, riding in her wheelchair with Lola and Joe in her lap. She wore her favourite white linen Ghost shirt over a black skirt. Her presence was heroic, though at times, she seemed absent from the proceedings, moving on in her mind to a different place.

The following weekend, Matt drove her down to his parents' house in Sussex with the twins. She wanted to sit in the garden, to be in the fresh air outside London, where the wind blew over the downs, from the sea. But soon, she could not breathe. They called an ambulance, which took her back to London, to Trinity Hospice. Joe was confused. He thought that a policeman had taken her away. I arrived at the hospice soon afterwards. 'I'm dying of the pain,' she said, clawing at her shirt. She was wearing black tights, and I wanted to take them off for her, to ease the pressure on the tumours in her liver, but I didn't know where to begin.

'Give her more morphine,' I said to the nurses. 'I don't want her to be in any pain at all, please, do it now.'

They increased the dose, and she seemed calmer. I sat beside her bed, where the windows were half-open to the garden. It was still light outside, not yet autumn. Late roses brushed against the glass. I stroked her face, as dusk fell. She had an oxygen mask over her face, and she could not speak to me, but she could still hear me. 'This isn't the end, Ruth,' I said. 'It's not the end. Wherever you go from here, I will still be with you. I'll always hear you, you'll always hear me.'

She nodded her head. 'I'm not leaving you,' I said. 'We'll still be together, I promise you that.' When it was dark, Matt came with the children to say goodbye. She knew they were there, and she took the oxygen mask from over her face, to kiss them. They were frightened – there were so many machines in the room – but they kissed her, and then Matt took them home again. My mother was there too (though I could hardly bear to meet her eyes, for fear of seeing what was reflected in my own); and later that night, some of Ruth's friends came to see her in the dark room. By then, she was unconscious. But I think she still heard them, as they wept by her bed.

She died in the dark, before dawn broke. My mother was beside her, grief etched on her white-wax face. My father arrived from South Africa, too late to see Ruth. He sat by her body and said a Jewish prayer, rocking himself. I sat on the other side of the bed, beside the window, and held my sister's hand. It was cold, but she still seemed alive to me. Her eyes were closed, but her eyebrows looked as quizzical as ever. I expected her to sigh, and open her eyes again, and smile at me. But she did not.

I miss her still. I miss her so much. I don't know where she is, however hard I have tried to find her. 'I'm here,' she says to me, inside my head. But which one of us is speaking?

## FRIDAY 30 MARCH

QUARTER TO EIGHT. Jamie comes into our bedroom. 'Time to get up,' he says. I'm awake, but am I still dreaming? I hear Kirsty's voice, as clear as clear can be. 'Come on, boys,' she says, and laughs, her full-throated laugh, head tipped back, red hair glinting in the morning sunlight. I'm not sure whether she's talking to her boys, or mine. 'You're dead,' I say. She laughs again. There is a wall between us now, but I can hear her laughter. Then I see a gap in the wall, and her hand reaching through it. Her hand is warm when I touch it, briefly. 'Come on, Mum,' says Jamie. 'Come on . . .'

## Sunday 1 April, April Fool's Day

'A pinch and a punch for the first of the month,' said Ruth, when we were small, but we never came to blows. Once, she scratched my stomach by mistake, and I still have the mark – which I'm glad of; not a scar, just a semi-circle of three little red spots, broken veins.

Early this morning, I dream that Ruth is still alive – that maybe she was never dead – and we are going out together to buy some new clothes, which is fortunate, because I am half-dressed. 'I'm really glad you're back,' I say to her, darting into the shop with a towel wrapped around my waist, foolish and furtive, trying to keep hidden from passers by. 'The thing is, I'm no good by myself,' I continue. 'Everything goes wrong. I'm like a gooseberry when you're not here – tagging along with other pairs of friends. Two's company, three's a crowd. I'm the third person foisted on to a couple who don't need me around . . .'

She doesn't say anything, but I know she's there. And then she's gone again, and I wake up, wondering if I can remember the real sound of her voice.

## MONDAY 2 APRIL

TOM'S SEVENTH BIRTHDAY. My father sends him a letter, reminding him that it will soon be Passover.

It has a terrible and a happy side to it [writes my father]. Moses our teacher lived about 3,500 years ago. He had a lucky start in life because he was saved from being killed when he was a newborn baby. By order of Pharaoh the king of Egypt, all newborn Hebrew baby boys were to be killed. This was because Pharaoh was afraid that the Hebrews were becoming too many, even though most of them were to become slaves working for the Egyptians, building pyramids and temples you can still see today.

Moses' mother put him in a little cradle lined with pitch or tar on the outside and floated it off like a little boat towards Pharaoh's daughter, a princess, who was having a bath in the Nile River with her maidens at the time. She adopted Moses and he was brought up like a prince, learning many languages and becoming very wise.

Moses knew he was a Hebrew by birth although an Egyptian by his upbringing. Moses was very sad and angry when he saw an Egyptian beating a Hebrew slave to punish him and make him work harder. He killed the slave-master and when it became known he ran away towards the wilderness of Midian in case the Egyptians found out and wanted to punish him. There he looked after sheep belonging to a priest called Jethro. He fell in love with Jethro's daughter, Zipporah, married her and had two sons, Ephraim and Mannaseh. Zipporah was black – an African.

Then a wonderful thing happened to Moses in the wilderness of Midian. A vision and a voice came to him and spoke to him out of a burning bush that blazed but was not consumed by its fire. Moses felt that God spoke to him about becoming the leader of the Hebrews, and taking them to the land of Canaan. The Hebrews believed that Canaan was promised to them by God when God spoke to Abraham, the very first Hebrew of all, about four hundred years previously . . .

Passover, which Jewish people – people descended from Abraham – celebrate, is a happy time that tells the story of how Moses led the children of Israel – Israelites descended from Abraham and his son and grandson Isaac and Jacob – out of Egypt.

Lots of love to you for your birthday!!!

Grandad

Somebody told me that every seven years, our cells are replaced – not all at once; just slowly, as time goes by, until they've disappeared, and our body is new again. (Does that mean that seven years after Ruth's death, the cells of my body will no longer remember her? No, impossible: each new cell must inherit the memory of the old.)

Tom was born in this house, in our bedroom, in the quiet time just before midnight – on a Saturday that fell between Good Friday and Easter Sunday, that year. Jamie was sleeping in the room next door, but at dawn he woke up and said, 'There's a baby here.' Afterwards, I felt such peace descend over us, like spring sunshine.

Three years later, just after Tom's birthday, I realized that I was pregnant again. But it did not seem possible to have a third child, as Ruth was dying. I lay in bed for several days, and the room spun around me, out of control. Ruth came to visit, and climbed into bed with me. I did not tell her what was happening at the time. It seemed too cruel to talk about another baby, as the tumours grew and made her stomach swell, while she wept over leaving her children motherless. The curtains were open, and we looked out of the window, into the sky above the rooftops. I felt like I couldn't think straight: there was a buzzing inside my head, like a badly tuned radio. Later, when I was in hospital, the doctor said that I needed to take deeper breaths. ('Breathe deeply, one . . . two . . . three . . . and then you'll be asleep, and before you know it, you'll wake up, OK?')

Now I'm looking out of the window again, sitting in this new attic room, the room that was not built when Ruth was still alive. It is windy outside, and the petals are being scattered from the damson tree at the bottom of our garden, but the new green leaves survive and a blackbird is singing and maybe I will make plum jam this summer.

## TUESDAY 3 APRIL

LAST NIGHT, I dreamt about the haunted house, but it wasn't haunted any more. I went upstairs to the attic, and there were still cracks in the walls, but no ghosts hiding there. I was glad to find all the extra space in the house, because I want Lola and Joe to have a room of their own when they come to stay. In my dream, I understand that the house isn't finished yet – I need to find a good builder, someone I can trust, who will fix the walls and mend the broken floorboards – and then there's the roof to consider, the roof which has still got holes in it. Maybe the ghosts flew away out of the roof, up into the night, jumping over the moon, laughing out there among the stars. Or perhaps they have gone to find someone else to live with, another house, another street.

In the morning, I say to Neill that maybe we should think about moving. 'Why?' he replies. 'I love this house, we're happy in it. Tom was born here.'

'But we're growing out of it, now that the boys are getting bigger, two boys in a small house,' I say. 'We don't need to rush into anything, don't worry . . .'

Before I get any further in making plans for the future (our castles in the sky), Tina Laurent rings. She has exciting news. Another EVP researcher, faraway in British Columbia, has picked out the word 'Picard' in a recent recording. Tina thinks that this is a good sign. Afterwards, I tell Neill. 'I don't think it's anything to do with you,' he says. 'I think it probably refers to Captain Picard from *Star Trek*. I expect most ghost-hunters believe in aliens. Spirits, spaceships, stuff like that – it's all on the other side.'

Perhaps the ghosts in the attic have gone to British Columbia. I don't think so, though . . . no, not really. I think we've just learnt to accommodate each other. And doubtless the ghosts have lives of their own to get on with, too.

## WEDNESDAY 11 APRIL

I'M GOING TO visit the Spell Check spirit in Stoke-on-Trent – the ghost in someone else's machine – and it's thanks to my new friend, Montague Keen. (My friendships with older men that have developed over the past six months – Dale, Monty; my father and his father, even, at a distance – seem to have added a certain ballast to my life, despite the fact that all of these men occupy odd, esoteric, possibly weightless realms.) I know that I told myself that the visit to Tina was my final venture into psychic technology; and here I am chasing spirits again: but after this trip, I'm stopping, I've promised Neill, I *promise*. ('About time too,' says my imaginary therapist. 'And by the way,' she adds – she? I never realized he was a she; though her voice has an unsettling habit of shifting sex mid-sentence – 'I think we have reached closure, you and me.' 'Well, thank you,' I say, 'goodbye . . .' 'Goodbye,' says the imaginary therapist, 'and look after yourself, my dear.')

We meet at Euston Station – Monty in tweed, me in jeans – and take the train together, north through the waterlogged fields of England. (The foot and mouth epidemic is in full swing, but the countryside bisected by the railway line still looks peaceful, as we speed past.) 'The Society of Psychical Research is extremely excited about this case,' says Monty, in a lowered voice, the very soul of discretion, because the carriage is packed with passengers and strangers surround us. 'This could be the Holy Grail of psychic research, the permanent paranormal object,' he continues, in even more hushed tones. 'But do remember, as I've said to you before, these things have a habit of melting away before our eyes.'

'I'm still hopeful,' I say. 'I always travel in hope.'

We're met at the other end by Jean, who is married to Dave Smith (the man who discovered the Spell Check ghost in his computer). Jean also lives, in a manner of speaking, with Dave's ghost, Lady Prudentia Trentham; because Lady Prudentia now speaks to Dave in his head, as well as on the computer, and accompanies him home at night. 'She came on holiday with us last week to our caravan in north Wales,' says Jean, matter-of-factly. 'We were just getting settled in, and Dave said, "Jean, she's here with us."'

Jean drives us out of the city and into the almost countryside, to Westwood Hall, the school where Dave works as an administrator, and the place where Lady Prudentia Trentham lived over 350 years ago; though it sounds as if she's still very much at home there. 'It's all to do with electricity,' says Jean, 'that's how her ladyship communicates. I don't like electricity, myself. We were always warned about it, as children. These days, no one seems to tell children not to put their fingers in plugs.'

Twenty minutes or so out of Stoke, we turn off the main road, past a nineteenth-century gatehouse. I half-hoped that we would pass through landscaped gardens to a stately home; but the original Westwood estate is now covered with rows of modern houses, and the Hall itself turns out to be a squat Victorian building, with lumpy sixties additions, built on the site of Lady Prudentia's long-gone Elizabethan mansion. There are dark, wet rhododendrons on either side of the drive, and a couple of glum teenagers that disappear on their skateboards as we drive past, although the school itself is empty for the Easter holidays. Only Dave is here today – ready and waiting to meet us in the entrance hall; him and the ghost in his head – a white-haired man in a pale blue shirt and matching trousers, who looks rather tired, washed out, even; as if he's been up most of the night with Lady Prudentia.

Above our heads, in this place that smells of school days and chalk dust, a light is flickering. 'Dave, that light's flashing,' says Jean, blinking.

'That's because the bulb's going,' says Dave, who used to be an architect, and seems like a thoroughly practical chap.

'Perhaps Lady P is trying to communicate through the Morse code,' says Monty, as the light continues to flicker.

'She sees everyone who comes through the door,' says Dave. 'And she picks up on what we talk about. She likes to be included.'

Jean goes off to make some tea, and Dave takes us into his office, where plans and photographs of Westwood Hall hang on the walls. This is the room where Lady Prudentia first made contact through the spell-check programme of his main-frame computer on 30 September 1998. 'She'd been trying to get someone to listen to her for years,' says Dave, 'ever since she died in 1642. She's scared the living daylights out of some people, as you can imagine.' In fact, Dave was writing a short piece on the history of the hall and its haunted reputation, for the benefit of the local schoolchildren, when Prudentia crashed into his spell check for the very first time.

Dave shows me a copy of that momentous communication, in which the spell-check screen offers the cryptic suggestion,

'Fernyhough', to replace 'Trentham'. 'Janet Fernyhough was a staff member who had felt as if she'd been pushed by something – or someone – invisible in the staff ladies' loo,' says Dave. The following morning, he continues, the word 'Dieulacres' appeared, as another spell-check substitute for 'Trentham'. 'Dieulacres was the name of the original Abbey lands upon which Westwood Hall was built,' he says, 'but I didn't know that at the time.' Since then, Dave has received thousands and thousands of spell-check messages from Prudentia, both on his office computer, and via his laptop at home, including the words 'death-is-a-gate'. 'I don't think she really knows how she communicates,' he says, 'but I do know she's getting better and better at it, though she does get tired.'

I've brought my own laptop here with me today, at Dave's suggestion, containing a new document in which I've written something about Lady Prudentia, to alert her attention. (Dave gave me a few details about her on the phone last night: she was from a leading Catholic family, the Eyres; she had two children, one of whom died in infancy; she came to live in Westwood Hall after she was widowed in 1628; she was persecuted for her faith and hounded by her neighbours; one of whom, says Dave, raped her – a crime that led to her death, and her subsequent desire to name the guilty man, however many centuries it took to get someone to listen . . . ) The plan this afternoon is for us to run the spell-check programme on my computer, in Monty's presence, to see what happens. Will her ladyship speak through my screen?

No, she will not. There are no anomalous words on my screen; and nor do they appear when Dave taps the spell-check button instead of me. We both write pleading messages, with inviting misspellings, crying out for Lady Prudentia's attention; but still, there is nothing, though an unexpected gap appears in the text – a space between the lines – when Dave is working on the screen.

'Dearre Lady Prudentia,' I write, after Dave hands the laptop back to me, 'please do comme through on myh computerr today?'

'Dearer, deader, deafer,' responds the spell-check box. I press the button again. 'Come, comes, coma, calm,' says the spell check. 'My, myth.' These words have a curious charm all of their own, but they do not seem to me to be Lady Prudentia's. 'She's not used to your computer,' says Dave, apologetically. 'It's different to mine. She's never worked on an Apple Mac before.'

So I have a go on his laptop, instead, which produces gratifyingly instant results. When I type 'Prudentia', Dave's spell check comes up with the word 'lady'; and 'Trentham' is first replaced with 'in', and then 'here'. 'Lady . . . in . . . here . . .' I say, gazing at the screen. 'That's brilliant!' Dave looks relieved, though a trace of disappointment flickers across Monty's face, as my computer continues to refuse to do anything interesting at all. I keep typing on Dave's computer, and I don't want to stop (will Ruth finally, please, send me an email, written in the spaces left by this determined ghost?). 'It's quite compulsive, isn't it?' I say, reluctantly pausing for another cup of tea, after the word 'your' has appeared at least half a dozen times in the spell-check box, in response to a variety of unrelated words.

'Oh, yes,' says Dave. 'I spend hours talking to her ladyship like this. When she's with me, I'm all of a glow, all of a tingle. She understands how I feel – and she's become a very deep and valued friend to me. In fact, I've started laying a place for her at the table when we eat dinner at home, and pouring her a glass of wine. I don't want her to feel left out, after all her hard work.'

He shows me a letterhead saying, 'Lady Prudentia Trentham' in a computerized copper plate. 'She did that,' says Dave, proudly. 'I typed out my name, in my usual typeface, and she re-arranged it on the screen into her name, before my very eyes. She wants her own headed writing paper, you see, and an office, and staff, and five computers. She's got big plans . . .'

Monty (the veteran of so many psychic investigations) reminds me that we've got to catch the train home before it gets too late, and anyway, he adds, Prudentia is beginning to repeat herself. ('She seems to have a rather autistic streak,' he remarks, under his breath, as another 'your' flashes up on the screen.) Dave says that before we go, he'll give us a quick tour around the surviving Elizabethan cellars of the house. We walk across the courtyard, and down a flight of worn stone steps where discarded sweet wrappers lie gathered in drifts – past the Victorian vaults, and beyond, into Prudentia's foundations. 'We think she was buried just behind this wall,' says Dave, his eyes shining in the gloom, gently brushing his fingertips against the crumbling mortar, as if it were her ladyship's cheek.

'Extraordinary,' says Monty, examining the ancient brick-work. I wait to feel the chill of Lady Prudentia's breath, but there is nothing (though the damp is making me shiver). 'Time to go,' says Monty, briskly, and Dave says he will drive us to the station. I ask if Prudentia will be coming along too for the ride. 'I take her with me everywhere,' replies Dave.

'Perhaps you could suggest that she has another go on my computer?' I say, when we reach the station.

'Oh, she will,' he says, 'she certainly will.'

'Goodbye, Dave,' I say, shaking his hand.

'Lady Prudentia would like you to come back,' says Dave. 'She likes you very much. She says you're part of the plan.'

I don't ask what the plan is. I've learnt by now to side step the issue, when time is running short. I'm still interested, of course, in other people's plans – just as I am in other people's ghosts. Sometimes they are far more compelling than one's own. (On the train home, Monty tells me about 'The Plan' – a different plan – formulated in the early years of the last century by various illustrious members of the Society for Psychical Research, which involved a peculiar form of Edwardian eugenics. Their scheme was to conceive a baby boy who would grow into 'a new Augustus' to lead the world. But the new Augustus didn't play ball, and after a career in the British army, retired from the world as a Dominican monk, without ever addressing The Plan. Now he's dead, and still silent on the subject, as far as Monty can tell.)

In fact, when I come to think about it, everyone that I have met in the last year seems to have a plan. Dale Palmer has a big plan, in the form of his website that will allow the dead to communicate down the wires; Gary Schwartz and Linda Russek have their plan for further research into the Grand Organizing Designer (otherwise known as God); Laurie Campbell is the medium for the very big plans of various deceased scientists (not to mention Freddie Mercury); Monty Keen and David Fontana are planning an extensive scientific investigation of the Spell Check ghost.

As for my plan . . . Well, what plan might that be? (I am reminded of Jack Hallam – my first and favourite EVP ghost – whose response to Judith Chisholm's request to please explain 'the plan' was that there was none.) I'm with Jack on this one. I have no plan. I have travelled in a number of circles, and failed to reach a clear destination; I have faltered and dawdled and often lost my way. I have taken one step forwards, and two steps back again, to where I started (even though beginnings look different when you return to them, just as conclusions also change). Yet in the end, Ruth has been by my side, for most of the time, often infuriatingly silent; but there – yes, here – all the same. Does she have a plan?

'Do you have a plan?' I say out loud, back home in the attic, just before I go to bed.

There is no answer, so I type it on to my computer screen. 'DO YOU HAVE A PLAN?' I hit the spell-check button. 'The spelling check is complete,' says the message in the box.

'OK,' I type. 'Are you riding your bicycle? Do you cycle in circles in the sky? Ruth, answer me, please.'

'There is no answer,' I write.

Maybe answers are not the point.

## FRIDAY 13 APRIL, GOOD FRIDAY

FRIDAY THE THIRTEENTH. The unluckiest day of the year; the day of the dead: mainly animals, now, hundreds of thousands of animals that have been slaughtered because of foot and mouth disease. 'A disaster,' says my mother on the phone this morning, almost crying. (When Ruth and I first left home, my mother acquired two pet sheep, sweet-faced, calm-eyed creatures called Holly and Mary, who followed her through the garden. My mother became a vegetarian, as did my sister; though years later, when the brain tumour clouded Ruth's once-clear mind, she came home from hospital, and ate her children's pork sausages. Then she went upstairs to the top-floor bedroom, and hung out of the window, shouting, 'I'm dead, I'm dead, I'm dead.' I do not know what became of Holly and Mary. I think they went to graze on a Welsh hilltop, long before my mother had remarried and moved to America. I'm not clear what constitutes old age when it comes to sheep, though surely they must be long gone by now, and my stepfather is dead, of course, and I know my mother misses him, but we never talk about him, which must be very hard for her. Perhaps one day we will find the right words.) I also avoid the subject of the dead cows and sheep with my husband and children, for fear of adding to the general air of morbidity that threatens to swamp us, but I can't stop thinking about a new-born lamb that is on the front page of today's paper: a small lamb in a muddy field, that will soon be killed alongside its mother; one lamb, amid so many. (Am I turning into my father, an Easter depressive, dwelling on death and disaster at holiday time?)

We are going to stay at a seaside hotel in Sussex, for a weekend with the children, which will conveniently incorporate a trip to my sister's grave. 'They might as well learn that Easter's not just about chocolate eggs,' I say to Neill, when he suggests that the graveyard visit could be a less than festive experience. But I guess it's probably time to pull myself together, pull us together; though it is they who pull me, my family, that I love, who love me, despite everything. (Much as I hate to admit this, could Gary Schwartz be right, in the end: that love is the only answer, when everything else stops making sense?)

'Oh please,' says Ruth, in my head.

'What's that supposed to mean?' I say.

'Good grief,' she says, and veers off to the left, on her bicycle.

'Wait for me,' I say.

'See you there!' she cries, over her shoulder, before disappearing into the distance.

This is a journey south that we've made many times before; so often, that I know it by heart. Over the Thames at Blackfriars Bridge, along the South Bank, then skirting past Clapham Common and Trinity Hospice, unless I'm feeling too gloomy; in which case we head for the South Circular. Today, however, I decide to make a change. 'Let's cross the river at Hammersmith Bridge,' I say.

'We always go over Blackfriars,' says Neill. 'Hammersmith is usually closed for road works.'

'It's definitely open today,' I say. 'Let's do something different.'

'OK,' says Neill, shrugging his shoulders, but smiling at me. 'Whatever you want.'

The way is clear today: no traffic jams, no hold-ups, no delays. (The radio this morning said that everyone has left the country, to avoid the incessant wet weather and the burning pyres of slaughtered animals, in search of foreign sun instead.) We sail over Hammersmith Bridge, ignore the signs to Mortlake, and pass a Good Friday church parade, heading in the opposite direction, led by a determined woman carrying a large wooden cross. I used to live just around the corner from here, in my first year after leaving university, in a little house overlooking the river. (Of those of us who shared the house: one is now a widow, and someone else is me. For a time, there was another resident of the house: Ruth, before she went on an archaeological dig to Peru. A week after she'd left for Peru, I panicked: this was the longest we'd ever gone without talking to each other. There were bombs in Peru, and terrorists. I phoned up the British Embassy for information. There was an echo on the line. The man at the other end of the phone was patient, though we seemed to be talking at cross-purposes. He could not send out a search party, he explained, for a person who was not yet missing. 'But she *could* be missing,' I said. After another week, a letter arrived from Ruth, saying that she was fine. I imagined her, up in the mountains, separated from the rest of the world by a rope bridge. What was she digging for? I can't remember; nor do I know what she found.)

'I'm losing my memory,' I say to Neill, after we've left the church parade far behind, and the turning that leads to the place where I once lived. 'This morning, I realized that I had forgotten something so important that it seemed the only plausible explanation was that I had a brain tumour.'

'What was it you'd forgotten?' he says.

'I can't remember,' I reply.

'It's just middle age,' he says, 'like middle-age spread.'

'Ruth will never grow old,' I say, forgetting (again) to be cheerful for the bank holiday, 'never get wrinkled and portly, like we will.' Silently, I wonder if she will never lose her memory, either. Do the dead remember us, as we remember them?

'Of course, how could we forget?' says the voice in my head.

## Saturday 14 April, Easter Eve

I GO TO A flower shop and buy pots of white roses and hyacinths – still living, still sweet scented, not the kind that might wilt the moment you turn and walk away – to take to

Ruth's grave. I also buy a large packet of Easter eggs; the ones that look like speckled birds' eggs, with solid chocolate inside. Her grave is close to the coast, beside an ancient flint church (though to get there, you must first pass a tangle of flyovers and a dual carriageway that leads to a small airport, where light aircraft lift off into the pale grey sky). My sister's headstone is on the far side of the graveyard; sheltered by a hedgerow, where wild flowers grow. She wanted her tumour-ridden body to be burnt first, at a crematorium near here, in the foothills of the South Downs, but to have a headstone in this quiet place – 'Somewhere for you to visit,' she said, not long before she died. We came here after her cremation: her friends and family and the children, carrying seedlings to plant around the grave for her. I've been back several times since, bringing seashells and flowers and other small offerings. On one side of her headstone is a Jewish prayer – I don't understand the Hebrew – and on the other side is her name, and her children's, and the dates of her birth and her death. What more can you say in stone? Wisteria is carved onto that side; lavender on the other. She grew wisteria up the front of her house (as I do, too), and lavender in the back garden, like me, like our mother.

The children help me scatter the Easter eggs between the flowers and the headstone. Tom traces his finger around the stone words. It is so cold – whipped by a sea breeze; almost sleeting. The churchyard is empty apart from the four of us. I'm crying, I can't help it, even though I want to be happy, but no one can see, because the tears are dried on my face by the wind as fast as I can weep them. I go over to the church, where I have often sought refuge before; but today it is locked. It has never been locked before. I rattle the door, but no one is inside to open it. So we walk back to the car. There is nothing else to do here.

'Look, Mum,' says Jamie, as we go through the churchyard lych-gate, pointing up to a nook in the roof. 'Can you see the birds?' Two white doves have built a nest there. 'That's something good, isn't it?' he says.

'Yes, yes, it is,' I say, feeling very tired.

That night, I go to bed early, in the unfamiliar hotel room where you can hear the shingle washed up on the nearby shore. (I used to like hotels, but this weekend I don't: other people's memories fill the room, and dust from their dead skin gathers under the mahogany bed.) Tom climbs in with me, and falls asleep in the crook of my arm; his gentle breathing overlaid with the waves outside. (Tom – whose second name is Louis, for my paternal grandfather that I never knew – Tom, with flame-red hair, like Kirsty, but with a seven-year-old smile all of his very own.)

## SUNDAY 15 APRIL

EASTER SUNDAY, JESUS is risen, and the newspaper's front-page lamb has been saved, for today at least, and christened Lucky. The children get up early to look for Easter eggs outside in the weak morning sun, running across the grass, Neill behind them, making sure that they don't get lost. After breakfast, we go for a walk along the beach, and find two very small dead sharks, washed up on the sand. 'Poor sharks,' says Jamie, forgetting that he was once frightened of what might lurk at the bottom of the sea, 'they look so little. Could they breathe again if we put them back in the water?' Tom collects shells, slowly, carefully, like Ruth and I did as children, and adults ('cowries are good luck,' she said, after finding one on our last holiday in Wales). He gives me fragments of mother of pearl, one bit at a time, into my pocket, as he unearths them from the wet sand. Jamie splashes through the shallows, setting the sharks free again in the waves. Neill circles my cold hands inside his warm ones, as we watch our children.

For a moment, Tom lifts his face to the sky. 'Look,' he says, as he always does, pointing at the criss-crossed jet streams left behind by aeroplanes on their way to other places, 'Ruth has drawn us kisses in the sky.'

At lunchtime, we eat chip sandwiches at the beach café, and then drive into Chichester to see the cathedral. We arrive after the Eucharist, but before Evensong: slipping in as visitors, rather than worshippers. We walk down to see the Graham Sutherland painting at the far end of the cathedral, of Christ appearing to Mary Magdalene on the first Easter morning. 'It's called, "Noli me tangere", I whisper to Tom. 'That means, "Do not hold me".'

'Why can't she hold him?' says Tom.

'Because he's going to heaven,' I say.

'I don't believe in God,' says Jamie. 'Neither does Dad.'

'I do,' says Tom. 'He lives here.'

Tom and I light candles for Ruth and Kirsty and Kimberley at the site of the Shrine of St Richard, balancing them in a tray of sand. They cost five pence each, and then Tom wants to light another one for the little boy in his class who died when he was four years old; and afterwards Jamie wants to light his own candles for his disappeared aunts.

'But you don't believe in God,' says Tom.

'That doesn't mean I don't believe in dead people,' says Jamie, so I give him some money and he makes his offering. By this time, Neill is lighting a candle at the other end of the altar, and we seem to have used up the entire supply in the cathedral, and I still need more for my grandparents and stepfather (so many ghosts that we bring with us today; yet so few amid the throng that must fill this church and others; the spirits that circle the living; in our houses and around the streets; all the dead people and the sheep, rising over the hills and up, up, up into the sky).

I usher the children away from the candles in the sand, shushing their mild protests, into the Lady Chapel. Tom and I sit at the front; Neill and Jamie stand at the back, as if making a point about their status as outsiders (even though we're all outsiders coming in). I close my eyes and say (not out loud, but inside my head), 'Please, God, give me a sign that Ruth is in heaven with you.' I open my eyes again, and Tom is spelling out the words on the altar. 'Oh . . . lamb . . . of . . . God . . . grant . . . us . . . thy . . . peace,' he says. 'But who is the lamb of God?'

'Jesus,' I say.

'Is Jesus here, too?' says Tom.

'I suppose so,' I say. 'Look, there's a picture of him on the cross.'

'Jesus is here and everywhere,' says Tom. 'We learnt that at school.'

'Can you feel him?' I say.

'I think so,' he says, thoughtfully, 'like a ghost, blowing on the back of my neck.'

We get up and leave the Lady Chapel, walk past our candles (that are still burning, even though they are so small), and down to the Arundel Tomb, where the stone figures of a medieval earl and countess lie together, holding hands. Beside the effigies is a copy of Philip Larkin's poem, 'The Arundel Tomb', and I read the last verse out loud for my children, and for me, too:

Time has transfigured them into
Untruth. The stone fidelity
They hardly meant has come to be
Their final blazon, and to prove
Our almost-instinct almost true:
What will survive of us is love.

## Monday 16 April

Easter Monday in the year 2001, and I'm walking on the treadmill at the gym, talking to myself without moving my lips. I have not come to the gym for months and months (there was always tomorrow); now, at last, seems as good a time as any. (Why? Why not? Today is a very good day to begin again.)

But I'm not running. I got tired of running, and staying in the same place all the while. I'm walking, not too fast, not too slow, at my own speed, in my own time, while the treadmill turns round in circles beneath me. I like to think that I'm walking towards Ruth, slowly, steadily, as long as it will take. I know that one day I will reach her.

Ruth, sweet Ruth, my sister, myself.

## Permissions

Permission to quote copyright material is gratefully acknowledged as follows:

Browne, Sylvia, *Life on the Other Side*, reprinted by kind permission of Penguin Putnam Inc./Piatkus Books.

Eliot, T. S., 'Little Gidding' from *Four Quartets* and 'The Hollow Men' from *Collected Poems 1909–1962*, reprinted by kind permission of Faber & Faber Ltd.

Skeptic's Dictionary, entries reprinted by kind permission of Robert Todd Carroll at www.SkepDic.com.

Ferenczi, Sandor, *Stages in the Development of the Sense of Reality; Love with Science* and 'Spiritism', reprinted by kind permission of Penguin Publishers.

Fontana, David, Keen, Montague and Ellison, Arthur, extracts from *The Scole Report* reprinted by kind permission of The Society for Psychical Research.

Frazer, James George, extracts from *The Golden Bough* published by Macmillan.

Freud, Sigmund, extracts from the *The Interpretation of Dreams, The Origins of Religion* and *Moses, His People and Monotheist Religion* and The Freud/Jung letters reprinted by kind permission of HarperCollins Publishers. Extract from *Totem and Taboo* reprinted by kind permission of Mark Pattison Associates.

Jones, Ernest, *Sigmund Freud*; *Freud, His Life and Work* and *Occultism*, reprinted by kind permission of The British Psycho-Analytical Society.

Lacan, Jacques, extract from *The Four Fundamental Concepts of Psycho-Analysis* translated by Alan Sheridan. Copyright © 1973 by

Editions du Seuil. English translation copyright © 1977 by Alan Sheridan. Used by permission of WW Norton & Company, Inc. and Hogarth Press.

Larkin, Philip, 'The Arundel Tomb' from *Collected Poems*, reprinted by kind permission of Faber & Faber Ltd.

Levi-Strauss, Claude, extract from *The Raw and the Cooked* reprinted by kind permission of Jonathan Cape Ltd.

Lewis, C. S., *The Voyage of the Dawn Treader*, copyright © CS Lewis Pte. Ltd. 1952. Extract reprinted by permission.

Opie, Iona, and Tatem, Moira, extract from *A Dictionary of Superstitions* reprinted by kind permission of Oxford University Press.

Salter, W.H., *The Society for Psychical Research: An Outline of its History*, reprinted by kind permission of The Society for Psychical Research.

Vaughan, Henry, 'The World', taken from *Poems on the Underground*, reprinted by kind permission of Cassell Publishers.